# Women's Lives in the Tudor Era

# Women's Lives in the Tudor Era

Amy McElroy

First published in Great Britain in 2024 by
Pen & Sword History
An imprint of Pen & Sword Books Limited
Yorkshire – Philadelphia

Copyright © Amy McElroy 2024

ISBN 978 1 39904 200 0

The right of Amy McElroy to be identified as
Author of this Work has been asserted by her in accordance
with the Copyright, Designs and Patents Act 1988.

A CIP catalogue record for this book is
available from the British Library

All rights reserved. No part of this book may be reproduced or
transmitted in any form or by any means, electronic or mechanical
including photocopying, recording or by any information storage and
retrieval system, without permission from the Publisher in writing.

Typeset by Mac Style
Printed in the UK by CPI Group (UK) Ltd, Croydon, CR0 4YY.

Pen & Sword Books Limited incorporates the imprints of After
the Battle, Atlas, Archaeology, Aviation, Discovery, Family History,
Fiction, History, Maritime, Military, Military Classics, Politics,
Select, Transport, True Crime, Air World, Frontline Publishing, Leo
Cooper, Remember When, Seaforth Publishing, The Praetorian Press,
Wharncliffe Local History, Wharncliffe Transport, Wharncliffe True
Crime and White Owl.

For a complete list of Pen & Sword titles please contact

**PEN & SWORD BOOKS LIMITED**
47 Church Street, Barnsley, South Yorkshire, S70 2AS, England
E-mail: enquiries@pen-and-sword.co.uk
Website: www.pen-and-sword.co.uk
or
**PEN AND SWORD BOOKS**
1950 Lawrence Rd, Havertown, PA 19083, USA
E-mail: Uspen-and-sword@casematepublishers.com
Website: www.penandswordbooks.com

*In memory of my Mum, Patricia Ann McElroy, forever in my heart and thoughts.*

Remember the poore, that for God's sake doo call.
for God both rewardeth and blesseth withall.
Take this in good part, whatsoever thou bee:
and wish me no worse than I wish unto thee.

*Think on the poore – Thomas Tusser*

# Contents

*Acknowledgements* viii
*List of Illustrations* xi
*Introduction* xiv

**Chapter 1**    Growing Up    1

**Chapter 2**    Adolescence    15

**Chapter 3**    Tudor Brides    25

**Chapter 4**    Lives of Wives    50

**Chapter 5**    Motherhood    71

**Chapter 6**    Working Women    90

**Chapter 7**    Recreation    115

**Chapter 8**    Woes of Widowhood    126

**Chapter 9**    Wills of Women    144

**Chapter 10**    Conclusion    153

*Notes* 166
*Bibliography* 173
*Index* 177

# Acknowledgements

Little did I ever think I would write a book, let alone publish a second, with a third and fourth in progress. Whilst writing this book, I underwent surgery for Endometriosis and it made me realise how grateful I am for the modern world I now live in. I genuinely have no idea how Tudor women coped with gynaecological conditions. That being said, thank you to the NHS who got me back on my feet so I could continue with this book. I cannot thank the Pen and Sword family enough for all they have done in making this a reality, in particular Sarah-Beth, Laura, Sarah H and Lucy.

To my best friend, Pops, I love you, you remain my biggest supporter, thank you for the unwavering love, support and encouragement, I would not be who I am without you. Colin, I remain surprised at your interest but thank you for consistently supporting me in this venture. Sarah, Ava and Will, I love you lots, keep up the reading Ava.

I have had so much support from both old and new friends since I began writing and would love to thank everyone but the acknowledgments would probably be longer than the book, so, thank you all. Having said that there are a special few who I could not omit here as I'm not sure how far I would have gotten without their help and guidance. MJ Porter and Tony Riches, I can't thank you enough for all the help you have given me with various things, Tony, you sir, are a legend. I will save the specific thank you for the next book but you can rest assured I am taking care of them. MJ, you have given me unwavering support from day one and I can't explain how grateful I am for your support, advice and words of wisdom, especially during the bad days. I owe Rebecca Batley a huge thank you for all the help along the way, both in the final months leading up to the publication of *Educating the Tudors* and throughout *Women's Lives in the Tudor Era*. You have been an incredible sounding board and gave me encouragement every step of the way. Special thanks for your support with images, source material and for the sneak peeks of your own work. Caroline Angus, not only are your own books amazing, but you took the time to give me advice when I was doubting myself, thank you.

There are a few who I would specifically like to thank for their help in writing *Women's Lives in the Tudor Era*: Dr Amy Louise Erickson, for responding to my query and whose book *Women and Property in Early Modern England* has been priceless in the writing of this book; Hana Cole, thank you so much helping me with a source I could not locate, your simple gesture of kindness meant I could continue and stop panicking, you will always have my gratitude; Tina, the Bookshop Fairy deserves all the thanks in the world for continually searching her treasure trove of books for me, if you haven't already, then check out the Old Curiosity Bookshop, it is wonderful.

As this book focuses on women, I must thank one of the most incredible women I have ever met. Helen Downing, you are a light in the dark, your support means a lot and your enthusiasm for my work keeps me going, you have never once doubted me so thank you, I hope you continue to follow your dreams. To my friends who continue to be my cheerleaders (even though some of you don't even like history, although I am beginning to think there is a secret Tudor fan in Lucy-Bug), thank you ladies. Pam, you are an inspiration for me to keep reaching for the stars, your friendship, kindness and unwavering support means the world to me, I know I say it a lot but thank you from the bottom of my heart for always being there. I could not possibly write acknowledgments without a mention of my self-proclaimed 'biggest fan', Andy, as always you are my IT guru and I'm always thankful for your advice and support. I also know two people that will be looking at this page to see if their names are here so, surprise Nikki and Jennie, you both make me smile on a daily basis and I am grateful to both of you.

Life as a Tudor woman is something we can only really imagine for the most part. However, if you are looking for more of an experience you can actually try it out. Old Hall in Norwich offers a Tudor Experience where you can stay in a Tudor manor, with Tudor furniture, including the beds! The venue hosts banqueting events and Tudor breakfasts or if you prefer to try things at home, you may wish to get yourself a copy of the wonderful host, Brigitte Webster's, *Eating with the Tudors*.

Thank you to those who are reading this and those who have read *Educating the Tudors*, I appreciate each and every one of you. I am so grateful to readers and bloggers; reviews really do mean a lot to writers and I continue to take on board feedback. For those who specialise in Tudor history you are all stars, yes that's you Heidi! Thank you to all those who have welcomed and supported me in the writing world.

Lastly, I am extremely grateful for all the institutes that have allowed me to use images from their digital collections: the Wellcome Collection, British Library, Yale Center for British Art and the Folger Shakespeare Library which I very much hope to visit one day.

# List of Illustrations

1. Mary I. Archer, Thomas, *Pictures and Royal Portraits illustrative of English and Scottish History ... With descriptive ... sketches.* (London: Blackie & Son, 1878). Copy supplied by the British Library from its digital collections. Public Domain image.
2. Complete copper alloy hooked tag, or dress hook. The object has an elaborate openwork disc-shaped body with an inner disc and a central circular depression. The inner disc contains a band of radiating lines. The tag end is rectangular and the hook is collared and complete, being triangular in cross-section. The Portable Antiquities Scheme, The Trustees of the British Museum, CC BY-SA 2.0 via Wikimedia Commons.
3. Fashions of the era. Costumes; Beards of the sixteenth Century; Dress of a Lady 1485; John Cassell. Public Domain image, via Wikimedia Commons.
4. Music Book and Instrument owned by Elizabeth I. Smith, J. F. (John Frederick), 1806–1890; Howitt, William, 1792–1879, *John Cassell's Illustrated History of England. The text, to the Reign of Edward.* Copy supplied by the British Library from its digital collections. Public Domain image.
5. Clothing comparison between peasants and the queen. Differing fashions. Elizabethan Era English Life, CC BY-SA 4.0 via Wikimedia Commons.
6. Lady Jane Grey. Wylde, Flora F. *The Tablette Booke of Ladye Mary Keyes, owne sister to the misfortunate Ladye Jane Dudlie; in wiche wille be founde a faithefulle historie of alle the troubels that did com to them and theire kinsfolke, writt in the yeare of oure Lorde fifteene hundred and seventie-seven.* (London: Saunders, Otley & Co, 1861.) Copy supplied by the British Library from its digital collections. Public Domain image.
7. Sir Thomas More with his daughter, Margaret More-Roper. Archer, Thomas, *Pictures and Royal Portraits illustrative of English and Scottish History ... With descriptive ... sketches.* (London: Blackie & Son, 1878).

Copy supplied by the British Library from its digital collections. Public Domain image.

8. Woodcut of Lawn Bowling. Scanned from *English Life in Tudor Times* by Roger Hart, NT: Putnam, 1972, SBN 853401608. Public Domain image, via Wikimedia Commons.
9. Table of Kindred and Affinity. Image © Ian Paterson. cc-by sa/2.0 – geograph.org.uk/p/537038
10. Wedding procession. The Happy Wedding, *le Gestes of ye Ladye Anne: a marvellous and comfortable tale.* Edited by Forsyth, Evelyn. Copy supplied by the British Library from its digital collections. Public Domain image.
11. 'The description of Woman's Age.' Verse by Thomas Tusser from *Five Hundred Points of Good Husbandry*, transcribed by Thomas Trevelyan in his commonplace book. Folger MS V. b. 232, fo. 19, by permission of the Folger Shakespeare Library.
12. Sixteenth Century Woodcut of a Lord and Lady. Unknown author, Public Domain image, via Wikimedia Commons.
13. A sixteenth-century room. Illustration from *Illustrated History of Furniture, From the Earliest to the Present Time* from 1893 by Litchfield, Frederick, (1850–1930). Public Domain image, via Wikimedia Commons.
14. Birthing scene. A woman in bed recovering from childbirth. A midwife washes the baby while another attendant looks after the mother. Woodcut. Public Domain mark, via The Wellcome Collection.
15. Birthing stool. *The expert midwife, or an excellent and most necessary treatise of the generation and birth of man ... Also the causes, signes, and various cures, of the most principall maladies and infirmities incident to women.* Rüff, Jakob, 1500–1558. Public Domain image, via The Wellcome Collection.
16. Woman on a settle with four children, by Hans Holbein the Younger. Public Domain image, via Wikimedia Commons.
17. Wylde, Flora F. *The Tablette Booke of Ladye Mary Keyes, owne sister to the misfortunate Ladye Jane Dudlie; in wiche wille be founde a faithefulle historie of alle the troubels that did com to them and theire kinsfolke, writt in the yeare of oure Lorde fifteene hundred and seventie-seven.* (London: Saunders, Otley & Co, 1861.) Copy supplied by the British Library from its digital collections. Public Domain image.

List of Illustrations  xiii

18. *The herball or, generall historie of plantes*, gathered by John Gerarde, ESTC S122353. The Wellcome Collection. Attribution 4.0 International (CC BY 4.0).
19. A woman sits spinning at a spinning wheel. Wood engraving. Public Domain mark, via The Wellcome Collection.
20. Interior scene, sixteenth-century hospital. Public Domain mark, via The Wellcome Collection.
21. Midwife assisting a woman in labour. A woman seated on an obstetrical chair giving birth, is aided by a midwife who works beneath her skirts. Woodcut. H. Speert, *Iconographia Gyniatrica – a Pictorial History of Gynecology and Obstetrics.* (Philadelphia, 1973). The original is a plate to: E. Roeslin, Rosengarten, 1513. Public Domain mark, via The Wellcome Collection.
22. Caesarean section. A baby being removed from its dying mother's womb via Caesarean section. Reproduction of woodcut, 1483. Public Domain mark, via The Wellcome Collection.
23. Woman spinning. Woodcut with woman spinning with a spinning wheel. Unknown author. Public Domain image, via Wikimedia Commons.
24. Headdresses. *The National and Domestic History of England … With numerous steel plates, coloured pictures, etc, Volume II.* (London Aubrey, William Hickman Smith, 1867–70). Copy supplied by the British Library from its digital collections.
25. Fashions. Smith, J. F. (John Frederick), 1806–1890; Howitt, William, 1792–1879, *John Cassell's Illustrated History of England. The text, to the Reign of Edward.* Copy supplied by the British Library from its digital collections.
26. Elizabeth I. Archer, Thomas, *Pictures and Royal Portraits illustrative of English and Scottish History … With descriptive … sketches,* (London: Blackie & Son, 1878). Copy supplied by the British Library from its digital collections. Public Domain image.
27. Monumental brasses of Sir John Bassett (1462–1529) of Umberleigh, with his two wives: (right) first wife Ann Denys; (left) second wife Honor Grenville. Monochrome negative image, detail from top slab of his chest-tomb, Atherington Church, Devon. Public Domain image, via Wikimedia Commons.

# Introduction

There are certainly a few women that spring to mind when we think of the Tudors, and most will likely be of royal or noble birth. There are those who are remembered for who they married, their achievements and even their deaths. But what about the women who lived a normal life? How did their lives differ to the upper ranks of society? Were the lives of women so different to those of men?

Equality of genders remains a topic widely discussed today although clearly society has come a long way since the Tudor era. Despite the incredible achievements of some Tudor women, men were viewed as the stronger gender. This unfortunately means there is much less literature and fewer records available on the female population. Most contemporary literature was written by men, even that which was aimed at female readers. The little that survives that is written by women is usually relating to the higher levels of society and largely consists of letters, diaries and books of advice compiled during their lives. This literature, therefore, does not represent the experience of all classes. Society largely saw women as either maidens, wives or widows, making marriage an extremely important aspect of their status. Although there were age restrictions for marriage, for women it was becoming a wife that marked their entry into adulthood rather than their age. Unless they had chosen a life of piety within a religious institution or had the financial resources to maintain themselves, those who remained unmarried were often criticised by society. It was thought strange if a single woman did not wish to marry and instead chose the life of a spinster. Therefore, for the majority of Tudor women, securing a husband, preferably an advantageous one, was one of the primary aims in life, an aim that was fully supported by the Church.

The societal expectations of women were influenced by biblical teachings such as the story of Adam and Eve, the early fathers of the Christian Church and texts from those believed to be an authority on the matter, in particular St Jerome, Aristotle and Thomas Aquinas. Women were expected to display the Christian virtues of modesty and chastity amongst numerous others. They faced constant reminders through church sermons and services that they had a duty to be obedient as a daughter and later as a wife. Educational treatises and medical theories relied upon in the sixteenth century expanded on earlier works and added support to the idea that women should be submissive and obedient to men. It was not just didactic texts that influenced how women were perceived, medical texts enforced these views. In medicine, the Tudors followed Galen's writings and believed the body was made up of four humours with men being hot and dry, and women being cold and moist which society believed made females weaker and gentler.

The philosopher Aristotle was of the opinion that the creation of women was an error and they were therefore an imperfect version of man. This was the mindset many women had to contend with during the Tudor era.[1] Due to these various attitudes, women were believed to be intellectually lacking compared to men and so found themselves barred from most formal education and employment opportunities. However much the Aristotelian theories were respected by a large portion of the male population, not all situations favoured men and women sometimes found their sex to be advantageous. Many men greatly respected their wives as much more than a piece of property. There are also exceptionally intellectual females known within the Tudor era: Lady Jane Grey, Elizabeth I and Margaret More-Roper being some of the most renowned who proved they were just as intelligent as their male counterparts. Admittedly the education they received was not perceived as the 'norm' for female education at the time, but they exceeded their expected abilities where many at the time would have expected them to fail.

There were clear boundaries between what was considered men's and women's work. In Tudor society the aristocracy, made up of the gentry and nobility was the highest level of society after the royal family. Most of the aristocracy had homes in both urban and rural parts of the country. The rest of society was separated according to status and role. In rural England, those who owned land and farms were known as 'yeomen', those with smaller farms were 'husbandmen' and those who did not own land and worked for wages were the 'labourers'. In towns and cities, the wealthiest were the merchants who were followed by 'craftsmen', 'journeymen' and like their rural counterparts, 'labourers'. The position of a husband dictated the role of his wife, and her duties and responsibilities to some extent. Men were the head of their household, to be obeyed by those within his house. The household itself, was typically the responsibility of women. Women were there to ensure her male relatives, whether that be her father or husband and children were looked after. Women also worked for wages if required, which it was amongst the largest proportion of society. It is overwhelming the amount of work an ordinary housewife would undertake on a daily basis. Imagine having to daily sweep earth floors, launder all of the families' clothes using whatever water source was available, after having to make your own soap to do so. She also needed to feed her family and any servants and on top of that care for any livestock they may have. It would be easy to assume that the wealthier you were the less work you did but as we shall see, even the extremely wealthy were rarely idle, the tasks just varied, as did their responsibilities.

Disparity in the treatment between the sexes is apparent in many aspects of Tudor life, from employment, inheritance, expectations of behaviour and even crime. If faced with criminal court charges the sentences imposed were thought to be much more lenient for women than their male counterparts. This was partly due to the belief that women were more delicate and gentler in nature and equal punishments would be too harsh. It was illegal to torture women, though through the ordeal of Anne Askew, a Protestant reformer, who faced the rack for her beliefs, we know that it did happen. Though they should not be tortured, the punishment for treason for a woman was burning whilst for men it was to be hung, drawn and quartered. It is almost impossible to say which is the crueller and more brutal. Women did have the ability to 'plead the belly' when they were incarcerated. Pleading the belly was a claim that they were pregnant and therefore could not be executed. For some it was true, for others they managed to become pregnant whilst in prison before they could be examined.[2] A pardon may be issued in these cases but it was certainly not a guarantee to escape punishment.

Women also faced serious disadvantages when they were the victims of crime. Women were viewed as less reliable witnesses, which made accusations of sexual crimes such as rape almost impossible to prove. The medical theory of the time did not help women as it was claimed a woman could not conceive a child unless both parties experienced pleasure and therefore it was not rape if a child was conceived. The law also stated that the act of rape was not actually a violation of the woman, instead it was a violation of a man's property, the man being the husband, father or guardian of the victim. The ordeal is intensified by the fact that if married, a wife required the consent of her husband to sue her attacker for the crime of rape. This was a course of action many men would refuse to take as the community may then make judgments about a man's wife and therefore him as her husband.

The legal system of the Tudor era ensured women remained subordinate citizens in both criminal and civil law. Common law determined that daughters could only inherit an estate if they had no brothers. The custom of primogeniture meant that estates passed to the eldest son; daughters were at the mercy of receiving a gift of inheritance or the generosity of their brothers whilst younger brothers were required to make their own way in the world. This may appear harsh to younger sons but those from wealthy families were rarely left poor, they just could not inherit the bulk of the family estate. Younger sons were able to inherit property from their mother. Primogeniture primarily aimed to ensure estates belonging to the nobility and royalty remained intact and were not torn apart by individual bequests. If there were no sons, then daughters could inherit and the estate could be bequeathed jointly if there were more than one daughter. This did not stop male relatives attempting to claim the estate for themselves, arguing that under the common law male heirs were preferred for inheriting property. Of course, there were men with daughters and no sons who preferred their estate remain in one piece and therefore sought ways to ensure it passed to a male relative rather than his daughters. A man could bequeath the estate to a male relative ensuring his daughters did not receive it. If a man wished his daughters to inherit, bequeathing an estate to female relatives was made extremely difficult if the property was entailed to a man's heirs. Fathers below the ranks of the aristocracy were more likely to bequeath their estate equally amongst his children, regardless of whether they were sons or daughters. If they possessed land and property, they may leave the property to the son and leave the daughter personal chattels. This meant the property could remain within the family whilst the daughter would receive an adequate value of goods as her own inheritance. There were four bodies of law regulating property ownership: common law, equity, manorial and ecclesiastical. One point of law all of these bodies agreed on was supporting a widow's right to an income after the death of her husband.

When it came to marriage, all were technically free to marry as they chose, but in a patriarchal society, where women were subordinate, they often followed through with their father's recommendation of a partner. For some, this led to a happy, loving marriage but others would find themselves in an unhappy union. Women were permitted to refuse a match but had to consider whether they were at risk of disinheritance, being outcast from their family or the refusal having a detrimental effect on the advancement of their family. As such it was sometimes felt women, especially those of aristocratic families, had little alternative than to accept the choice made for them. Couples most often married within their own social circles and parents would usually try to secure a partner around the same age as their child. For the wealthy, marriage was a way to secure further wealth and influence. The exception was widows who could marry as they chose or remain unmarried if they preferred.

Following marriage, varying social aspects of life were presented to women; events such as attending another's childbirth which were not commonly attended by unmarried women. Childbirth was the next step in the typical life of a Tudor woman. Once married, a wife was expected to provide her husband with children and those of aristocratic families specifically hoped for male heirs to continue the family and preserve the estate intact. The period leading up to and following childbirth differed between the social ranks, but all sought to ensure the birth went as smoothly as possible. All women understood the dangers they faced in pregnancy and childbirth. Pregnancy and birth were a time of both joy and trepidation for all the family. Motherhood changed a woman's life again; she became responsible for the care of her child and their initial education. For some mothers the most difficult decision could be having to send their child to another household at an early age. This did not mean they did not care for their child but simply that they needed to secure a good upbringing or needed their child to assist in providing an income for the family.

Whilst there is a wealth of information about the queens of England and some aristocratic ladies, in comparison, there is a lack of evidence on how the rest of the female population lived on a day-to-day basis. The majority of women were illiterate or could read but not write, therefore we are left with little to piece together the lives of everyday women. Much of their lives was centred around religion; learning psalms and prayers, education, social events and the major life events. *Women's Lives in the Tudor Era* aims to look at the lives of such women, the milestone events in their lives and how those important events varied according to class and wealth.

> Note on money: Tudor money is written as l s d.
> l = £.
> s = shillings, 20s = 1l.
> d = pennies, they also had half and quarter pennies. 240d = 1l.

The Tudors also had other coins; they commonly used marks which were two thirds of 1 or 160 pennies.

£1 from the year 1500 is equivalent to approximately £963. In 1500 this could purchase one of the following: 2 cows, 9 stones of wool, 2 quarters of wheat, 33 days of labour from a skilled worker.

By 1600 this reduces to £241 in today's value. In 1600 this could purchase one of the following: 2 stones of wool, 20 days of labour from a skilled worker.

These values are based on inflation rates only. In terms of income, £1 from 1500 would be equivalent to approximately £21,000 and from 1600 approximately £6,400.[3]

# Chapter One

# Growing Up

The birth of a daughter was typically not as celebrated as that of a son. The occasion largely went unrecorded, unless the child was of aristocratic or royal blood, and even then, it was not guaranteed to be recorded. That is not to say parents did not rejoice at the birth of a daughter, all children were seen as a blessing from God. It just so happened that due to the custom of primogeniture and law, the birth of a male provided the much-desired heir to pass on the family name and estate. Daughters placed a financial burden on their parents as they would be expected to pay a sum towards their marriage as we shall see later on. Although there was a financial implication of having daughters, through their marriages, they also brought opportunities of family advancement through the creation of beneficial connections and alliances.

All children were baptised within days of their birth and could be baptised on the day of the birth if the need arose. A baby was usually only baptised on the day of birth if there were concerns for its survival, as it was deemed vital to ensure the child's soul was protected if the child should not survive. From birth, boys and girls were treated differently although, up until the age of around 6 or 7, all children would remain in the care of their mother. If a child was born to a wealthy or aristocratic family, the child would be cared for within the household nursery, under the supervision of their mother. A household nursery would have a number of servants to assist with the care of children, including wet nurses, cradle rockers and maids, all of whom were chosen with care to fulfil very specific roles. Boys and girls would be swaddled for the first few months of their lives before being dressed in a similar manner in what was effectively a dress. This may raise the question as to why boys were dressed in what we may perceive as feminine clothing? Although this question has no definitive answer it is likely to have provided ease when toilet training children. After this, young boys and girls would be treated as miniature adults; the young girls beginning to dress in a similar manner to their mother. Those growing up in a nursey full of servants would naturally form bonds with these women and could remain close to them throughout their lives. Elizabeth I is known to have remained close to Kat Ashley and Blanche Parry, whom she had spent a portion of her childhood under the care of.

Growing up as a little girl in the Tudor era had some of the same experiences as children do in modern day England. They were taught to walk, talk and played with toys. Children of the Tudor era had imaginations just like children today and could likely make various games from their surroundings. Toys and games for children were widely available but the quality would depend on the wealth of the family. Not all parents could afford to buy toys new, so they often made them from various materials. The poorest families might even provide substitute items as toys for their children to play with. Young girls may have dolls; these would be handmade from wood and often painted. Boys may have wooden swords, shields and play at being knights of the realm. Imitating the females in their household, just as little girls do today, was a good way to learn how to behave and become an adult lady. The number of people in close proximity to them would depend on their family wealth and status. Humble households were mostly nuclear, having the parents and children residing together. Girls in these homes would have their mother, older sisters or possibly nearby family and neighbours to play with, imitate and learn from. Aristocratic households could have large numbers of servants, maids, governesses and sometimes other family members residing or visiting with them. Larger households perhaps gave little girls much more opportunity to play alongside other children or different women, further enabling them to imitate being a grown up. Many aristocratic men had business dealings or positions at the royal court, requiring them to be away from home frequently. Wives of those with positions at court had the opportunity to travel with their husbands, or at least visit. Nursery staff would take on the responsibility for the majority of childcare as very few children accompanied their parents to court. Children, in these circumstances, could go months at a time without seeing their parents, though the servants would certainly provide regular updates to the parents and by return, receive instructions in caring for the children. That is not to say there were no children raised at the court. Royal wards and children of courtiers could be brought up there. Parents had the option to bring their children but would be responsible for their maintenance. Jane Dormer, who lost her mother as a child, received her initial education at home. She was offered a place in the household of the future Edward VI when she was still a young girl. She would later join the household of the future Mary I and would spend time serving the princess and reading with her.[1]

Girls, regardless of wealth and rank, would need to learn how to maintain their personal hygiene, dress and present themselves modestly. When waking, most would wash their hands and faces within their chambers before dressing and would wash again before going to bed. Cleaning teeth was also performed by the Tudors; in the morning this was a rinse of the mouth with cold water but after eating they would use toothpicks. The more extensive methods of using one of the numerous powders such as soot or chalk would perhaps depend on the availability of the ingredients to the family but if they could be obtained, children would be taught to clean their teeth using their finger or a tooth cloth. Perfumed waters could be used for washing but the majority would just use a bowl of water to rinse away surface dust and sweat. Handwashing before, during and after meals was important, most did not have forks so would need to use their fingers and a food dagger to eat.

When it came to presenting themselves, Tudor females were expected to exhibit humility and kindness and of course be the dutiful daughter and later wife. To present herself with modesty she would need to learn how to construct the various layers of women's clothing, and this could be complex if she were wealthy and wearing the most fashionable pieces. It may appear strange to us today but they also had to learn what colours and fabrics they were allowed to wear, according to their status. The Sumptuary Laws dictated for instance that only royalty could wear the colour purple and differing furs were accorded to different ranks. They would wear a shift which was an under gown and hose made of linen or wool. Over this would be the kirtle which was a dress that was laced. A gown could, but was not required, to be worn over this, showing a part of the kirtle underneath. The wealthy would have various kirtles, gowns and sleeves of differing materials to mix and match making their dresses look different whenever they changed an aspect of it. A Tudor woman should ensure her kirtle reached her ankles, to avoid showing any flesh, though those working laborious jobs may have their dress a little shorter to avoid the hems becoming dirty and cumbersome whilst working. Many would not add the additional layer of a gown unless they were attending church or a celebration and instead would wear an apron over the kirtle to keep it clean whilst performing their daily tasks. Young girls who would grow up privileged enough to have the services of maids to help them dress would still need to know how to construct all the layers, as they may find themselves in service to another woman and be required to assist dressing her. The length and layers of clothing were not just to provide modesty but also acted as a barrier between the air and skin. The Tudors believed linen could wick away sweat and dirt from the body and used it for the layer next to the skin. The outer layers would stop anything that was airborne and capable of causing illness, from reaching the skin. It was a lesson for young girls to learn that they needed to change their linen shift as often as possible to keep themselves clean and smelling fresh.

A female's hair also played an important part in how they were perceived and acknowledged. Unmarried women could wear their hair loose to show they were a maiden, though it was not a requirement and they could choose to cover their hair. Whilst married women were required to cover their hair. The hair covering would depend on their wealth. The upper classes could afford the beautiful headdresses we associate with the likes of the queens of Henry VIII, whether they were the French style hood or the traditional English gable hood. Those less affluent may wear plainer headdresses or even a simple linen coif; much more practical for those aiming to keep hair away from their face whilst working. However the hair was worn it was still important to take care of it. The Tudors did not wash their hair as we do today, it was not a regular occurrence. They did, however, comb it, usually at least once a day. Young girls would need to learn how to comb their hair, removing knots, and how to rid their hair of lice, if required. Young females of all classes were taught decorum from an early age. This included showing deference to their elders and how to conduct themselves in specific situations, particularly whilst at church or in the company of those of the higher social ranks. The extent to which they practised this type of behaviour would be determined by their rank and the social circles they would be expected to be in the company of. Decorum for a young girl included not only how to make the perfect curtsey according to a person's rank, but also how to sit demurely, walk correctly and the art of accepting a gift whilst showing deference. This was more complex for those who would be placed in circles of ranked society.

The initial responsibility of a child's education lay with the parents, in particular the mother. Religion was at the centre of Tudor life and therefore, irrespective of wealth and class, it was of the utmost importance to a child's education. It was a mother's or her substitute's duty to introduce her daughters to her prayers, instil piety and obedience. The scope of the education a mother could provide ultimately depended on her own literacy skills and education. Children would mostly learn to talk through imitation, learning their ABC, nursey rhymes and their prayers. Early in the Tudor era, prayers were recited in Latin. As a result, unless they were taught Latin, even if children were taught to read, they would be unable to read the prayers for themselves, making reading unnecessary for a large portion of society. This also meant that until prayers began to be spoken in English, a large proportion of the population did not actually understand what they were saying whilst praying, they were simply reciting what they had heard from their parents or at church. The first prayer they would be taught to recite would be the Lord's Prayer. Prior to the Reformation, the Church required children to be educated to recite the Lord's Prayer, Ave Maria and the Creed. Post-Reformation required them to instead memorise and recite the Catechism. Not all responsibility for this lay with the parents, priests were also expected to assist teaching local children to learn their prayers by rote. From thereon, their days would begin and end with prayers, first thing when they awoke and last thing before they slept. Prayer was something that would continue for the remainder of their life. Different prayers were used for many aspects of daily life; morning and evening prayers, those which could be said before eating meat or to pray for a good harvest and so on. Morning and evening prayers were largely a private affair, most people would pray before they did anything else in the morning. For the wealthy, they could use their book of hours or a primer to assist in their daily prayers whilst the humbler classes would recite prayers they had learned by memory. Advice books of the time enforced the importance of parents instructing their children in religion.

> Take them often with you to heare God's word preached, & then enquire of them what they heard, and use them to reade in the Bible and other Godly Bokes, but especially keepe them from reading of fayned fables, vayne fantasyes, and wanton stories, and songs of love, which bring much mischief to youth. For if they learne pure and cleane doctrine in youth, they poure out plenty of good works in age.[2]

Aside from the shared learning of religion, though admittedly the extent differed extensively, the education of girls was far more practical than that of their male counterparts. All girls learned needlework of some fashion. Girls would begin to learn needlework using a sampler which was a piece that they could use to practise different types of stitches. Needlework schools were available in some areas where the parish or a wealthy patron would pay for poor children to be taught a skill. The aim was to ensure the children could find employment and therefore not become a burden to the parish by requiring alms. The needlework schools were considered as an equivalent of the writing schools that were available for boys. Girls who were not needed to labour away from home for their upkeep could remain with their family longer and continue to attend school. Outside of school hours, girls could persevere in improving their needlework skills and help their mother where needed with household chores, or caring for their younger siblings so their mother could work. As a young girl developed her skills at school, during her lessons she may work on pieces that would benefit her family and continue with these at home. By working on useful pieces or new samplers, girls could improve their ability to help at home by relieving her mother of small needlework tasks, benefiting both her mother and her through practise. Girls who did not attend a needlework school were by no means unskilled, they learned from their mothers, governesses, maids and other women they spent time with. By the age of 6, a young Elizabeth Tudor, the future Elizabeth I, was so accomplished she had sent Prince Edward a shirt that she had embroidered herself.[3]

If a young female was fortunate enough to receive any kind of formal education, following the initial lessons from her mother, she may start in a dame school which catered for boys and girls. Dame schools were usually set up by a woman who had the necessary resources to endow the school or at least offer a room in her home for the specific purpose of educating children, either teaching herself or employing another. Alternatively, a patron may secure space and employ a local woman to teach. The dame school was a little similar to needlework school, teaching skills such as sewing and spinning which could be practised at home. Spinning used a wheel to spin flax or wool into yarn. The women employed as teachers were largely literate and could teach the children to read, sometimes teach basic arithmetic and if she were able, offer writing lessons. Children could attend a dame school until around 7 years old, however, in the Tudor era there was no strict age limits for any educational establishment, they were more like guidelines than enforced rules. A dame school may have been the only school a young girl attended if her family needed her at home for her labour, but she will have learned a skill she could improve upon through practise and sometimes basic literacy skills. Having a skill allowed young girls to earn an income to supplement that of her household, therefore contributing to her own upkeep.

Young females may also have the opportunity to attend a petty school up to the age of around 14. Attendance at a petty school was usually at the discretion of the parents. As with all schooling, some parents were not always able to spare their daughter's labours at home, making attendance irregular for many. For instance, a young girl may have been required to help her family during seasonal events such as harvesting but was able to attend school at other times. Petty schools aimed to provide pupils with a solid foundation in their understanding of religion. The lessons depended on what had already been taught by the girl's mother but could begin with the very basics if the mother did not have the skills to teach. This could include learning their ABC then learning to read. Religion was the basis of all early education with even the ABC including the saying of a prayer 'Christ's cross me speed'.[4] In order to fulfil the aim of providing elementary grammar skills and a sound knowledge of religion, the schools would use a primer of prayers and psalms to teach the children how to read and where the skill of the tutor allowed, to spell. As a result, the children were learning to read using religious texts, therefore accomplishing both aims through the same task. Many had little use for the skill of writing but the ability to read offered them the capability to at least read their prayer books and as adults, teach their own children. The most fortunate petty school pupils could be offered lessons in basic numeracy skills, which of course would assist females later in managing their household budget.

For the majority of Tudor girls who received any kind of formal education this was the extent of it. A formal education was only possible if the family was able to support the child attending school, whether in terms of paying fees or managing at home without the additional labour. Though petty schools were free to attend, parents or guardians remained responsible for providing their daughter with the necessary equipment, this could be parchment and a quill or a hornbook. A hornbook was a wooden board with writing on such as the ABC or prayers, which was then covered with a sheet of horn to protect the words. Although ink could be made at home and a quill fashioned by anyone, parchment remained expensive. Therefore, hornbooks were more common amongst the humbler classes who would be attending petty schools. The parents may also be expected to make a donation towards the school. The extent and quality of the education delivered within petty schools after the basics had been taught, depended on the tutor. A tutor may well be an accomplished scholar, able to teach the children from a variety of literature. Others were humble men who had received a basic education and were passing on their knowledge in religion and grammar to local children.

Some towns and villages had no school but had the benefit of a parish priest who would use the parish church to provide a makeshift school for local children, teaching a similar curriculum as the petty school; the ABC, prayers and if possible basic reading and writing skills. Sometimes the parish priest received a token payment from those in the parish wealthy enough to make a donation. Alternatively, a wealthy resident may employ a schoolmaster to teach local children, providing him with a home as an incentive for taking the position. After 1529, education provided by parish priests increased following the Convocation of Canterbury. The Convocation ordered that all parish priests, when not engaged with their religious duties, should focus their attentions on teaching parish children to read and write.[5]

Prior to the Reformation, monasteries and some convents were able to provide education for children, though girls would not attend a monastic school. Convents were poor in comparison to monasteries and the nuns not educated in the same manner as monks. This perhaps meant that the education they could offer was not of the same standard as that provided to boys at the monasteries. That is not to say it was not a good education, it just differed according to the expectations at the time of what females should learn. Education offered by the convents usually centred on religion and practical skills. Many of the nuns would have been literate following their own training and were therefore well prepared to pass on their skills to children and novices. On occasion convents would teach French; this was the language widely known by the aristocracy and the ability to speak French was an indication of social status. Not all convents admitted children of humble origins for educational purposes but those that did, would accept only a few children (boys only up until the age of 14) for the sole purpose of education. The convents funded the children's lodgings and board using charitable contributions made to them. Other convents did not receive sufficient contributions, and therefore had to insist on parents paying for their daughter to be housed and educated there. Requiring fees for the maintenance restricted admittance to the daughters of the wealthier classes. As convents usually provided training for those entering and planning to take vows, they were limited in the number of children they could accept who were not intending to take vows. St Mary's in Winchester had the largest number of girls in its care in 1536 with a total of twenty-six, all of whom were the daughters of the aristocracy or wealthy gentlemen.[6] It is not known how many of these girls had entered the convent purely for educational purposes or had chosen a religious vocation, but it is apparent the aristocracy believed the convents provided adequate education for girls. The support for female education is evident throughout the Tudor period, though the reasoning for it was not always the same. Thomas Becon believed female education and schools specifically for girls were necessary so that women would have the capability of later instructing their own children in religion.

> Who seeth not now then, how necessary the virtuous education and bringing up of the woman-kind is? Which thing cannot be conveniently brought to pass, except schools for that purpose be appointed, and certain godly matrons ordained governesses of the same, to bring up the maids and young women in the doctrine and nurture of the Lord. And verily, in my judgment, they do no less deserve well of the christian commonweal, that found and stablish schools with honest stipends for the education and bringing up of the women-children in godliness and virtue, than they which erect and set up schools for the institution of the men-children in good letters and godly manners.[7]

Towards the end of the sixteenth century, after the convents had been dissolved, there was a scattering of boarding schools for girls. They included one in Windsor which was endowed by a woman, but they by no means replaced the opportunities previously offered by convents, in terms of the numbers of pupils across the country. These schools may have been set up in an effort to minimise the loss of educational opportunities as a result of the dissolution of the convents. It was perhaps also partly the result of the influence of the humanists encouraging female education. By this point, England had experienced two reigning queens, Mary I and Elizabeth I, both of whom were highly educated. Due to the nature of society attempting to emulate those of royalty this likely also impacted the increase in favour of female education.

Girls of the middling and upper classes received formal education in varying degrees. For some this would mean learning a similar curriculum to those who attended petty school. The difference being that the wealthier classes would most certainly learn to read and write competently in English. There was no 'correct' spelling during the early Tudor times, a variety of spellings were used for the same words so although spelling and writing could be taught, it was not with the same detail as we would expect in modern day schools. It was not until later in the sixteenth century that spelling became more standardised. There was a multitude of literature available on education, including work by the renowned scholar Desiderius Erasmus, who published *Civilitie of Childhood* in 1532 along with his previous book dedicated in 1517 to a young Henry VIII, *The Education of a Christian Prince*.[8] Much of the literature could be used by tutors and pupils but due the literacy levels not all could read and therefore, the middling and higher classes were those who benefitted most from the increasing amount of literature.

For all classes, religion remained an integral part of education, therefore prayers and psalms would be taught. Some may receive further instruction, providing their parents were accepting of female education. This could include the study of the aforementioned along with multiple languages, history, arithmetic and philosophy and further study of Christian doctrine, amongst other subjects. Of the languages, French was the most popular language for aristocratic girls to practise due to it being spoken frequently at the royal court as it was the language of diplomacy. Those who studied to this extent would have had a tutor or an educated family chaplain providing their education. Despite the spread of humanism and the success of some females, they were not allowed to attend grammar schools or universities. Tutors were therefore a valuable commodity to those wishing to learn but also incurred a cost. To receive a decent education as a female in Tudor England was only possible if their parents were willing to meet the costs. Girls like Lady Jane Grey and the Cooke sisters who received an education which was equivalent to that of a male of their rank, were the minority.

Households that took in children to polish their education would usually share a tutor, provided by the host or paid for by the parents to attend on their child at their temporary home. Those who remained at home may share some, not all, lessons with siblings like Henry VIII shared with his sister Margaret. The tutor could also split his time between pupils in the same household. William Hone was tutor to both Henry and his sister Mary but it is highly unlikely they were taught together due to the age gap. The royal siblings also shared a tutor in French. Giles Duwes taught all of the children of Henry VII and Elizabeth of York. Mary not only received instruction in French from Duwes, but also had a French companion named Jane Poppincourt join her household when she was only 5 years old.[9] Having a French playmate and a grandmother like Margaret Beaufort, who had the ability to translate French literature into English must have helped Mary master the language. Her skill in the French language would have been extremely beneficial for Mary who would later become Queen of France. It would certainly have assisted her in welcoming ambassadors to the court of her parents and later her brother.

Music and dancing formed part of a girl's education for the middling and upper ranks of society. The very wealthy would employ tutors to teach their children how to play instruments and dance masters to perfect the most fashionable dances of the time. This was not something which ended with childhood, women would continue to practise music and dance well into their adult life. Their skills with a variety of instruments were an indication of their status and was respected amongst the upper classes. Girls wishing for a place at the royal court would need to excel at music as they may be called upon to play for the royal family, providing entertainment whenever required.

Amongst the working classes, many young girls were not fortunate enough to experience any kind of formal education but would usually learn nursery rhymes and prayers by memory. Impoverished families may require young girls to start work at an early age, likely within their own household, but laws of later Tudor England stated that poor young females may be put to work by the authorities. Sometimes those as young as 6 or 7 could be sent to work for a master or mistress as an apprentice.

> And be it further enacted, that it shall be lawful for the said Churchwardens and Overseers, or the greater part of them, by the

assent of any two Justices of the Peace aforesaid, to bind any such children as aforesaid, to be apprentices, where they shall see convenient, till such man child shall come to the age of four and twenty years, and such woman child to the age of one and twenty years or the time of her marriage.[10]

For girls this young, the work could include serving another family, working in the fields during times of harvest, weeding, or what may have been more enjoyable to them, feeding and caring for the family's livestock. For some families, their livestock may have been a single pig or a couple of chickens to provide eggs. Children could assist their parents or mistress in tending to gardens, collecting produce for the kitchen, planting new vegetables or picking flowers for the mistress of the household to dry and use later. If a child grew up on a farm, or secured work on another farm, there was much work that could be done by them: keeping crops safe by acting as real-life scarecrows; feeding and mucking out animals; collecting eggs; helping prepare the soil for the planting of crops; and assisting with the harvest. The more difficult tasks, which may be reserved for slightly older children, were perhaps collecting and carrying water and milk or venturing to and from the market with produce. For the destitute, very young children even faced the prospect of being sent out by their parents to beg.

Parents wandering the country in search of employment were seen as vagrants, and were not welcome in most parishes due to the burden they imposed if employment was not forthcoming. If a vagrant mother was to give birth in a parish other than her own, the child as well as any other dependent children could be removed from her and settled within the parish. For some children this may be the last time they had contact with their parents and siblings as the children were apprenticed or placed in other households as servants. Regardless of whether they had to help in their own household, were sent to another or apprenticed by the parish authorities, having to start work from such an early age left no time or ability to gain any form of education other than the little they could gain at home from their mother. Some apprentices fared much better and found themselves bound to a master or mistress that encouraged education. All apprentices would at least be taught deportment and manners as this could impact the trade if an apprentice was rude or not socially aware of expectations. If a master or mistress had their own children, they would perhaps allow the apprentice to share some of their lessons, at least basic numeracy and learning to read and write. This experience could provide a pauper child with the skills to improve themselves beyond their expectations.

The age of 6 or 7 marked the end of infancy for a Tudor child and at this stage they would begin to learn the expectations of them as an adult. By this age, young girls should be capable of taking care of their own personal hygiene; washing their hands and face, cleaning their teeth and maintaining their hair, at least to a basic standard. This was an age where the disparity between the lower and upper classes became more apparent, and the following years would be completely unalike for young females of differing classes and wealth. For the humble classes, this meant they were put to work either in their own household or with another, though it was more common to keep children at home until adolescence, if the family could afford to do so. For families who relied on parish relief, this was the age when the parish could place a child in the household of another in order to reduce the financial burden on the parish. A child placed in another household became a servant and was expected to work from such a young age as a means of providing towards her own maintenance and upkeep. Some children may have been lucky enough to have a kind master or mistress who could afford to allow them a little more time as a child and allow them to gain more of an education. For others the labour of a child was much needed assistance for the household at very little cost to themselves.

The girls who were placed in these households would begin learning to clean, launder, cook and the general running of a household. If a family was able to, they themselves may arrange a placement for their daughter in a household of a better standing than their own. Here she may begin learning housewifery, including, how to manage servants, understanding the produce of the home and arranging hospitality for visitors when required. One aspect of this was learning the etiquette of seating arrangements. Seating was not so simple as guests arriving and sitting where they chose but was organised according to rank and importance. The head of the household would take precedence at the top table unless they were joined by someone of greater rank at which point, they would share their table. Other guests took up the rest of the tables with their status considered, those of least importance being placed the furthest away from the top table. If you got this wrong you could certainly cause great offence so it was an important lesson for young women, especially those who may be hosting the aristocracy later in life. A large portion of girls were sent to households of relatives, even if distant relatives, and would in effect be serving their own family. There was no shame in serving your own family. Due to the ranks of society, it could be advantageous to find a placement within a relative's household if they were of a higher social standing, even queens had their sisters and other female relatives serving them. For daughters of wealthy and aristocratic families, this age often meant little, as they could continue their comfortable lives until they were older, unless it was thought beneficial for them to be sent to another's household at this point. Lady Jane Grey was only 9 years old when she entered the household of Kateryn Parr where she continued her education. If they remained at home the period of childhood was extended, though they would assist their mother, thus learning in the process.

Households with additional facilities such as dairies, livestock, and stillrooms presented additional opportunities to learn skills. Girls working or residing in these households could learn medicinal remedies as well as their application, the care of animals, the making of dairy products and usually the brewing of ale. We may think it surprising that young girls would be learning to brew but during the Tudor era, ale was the most common drink. Water was not popular as it was not guaranteed to be clean; milk was sometimes drunk but usually by the young or sick. Milk was primarily used for making butter and cheese therefore usually only the whey was left to drink. Fruit juice was almost non-existent and wine was the preserve of the wealthy. Ale could of course be brewed to be very weak, known as small-ale so children would not be drunk but it remains surprising that children drank ale from a very young age. As ale was so popular it made sense for young girls to learn to brew early so she could assist her family and also know how to provide for her own family when she grew up. In a sense of how we perceive childhood today it would be fair to say that the humbler the child, the earlier they had to grow up in the Tudor era, taking on the responsibility of working and contributing to their family from a very young age.

## Chapter Two
# Adolescence

Adolescence in the Tudor era was the end of childhood, though the term 'adolescence' itself was not used at the time. Contemporaries believed adolescence began around 7 years old for girls and ended at around 14 years old, though as we shall see some adult decisions could be made before they reached supposed adulthood. By this point some girls had already left home to begin their working life. Tudor girls who had been privileged enough to remain at home past the age that others had been set to work, would now usually be sent to another household in their adolescence. This was a custom known as 'putting girls out'. For the middling classes this meant a period of domestic service which may end upon marriage unless they married someone within the household and were both permitted to continue their placements. For the upper classes the experience could consist of a period of training to ready them for their future as a wife and the lady of their own household. A lot of this training was through observation as they had done at home. The governesses or gentlewomen who supervised young ladies in the absence of their mother were ideal role models for a young girl to learn her skills in becoming an adult. Many would have started this training much earlier in their lives at home but this age provided the opportunity to develop and perfect her skills. The aristocracy would take every opportunity available to place their daughters in households of higher-ranking families, sometimes their own kin. The aim was to not only provide training for their daughter but also enable the daughter to create her own network of friends, alliances and possibly gain assistance in arranging a marriage for herself in the future.

Even the humblest of households often had servants. Domestic service was not restricted to the middling and upper classes although the experience may differ substantially in respect of the tasks expected of servants whilst employed or apprenticed. Some humbler families with multiple daughters could afford to keep one daughter at home whilst others were sent to other households. The remaining daughter would be expected to work within the household, whether this be providing childcare for young siblings, or contributing to the housework; laundering, cleaning, working in the dairy or caring for livestock. She may also be asked to deliver produce to neighbouring estates if her family had the good fortune to be asked to supply them with particular items. These daughters would not receive payment for their work as she was contributing to her own family and upkeep but if she did have spare time, she could supplement this with casual work within another household. This opportunity may result in further employment when she eventually left home or would at least give her the skills to manage her own household upon marriage. The position secured when joining another aristocratic household was dependent partly on the relationship between the two families. Some young ladies joined as servants, taking up the role of a lady's maid to the mistress whilst others would be accepted as family and treated almost like a daughter of the mistress. If the latter, she would no doubt still be expected to learn from her experience during her time there and assist her mistress but would be treated as family as opposed to a servant. It would be a rare household where young ladies would have their own chambers. Even the households of the wealthiest families would have a chamber that was shared by the young ladies residing in their household. Servants would have been separate from those who had joined to learn from their mistress. Servants would reside in servant quarters if they had the available rooms, but as with those of rank the females would be kept separate from the male servants. Catherine Howard resided in a shared chamber with other girls, when she lived with her step-grandmother, Agnes Howard, Dowager Duchess of Norfolk. The aim was to ensure the girls remained chaste and access was often barred at night with the mistress of the household having the door locked and the key returned to her.

Regardless of class, all young females who experienced work or training in another household would learn the art of housewifery. Entering the service of another household gave young women the opportunity to learn all the skills they required later in life to be the mistress of her own household and a good wife to her future spouse. Skills ranged from the daily tasks of keeping a home through to managing servants and where possible, the care of children. If they happened to reside in a household with babies or young children it was an additional opportunity for young ladies to learn how to care them, and the expectation was she would have her own when she married. Whether residing at home, or in the household of another, young ladies would benefit from any opportunity to expand their skills. At this point she could learn how make a breech cloth (nappy) and how to bathe, feed and swaddle a baby, including the preparation of swaddling bands ahead of the birth. She would be able to observe how their mother or nursery staff interacted with babies or children once they were relieved of their swaddling bands. Those intended for a household where she would be required to manage her own household accounts would benefit from observing her employer when she undertook her accounting duties. As mistress of her own household, she would require basic numeracy skills but also the ability to understand the accounting process. Girls would not usually undertake this task whilst in service but could try and learn as much as possible, in preparation for their own home.

Cooking was a skill which was required by all women. Adolescent girls would be expected to learn at least the basics of cooking even if she could not manage to learn to cook full meals. The very wealthy may never need to rely on their own skills in the kitchen but they would be unable to manage kitchen staff, plan meals for the household or accomplish the hospitality expected if they had no knowledge of the workings of a kitchen. Some who could afford to employ cooks still enjoyed spending time in the kitchen and would often cook themselves, whether for their own family or preparing food as gifts. Lady Lisle, wife of Arthur Plantagenet, 1st Viscount Lisle, prepared marmalade and conserves as gifts for others, including Henry VIII. Anne Basset, daughter of Lady Lisle wrote 'Madam, the King doth so well like the conserves you sent him last, that his Grace commanded me to write unto you for more of the codiniac (quince marmalade) of the clearest making, and of the conserve of damsons; and this as soon as may be.'[1] These skills were possibly passed on to her daughters when they were adolescents. There are certainly many recipes for the preservation of fruit at the time. Basic cookery skills were not just beneficial for the kitchen but also for concocting herbal remedies which was certainly a practical skill the majority of Tudor women had experience in. Knowing how to treat common complaints and illnesses was also a valuable skill for a woman and her family. The knowledge and skill in this subject was respected amongst society and young ladies, if they hadn't already, could begin experimenting, practising and observing others in the preparation and making of a variety of applications. To develop skills of this nature, girls would need to learn to differentiate between plants, understand their benefits and if applicable identify dangerous species. The next steps would be to learn which part of the plant was to be used for specific recipes, and how to treat the plant, for example, if she needed to boil or dehydrate it. Lastly, they would need to learn how to store the ingredients and build up their own knowledge of recipes.

The highest achievement in service would be to secure a position within the household of a duchess, princess or even the queen. To achieve this, a girl had to be noticed and be likeable. This meant adolescence was a time to shine for daughters of the aristocracy. The appeal of serving as a maid or lady-in-waiting in an aristocratic or royal household must have been a glittering prospect. They would have the chance to mingle with those who could provide opportunities for them and their families as well as the chance to receive gifts of clothing and jewels amongst other tokens of affection. These young ladies would need to take advantage of all opportunities to present themselves in a manner that would recommend them to the households of those in the ranks above their own. For this reason, social etiquette was vital for aristocratic children. As little girls imitated their mother, young ladies who had been sent to another household could learn much by watching and imitating the behaviours of the lady of the household. They would need to ensure they were aware of how to greet those of differing ranks, to show obeisance to their elders and how to behave around their social betters. Girls will have learnt to curtsey from a young age but this training did not cease on mastering a curtsey or other shows of deference. There were other skills young ladies needed to master: witty conversation, topics to avoid as a female, mingling with the opposite sex without causing any scandal and, if she wished to head towards the royal court, the art of courtly love. Music and dancing practice that began in childhood would continue on a regular basis. Adolescent girls who were not yet in service but were instead placed in another household to learn, would certainly continue with lessons in music and dance, sharing tutors and dance masters with other residents and possibly the mistress herself. Some employed dance masters from abroad to teach them (and any girls residing with them) lessons in the latest, most fashionable dances. Practice at dancing was not just a form of entertainment to the aristocracy, it was an important aspect of a girl's education in order to make her more attractive and noticeable to the opposite sex and higher-ranking women who could take her into their service. Music and dancing were both regular pastimes at aristocratic and royal homes and offered an opportunity for young ladies to show off their skill, partake in entertainments and meet prospective partners in an acceptable setting. There were a variety of instruments available at the time, the most common amongst aristocratic girls were the lute, clavichord and virginals.

Boys could be educated in all manner of subjects from history, warfare and law amongst a wide variety depending on his career aims. Girls would need to be educated to some degree within the upper social ranks as she would be expected to participate in intellectual debates, entertain guests within her home and of course converse with her husband when she married. Girls did not require the same level of academic education as their male siblings but the upper ranks of society would be expecting a degree of intelligence when socialising. There was no better time to learn and practice all of these things than when a young lady's own family or that of her mistress had guests come to visit. Hospitality was the remit of females and therefore, adolescence was a good time for females to learn how a household would prepare for events, which could range from small dinner parties with a few guests, to large gatherings catering for many.

Whether they remain in their own home or were sent to another household, daughters of the aristocracy would experience a range of visits from different rank guests. Rather than being able to join the visit as a guest, she would need to learn how to behave as a hostess, how to greet each person by their rank, the order of the serving of food and drink and ensure she behaved modestly. It was not just the visit itself that she would learn how to navigate but also the planning beforehand, the teaching of which would be passed on by her mother, other female relatives or the mistress of the household she was training at. Arranging a party or visit may seem easy enough for us today, but to plan a successful event in the Tudor era, a hostess needed to guarantee provisions were ordered well in advance to secure delivery in time. Entertainments would also need to be booked as musicians or other entertainers may have needed to travel a fair distance to appear. There was also the consideration of board, ensuring all who were due to stay had adequate rooms and bedding; if the household did not have sufficient materials such as bed linen, they would need to borrow from friends or family with plenty of time to prepare the rooms. Party planning in the Tudor era was something that aristocratic females would need to learn in order to impress their counterparts but also to help her husband with his own interests by impressing his guests and behaving with impeccable decorum. Learning these skills from a young age could be extremely beneficial to those who would later mix in the highest circles of society. Once all guests had arrived and were settled, young ladies could then take advantage of the situation and show off their skills in entertaining conversations and dancing. If a young lady impressed the guests, she may have been rewarded with the opportunity to move to a more prominent home and could from then on work her way up through society if she wished, although on occasion the girls chose to remain with a specific mistress if they had formed a bond.

All classes would develop their skills in needlework during this time in their lives. Females of the lower classes would be learning how to mend and sew clothing and knit warmer clothes and accessories for the colder months whilst wealthier young females, although they would still learn how to mend and make clothes, would also increase their skills by learning to embroider. Embroidery was a pastime as well as work and was often used as a way to pass time, particularly when poor weather halted outdoor pastimes, but also for charitable donations. Women were often working on pieces for the poor, gifts for individuals or for churches, including altar cloths, book bindings and fashionable accessories such as gloves and sleeves.

Although a formal education was not deemed necessary for girls, those fortunate enough to have parents who believed in a full education for females, could expect to continue their education throughout adolescence. Lessons could start as early as 8:00am and their day spent in various lessons of literature, languages, music, and dancing until late afternoon. Arithmetic was another important subject for the girls to learn how to manage the household accounts. They were allowed breaks in between lessons, the main being the midday meal for wealthier households, and once their daily lessons were over, they may choose to spend time on other pursuits whether they be reading, riding, more dancing or needlework. Reading was an encouraged pastime during the Tudor era, though not all genres were recommended by scholars, particularly for females. The Bible was the most popular of the era, followed by John Foxe's, *Book of Martyrs*. There were various subjects available; languages, gardening, mathematics, chivalric stories and the works of the saints. A little bit of law would not go amiss in case a woman ever had to manage her estates and understand her rights in relation to property. Religious literature and stories of morality were the most recommended followed by conduct books, whilst romance was frowned upon. Although there was a group of scholars who began to encourage female learning during the Tudor era, it was not welcomed by all. Those who were encouraged to learn by their father may face criticism from their mother who believed they did not require such a comprehensive education.

Some fathers took the opportunity to send their daughters abroad in an effort to further their education, polish their social skills and practise their lessons in languages. A placement in a foreign court was hoped to pave the way for a position in the English royal court. Lady Lisle sent two of her daughters to the households of the French nobility and the Boleyn sisters spent time at the French court. Mary Boleyn travelled to France in 1514 when she was approximately 14 years old. Her father, Thomas Boleyn had secured her a position as a chamberer for Mary Tudor who was travelling to France to marry the King of France, Louis XII. Though her time in France was fairly short-lived as a result of Louis XII dying a few months after the wedding, it was an experience that set up Mary for a role as a maid of honour when she finally reached the English court and would have been the most excellent opportunity to perfect her French language skills.

Latin remained the language of the Church and law. It was mostly studied by men but later in the Tudor era, some females also began to study Latin. The study of Latin enabled women to read the scriptures and religious doctrine. It also opened up opportunities to read the classics such as the works of Cicero and Aesop's *Fables*, that were becoming more popular with the Renaissance and the humanist curriculum. Prior to this, even the most pious of women had not fully understood the prayers they recited, nor the prayer books they used during services. Any legal documents drafted in Latin had to be read to them or translated, placing a reliance upon men. The increase in women learning Latin meant they could become more independent, amongst the aristocracy at least. They had the ability to read and understand legal and religious literature without the assistance of a man.

Young females were not expected to, nor allowed to enter academic occupations and therefore academic education was viewed as superfluous. As with all things there were exceptions to this. Elizabeth I is well known for her intellectual abilities as well as Lady Jane Grey and of course, Margaret

More-Roper, the daughter of Sir Thomas More who championed female education. Lady Jane Grey was an avid reader whom the scholar and tutor Roger Ascham praised for her intellectual abilities; her education was partly due to her own keen interests rather than her parents' encouragement. When visiting Lady Jane, Ascham found her reading Plato's *Phædon Platonis* [On the Soul] in Greek whilst the rest of her family were out hunting and when asked why she had not joined them she replied 'I wisse, all theire sporte in the Parke is but a shadoe to that pleasure, that I find in *Plato*: Alas good folke, they neuer felt, what trewe pleasure ment'. Ascham asked how she came to be so interested in learning, Lady Jane explained 'One of the greatest benefites, that euer God gaue me, is, that he sent me so sharpe and seuere Parentes, and so ientle a scholemaster. For whé I am in presence either of father or mother, whether I speake, kepe silence, sit, stand, or go, eate, drinke, be merie, or sad, be sowing, playing, dauncing, or ding anie thing els, I must do it, as it were, in soch weight, mesure, and number, euen so perfitelie, as God made the world, or else I am so sharplie taunted, so cruellie threatened, yea presentlie some tymes, with pinches, nippes, and bobbes, and other waies, which I will not name, for the honor I beare them, so without measure misordered, that I thinke my selfe in hell, till tyme cum, that I must go to M. Elmer, who teacheth me so ientie, so pleasantly, with soch faire allurements to learning, that I thinke all the tyme nothing, whiles I am with him. And when I am called from him, I fall on weeping, because, what soeuer I do els, but learning, is ful of grief, trouble, feare, and whole misliking vnto me: And thus my booke, hath bene so moch my pleasure, & bringeth dayly to me more pleasure & more, that in respect of it, all other pleasures, in very deede, be but trifles and troubles vnto me'.[2] This recollection by Ascham also gives insight into how Lady Jane spent her time sewing, dancing and practising music. It is apparent her parents had high standards to be punishing her and perhaps her sisters for anything other than perfection, therefore Lady Jane found solace in her books and under the tutelage of her tutor Master Elmer. The fact that Lady Jane studied Greek, Spanish, Latin, French and Italian as a child and in adolescence advanced to Hebrew, Arabic and the ancient language of the Chaldeans (Chaldee), is a remarkable accomplishment for a girl in the sixteenth century and is certainly not standard practice for girls at the time.[3]

During these years of adolescence, families of young females may begin seeking a husband for their daughter. To secure an advantageous match young females would be expected to be the image of Christian virtues. According to an Antwerp merchant residing in London, unmarried young females in the Low Countries had more freedom than those in England, which shows families were anxious to ensure a young female's reputation could not be tarnished by reducing opportunities for young females to misbehave or do anything they may later regret.[4]

It should be noted that wardship was existent during the Tudor era. Wardship gave the monarch the right over custody of heirs and heiresses who were minors. Therefore, if a child lost their father or both parents, they may become a ward of the Crown. The Crown had the right to the child's income from their lands up until they came of age so could be extremely profitable. The guardian had the responsibility of managing the estates of the young ward and ensuring they were taken care of, so although it could be profitable, it would be a lot of work to hold responsibility for all wards. They also had the ability to arrange marriages for wards, which again could be valuable. Therefore, the Crown could sell wardships, handing over responsibility but also access to their income to the buyer. The individual that bought the wardship would gain management of the income as the Crown had, and the right to select a marriage partner for the heir, usually their own child to further their own ambition. There were few heiresses during the Tudor era due to the practice of primogeniture resulting in very few girls inheriting their fathers' estate. This made the purchase of female wardships much more competitive and as a result, lucrative. To obtain the wardship of a young heiress could provide financial support to the guardian until she came of age and they could betroth the girl to their own son, if they had one, connecting the two families in the process. This also meant that the guardian had control over the bride's dowry which would ultimately be paid to them. If they had no son, they may choose to sell on the wardship at a profit to another family who did have a son the girl could be betrothed to. Towards the end of the Tudor period, wardships were largely sold to the family of the child. For young females who had been under a wardship they became free at the age of 16 unlike their male counterparts who were required to reach the age of 21 to end their wardship.

As childhood was short for impoverished young females, so was adolescence for many wealthier or aristocratic young females. Their adolescence ultimately ended with their marriage, which for this group of society occurred earlier than their humbler sisters. For those who did not have marriage in their future, they might enter a convent. Females appear to have entered convents at various ages. Dame Matilda Lee took her vows before adolescence at the age of 12 but others joined convents at an earlier or much later age.[5] Convents would provide training for its novices and a girl may further her own education once settled. If a family could not afford to pay for a daughter to enter a convent, she may still be accepted, but without a donation to the convent, she could only progress as far as a lay sister. This made her the equivalent of a domestic servant within the convent. She would not reach any higher than that but for those who truly wished for a life of piety this was still a suitable option for them.

Adolescence was an important stage in life for Tudor women, particularly those of the aristocracy. It was a time to practise and perfect the skills they had been learning since childhood. The range of skills could be as basic as perfecting a braid in the hair so it could be coiled under a headdress through to mastering a difficult piece of music to be performed in front of guests. If a young lady could impress those around her, she may find herself appointed to the royal court. For others, it was a time to start earning an income, learning how to manage a household and prepare herself for married life. For parents or those responsible for the young lady this was the time to focus on ensuring she was aware of her own respectability, knew how to behave around the opposite sex as well as avoid any situations which may cause her to be regarded as unsuitable as a bride.

> Be occupied wither doing some profitable thyng for your family, or elles readynge some godly book, let them not reade bokes of fables, of fond lyght love, but call upon God to have pure hartes and chaste, that they might cleve only to thyr spouse.[6]

## Chapter Three
# Tudor Brides

To find a suitable husband and marry was the aim of the majority of females in the Tudor era. Marriage was an expectation of society as well as being one of the seven Holy Sacraments, therefore being extremely important to the Church. In modern society, we would expect a marriage to be an arrangement made fundamentally between the couple, with little interference from others unless their input was requested. During the sixteenth century, a marriage could involve not only the couple but also kin, friends and even whole communities. By the time of their marriage young females had spent years learning what the expectations would be of them when they became a wife. The expectations of a wife were enforced by parents, the Church and the available conduct literature at the time. There could be no doubt that all brides came to their wedding on the understanding that they would obey their husband. The specific expectations of a wife were dictated by the social standing of the couple. As most people married within their own social ranks, they will have been aware of their anticipated role from an early age.

Although individuals were thought of as children until around the age of 14, females came of age at 12 years old with regards to consenting to marriage, whilst males did not come of age until 14. Despite being regarded as old enough to marry, a male could not inherit his estates until he was 21 years old, unless exempted by the monarch. Families could arrange marriages in the form of pre-contracts and betrothals prior to this point, but the families must wait until the children came of age to give their consent before a wedding could proceed. Marriages at such a young age were more common amongst the aristocracy and royalty where families aimed to use the marriage of the children to secure alliances, improve social status, expand dynasties and increase landholdings. The objective behind an early marriage was that if a female married once she was able to reproduce, it gave her more opportunity of producing an heir for the family. It also meant that the economic and social advantages that were hoped to result from the marriage, could be realised sooner. On occasion, young girls were sent to reside in the household of their intended groom so the children could grow up together. Alternatively, the couple would remain living with their own parents until they reached the age where they could both consent to and consummate the marriage. Three daughters of Sir Thomas Howard married young, all three being less than 16 years old, two of them marrying their fathers' wards. Following their weddings, all three daughters remained living in the family home and were treated as dependent children due to their youthful age. Two of the grooms moved into the home of their brides whilst the third groom remained living with his own parents until he was older.[1] Although young females could legally consent to marriage at the age of 12, even the wealthy and aristocracy did not commonly marry at such a young age. In the sixteenth century, the average age amongst the aristocracy was 20 years old for women, and 22 for men.[2] Amongst the lower classes the average age was higher at around the mid-20s. Females who married prior to the age of 21 required parental or guardian consent. This requirement was later confirmed in 1571 by the Convocation of Canterbury which stated that a marriage could not be contracted without parental consent. Lady Margaret Beaufort, mother of Henry VII, was married at the age of 12 to Edmund Tudor. Lady Margaret gave birth to Henry when she was only 13 years old. It is possible the birth resulted in her either being unable or unwilling to have any more children. Scholars also felt that the ages of 12 and 14 were much too young to be able to consent to or consummate a marriage. The esteemed scholar, Juan Luis Vives, advised an age of 18 years old as the earliest age for marriage.[3] The majority of working-class women waited until their mid-20s to marry. This was perhaps not through choice but it did give them time to get to know their prospective partner, mature and most importantly, understand the consequences of marriage. A later marriage age also enabled women to work and consequently save money towards their wedding and the setting up of a marital home.

The process of securing a marriage began with the search for an appropriate match. This could be a long process in itself. As with many subjects that were written about at the time, there was advice on the characteristics men should look for in a prospective bride, there was not however, the same advice for women, or at least no record of this advice. Instead, the advice for females was largely focused on how to make themselves agreeable to a potential husband. Robert Cleaver wrote that men seeking a wife, should seriously consider a female's reputation, her appearance and dress, her intelligence and the company she kept. The topics women spoke about was an important factor for men to contemplate as were those they chose to remain silent on.[4] Parents or guardians usually led the search for a suitor, particularly amongst the wealthy and aristocratic ranks of society. It was not unusual for other family members, friends and acquaintances to also make suggestions and sometimes make enquiries on behalf of the family before the potential couple were even aware of a possible match. It was often a wise step to include others in the search as they may have information about the prospective suitor including financial information or whether they were in favour with the nobility and the monarch. Parents with connections at the royal court may ask them to keep an ear to the ground for potential suitors for their daughter and may travel to court hoping for the opportunity to find a new son-in-law. Parents usually had their own preferred qualities in a potential son-in-law, one of which would be the land he held or would later inherit. Fathers would sometimes specify a sum of income they expected of their future son-in-law before they would even consider a marriage to their daughter. If the father were to die before a daughter married, the sum may be specified in his will, whilst others specified dowries would only be settled if the daughter married someone of their own rank or above.[5] One of the most interesting wills of the time is that of Sir Anthony Denny, a close friend of Henry VIII. His will goes into much detail on the education and religion of his children who were all minors at the time of his death in 1549. Denny made arrangements for each of his daughters to receive 20 marks per year whilst they were minors. They were later to be gifted 600 marks each for their dowries, with Denny stating his preference that he would like them to marry the sons of his heirs who were his wards at the time, 'one liking the other to be joined in matrimony'. He also specified that his widow was to have custody and the care of the children following his death, requesting she was to ensure there were 'tokens and agreement of faithful love' between the couples before they could marry. This is strong evidence that regardless of the financial situation, Denny as a father, was attempting to ensure his daughters would have happy marriages.[6]

Some friends and family members may introduce the couple whilst in a social setting before any serious negotiations began. It was not unheard of for men to initiate the matchmaking, all that dancing practice whilst they were younger may pay off, if a young lady was noticed during a court entertainment. If she proved herself to be an elegant dancer that behaved modestly, she would most certainly catch the attention of at least one courtier, particularly if she were new to court. A suitor may then try to find out who the lady was and her marital status. If more than one man showed interest, the lady's family could consider her preference as well as the settlements offered by the parties. This was dependent on whether the family had any interest in progressing a courtship with any of the interested parties. Another reason to excel at dancing would be to be noticed by the monarch and as a result be chosen to partake in courtly entertainments. Those who regularly took part in entertainments and masques were the people who would be in favour with the monarch, but were also noted by visiting guests, ambassadors and diplomats from abroad. Those in favour with the monarch would be attractive to other courtiers who were hoping to improve their own prospects. Mary Tudor, Anne Boleyn and Mary Boleyn were regular participants in court entertainments.

Those searching for a potential spouse would have to ensure there were no impediments: age, consent if under 21, a pre-contract, or prohibited degrees of consanguinity or affinity. There had been restrictions on who could not marry since the ancient times but during the Tudor era a table was published providing a list of the prohibited degrees. The *Table of Kindred and Affinity* clarifies the relations between people, whether by birth (consanguinity) or marriage (affinity), which are prohibited within marriage. Initially, the banned relations were up to four degrees of kinship. By 1540 the degrees had been reduced to two.[7] The degrees were based on the common relative, for instance, siblings were first degree, cousins, second. Once past the fourth degree a couple may marry but could benefit from applying for a dispensation allowing them to marry to further quash any doubts of the relationship. Examples of excluded relationships included sister-in-law, daughter-in-law, aunt and niece amongst others. Godparents were also forbidden as spouses until 1540, as the Church considered them to be spiritual kin to their godchildren. Godchildren could also not marry the children of their own godparents.[8]

Once a match had been found and the parties had agreed in principle that they were happy for discussions to begin, the next stage could proceed; the financial negotiations. Every marriage regardless of social status involved a transfer of property in the form of a marriage settlement. Marriage settlements were usually a negotiation between the families of the couple, most often between the fathers or their representative. Of course, if a suitor was found and the potential parties informed, the negotiations may not go any further if one of them were to refuse the match.

There were four financial aspects involved in the majority of marriage settlements: the *dowry, jointure, dower* and the last will and testament of the husband. The *dowry*, also referred to as the 'marriage portion', was the payment made by the bride's family, usually by her father to the groom or his father, or alternatively the woman's master if he was kind enough to gift a dowry for his female servants.[9] The dowry had no specific format and could consist of property, land, chattels, even livestock up to an agreed amount which had been negotiated between the parties and could be paid in instalments. The amount varied greatly according to wealth and status, the average sum for the daughter of the nobility was more than double that of the gentry.[10] For some families, the dowry placed great financial strain on them. As soon as a daughter was born, the parents were aware they would be required to fund a dowry if their daughter survived to adulthood and wished to marry. For those families with multiple daughters the cost implications could be immense. For some young women with no dowry, and few eligible men to choose from in her immediate area, the seeking of a spouse may mean she had to move around the country. These women may work at different households until they found a prospective spouse. In the meantime they had hopefully managed to save some of their wages towards her own dowry and contribute towards setting up a marital home.

For many girls, her dowry, was in effect, her inheritance, received early or, if her father had already passed away, was given as a specific bequest that her inheritance be paid in the form of her dowry, when she came to marry. Only the very wealthy could afford to provide appropriate dowries as well as generous bequests of inheritance for their daughters. Once the dowry was paid, the groom was not obliged to use it in any beneficial way for the bride, it was his or his fathers to do with as they wished. Quite often it was a sum of money which was much needed to maintain the groom's family estate or pay a debt. Although the concept of a dowry appears straightforward, it was not without problems. The first instalment was often paid either on the date the marriage was contracted or on the day of the wedding. If a couple were betrothed at an early age and the families agreed to pay the first instalment at that point, one or both parties could renounce the match when they came of age to consent. There was also the possibility that one of the parties may die before the marriage could be consummated. If the first instalment was paid months or even years prior, there is a possibility the groom's family would not have the resources to return the dowry. Under these circumstances a bride's family was within their rights to sue for the return of the dowry. To so do, could place in them in a predicament if they were marrying their daughter into a powerful family. What if one of the families was to be approached with a more beneficial match for their child? According to ecclesiastical law, the dowry was to be returned if the marriage did not go ahead with most marriage contracts stipulating that the dowry was to repaid if one of the parties died or did not consent. To breach the contract for a better offer simply meant the more preferable marriage could not go ahead as one party was already pre-contracted, therefore, it would not be a common occurrence. They could attempt to obtain a licence or dispensation to marry another and return the dowry but neither were guaranteed.

The *jointure* was the property and income from land that the groom or his father was settling on the couple to assist them in setting up a marital home and maintaining themselves. The property was settled on the couple in a joint tenure and therefore, if one party died the other would retain rights of the property alone, usually for their lifetime. On the death of both parties the property would revert back to the original estate or to their children if the husband had inherited the estate. The jointure was usually calculated to be an adequate proportion in value per annum of the dowry, with ten per cent being a common figure, but could certainly be negotiated.[11] If a bridegroom was marrying into a higher-ranking family, the bride's family may negotiate for a much higher jointure as the advantages were greater for the bridegroom. Alternatively, this also meant the dowry could be negotiated to be much higher if it was the bride that was marrying upwards in rank. If the bride's family were not forthcoming in paying the instalments of the dowry, the jointure could be withheld. If the groom were to die before the dowry was paid in full, the bride's family may be tempted to cease payments but the consequences could be dismal for the bride. As a new widow, she could be left with no jointure or alternative income and now on bad terms with her in-laws.

The Tudor era could be turbulent and some families forfeited their lands to the Crown for taking part in rebellions. The actions of men certainly impacted their wives during these events. Sir William Gascoygne had petitioned Thomas Cromwell in 1537 on behalf of his daughter, Dorothy. When she had married Sir Marmaduke, her father had paid 1,000 marks as her dowry. Marmaduke was the son and heir of Sir Robert Constable, who, having taken part in the Pilgrimage of Grace had been attainted for treason and as a result, had lost the family lands to the Crown. Gascoygne was understandably concerned about his daughter's future as well as his own ability to maintain her if the lands could not be retrieved. It appears in this case there was some empathy shown and Gascoygne was granted the wardship of the jointure lands and the income from them until his son-in-law reached the age of 16.[12]

The *dower* was the arrangement made for income the bride would receive to maintain herself and any dependent children if she were widowed. The jointure and dower were interchangeable with the dower being an entitlement under the common law if no previous settlement had been arranged. During the Tudor era it became much more common for jointures to be used as opposed to dowers. The reason being a dower left opportunity for non-payment upon the death of the husband. His family could easily cease payment whilst it was much more difficult to take back property which had been settled within the jointure. Amongst the aristocracy there was also a risk that the estate may not be able to maintain a generous dower in the future without having to split the bulk of the estate. Splitting up an estate was something the aristocracy were averse to doing, particularly with the added complexities of primogeniture. It was much more secure for a bride to have a property and land assigned for her to use for life, than an agreed amount which may not be affordable when it was later required. For the humbler ranks of society it likely made little difference as they often had little to leave upon their death.

Lastly, the last will and testament of a husband, in which he could bequeath his wife much more than the agreed dower and jointure, providing his estate was not entailed. The agreement of the marriage settlement could take months to finalise especially where wealthy families were involved. All four aspects did not apply to every couple, many did not have the financial means to pay a dowry or jointure and instead were more similar to today's arrangements of a couple saving for marriage then pooling resources. Often a couple would meet through their employment within the same household and would continue residing there, although following marriage they may be offered a larger room as a couple to share, as opposed to sharing rooms with other servants. Alternatively, if this could not be accommodated or the couple chose to, they could move to their own home.

All families wished their daughters to have a financially secure marriage. For the majority of the population this often-meant marriage to a man who had secured employment and possibly had a home of his own. For the aristocracy it was much more complex. Although they primarily wished for a financially secure match, if it were possible, as an added benefit, they would aim to marry their daughters into families that were wealthier, more powerful or higher ranking than their own. However, they did not restrict themselves to matches within the ranked elite of society. Aristocratic families who were perhaps financially struggling to maintain their lifestyle could seek a match outside of the aristocracy particularly for a son. To obtain a match for a son would mean the bride's family would be required to provide the groom's family with a dowry. The dowry could be a substantial sum, particularly as their daughter would be marrying into the aristocracy and therefore creating a wealth of opportunities for her family. It also meant her children would be born into the ranks of the aristocracy, an opportunity that could be extremely tempting to some families. The arrangement would give the groom's family a cash-injection whilst they lost little in return. Their son remained the heir to estates, though they may be asked to show favour to other family members with regards to their business ventures. Aristocratic fathers hoping to marry their daughter off may also look outside of the social elite as there was potential to reduce the amount of the expected dowry. A man marrying into the aristocracy could gain much, particularly if he married an heiress, in terms of influence, title and estates so may be willing to forgo a substantial dowry from the bride's family. They may even be willing to pay a reverse dowry on the understanding that if the father of the heiress later had a legitimate son, the payment would be returned. The payment of a reverse dowry was not restricted to those outside of the aristocracy marrying into the ranks but also amongst their own ranks where the groom would be benefitting from marrying a heiress. The purpose was to ensure the bride was secure in her inheritance, therefore her family could keep the payment on her behalf for her future if it were required.[13]

For the humbler classes, there may be little involvement from family in the arrangements for marriage. They had much more freedom to meet prospective partners through work or social events such as fairs, church festivals and the market. Some of the negotiations were not required as neither party had little to offer. These couple may spend time getting to know one another before agreeing to a betrothal with a gift being exchanged as a form of acceptance that they will marry when possible. This could be months or even years from the point of betrothal dependent on the time the couple needed to save enough to set up their own household.

Whilst a couple was saving, or in other cases where lengthy negotiations were progressing, the couple could get to know one another. They were able to spend time in each other's company; this was in effect, Tudor courtship, and the sole aim was to end in marriage. The couple may visit each other to eat, read or attend the same entertainments, although they would be unlikely to spend time together in private. A chaperone would usually be present, for example, a girl's mother would listen if one of them were reading to the other and family members or friends would be present for dinners eaten together. It was only at public entertainments where a couple may sit or dance together without requiring a chaperone. There were some who chose to ask their parents or other family members to meet a suggested match before they themselves did, at a dinner for instance, to get a family opinion. If the family provided a good account, they could then make arrangements to meet themselves. The future couple and their families would use this time to clarify specifics within the contractual agreement, consider other prospects and seek familiarity with their intended spouse and family. Courtship for the Tudors was serious, the goal was to find a spouse and amusing oneself through false affections was frowned upon by society. Couples from humbler origins who met and arranged their own marriages usually had a much longer courtship than their wealthier counterparts, who largely depended on others to make arrangements on their behalf. The implications of having to work and save towards their marriage meant they had more time to get to know their intended spouse and ensure future intentions were indeed honourable.

Throughout the courtship, tokens and gifts could be exchanged between the couple. Tokens varied according to wealth and could be anything from gloves, jewels and books. The acceptance of the gifts was a sign of intentions, if a ring was proffered and accepted this was usually a sign both parties consented to the betrothal. For the literate, this period may be the time to exchange letters, getting to know one another better and making enquiries as to what their possible future together held. Most wealthy and aristocratic daughters left negotiations to their parents but would likely be keen to give their opinion on their intended, particularly after a period of getting to know her prospective spouse. A young lady would most likely wish to know where she was to live, what the place was like and its surroundings, as well as the situation regarding the number of servants and maids she would have, whether she could take her own and all manner of things relating to her new home.

At the end of the courtship if both parties were content to marry, they could make the agreement formal, known as a betrothal, contracting or handfasting amongst other terms. This could be done very publicly with witnesses or in private. Whether the agreement was binding was a matter of debate during the time, witnesses were often used to avoid any arrangement later being reneged. There were cases where one party or the other would refuse to marry stating they had never been contracted; therefore, many chose to eliminate this prospect as much as possible. Some even chose to obtain the services of a priest to witness the formality and would speak words of promise. 'I, R., do promise to thee, F., that I will be thine husband, which I will confirm by public manner, in pledge whereof I give thee mine hand'. The woman would then repeat the words and the couple would pray together with the priest.[14] The tradition of handfasting was similar in that promises were made by the plighting of troths, holding of hands and the exchange of rings. The betrothal, however it was made, could be made conditional, for instance, an heir may promise to marry upon inheriting his family estate. Someone of a humbler family may promise to marry at the end of his apprenticeship as apprentices usually had a stipulation within their contract that they could not marry until they had completed their term. For those that made this promise, it was binding. From this point the marriage was agreed, unless there were reasons relating to affinity, pre-contract to another, or consanguinity. Of course, there could be those who decided against the marriage after a period of courtship, and at this point negotiations would cease and the marriage would not go ahead. Couples who had consented could proceed with their marriage. Church weddings became the most common form of wedding as it largely removed the possibility of later being denied but it was not a requirement.

Those choosing a church wedding could, at this point, have the banns read announcing the intended marriage. The period of time between the making of the contract and the banns being read varied. There was no requirement to marry within a specified time and couples had their own reasons for delays which could be needing to save or even the time it would take to organise a magnificent wedding. The banns were required to be read three times, usually three Sundays or holy days in a row. The reading of the banns provided an opportunity for the Church to ask if anyone knew of an impediment to the planned marriage; the impediments usually being a pre-contract to another, inappropriate degree of affinity or lack of consent. The banns were to be read in the couple's parish or if they each resided in a different parish, they would be read in both. If they were to be read in two different parishes, the marriage could not take place until the parish holding the ceremony received confirmation from the other that the banns had been read on three occasions and no objections had been raised.[15] Being read in the local parishes of the couple ensured those who knew them were made aware of the proposed marriage and members of the local congregation were those most likely to be aware of any impediments. To ensure a maximum audience, the banns were usually read following the usual service whilst the congregation was present. Those who knew of any impediment could then inform the priest of their objection to the matrimony. The reading of the banns in the local parish also had a social aspect; it gave local people time to start preparing for an upcoming wedding, whether they were helping arrange the celebration or to organise their own outfits and gifts in time for the celebrations. It also confirmed to all that the couple had agreed to marry. The alternative to having banns read was to obtain a licence from the Church to dispense with the banns. Obtaining a licence incurred a fee so was usually only pursued by the upper classes and could enable them to marry in a parish other than their own. This gave couples or their families much greater freedom where they could marry, though they were encouraged to marry in a chapel or church of their own parish during the canonical hours of 8:00 am to 12:00 pm. The licence did not just make the banns unnecessary but could allow the couple to marry on what were usually prohibited days.

At the lower end of the social scale, there were some who knew they could never afford to marry. For some couples, the contract or betrothal was sufficient for them to begin life as a married couple, without going through a formal wedding ceremony. This was a risk if their marital status was ever questioned and left the door ajar for those who may later regret the decision to betroth themselves. Others chose to forgo the contract and instead proceed to the wedding without a prior betrothal. Those whose marriage was later questioned in terms of a previous contract to another or prohibited degree of affinity could be declared invalid. As a result, any children of the union would be declared illegitimate. It was not until the eighteenth century that the law dictated that a marriage was only valid when performed by a priest and in the presence of witnesses. Prior to this, canon law dictated that a marriage was valid providing there had been a public declaration by the couple, made in the present tense, that they considered themselves to be husband and wife. Weddings which took place without the involvement of the Church were known as clandestine marriages. Couples who exchanged vows without a priest were still legally married, provided neither was later objecting to this fact. They could even forgo witnesses though the majority would at least have witnesses to protect themselves against any later claims the marriage was invalid or did not occur at all.

Few Tudor women married for love; the majority of young females were expected to accept their father's choice of groom. As consent was required for marriage, in theory, a young female could not be forced to marry, she could however be coerced. Some were coerced through the threat of having her dowry withheld unless she married the individual that had been chosen for her. Forced marriages were frowned upon by the Church and society, though a bride marrying without her father's consent was seen to be committing a greater sin by disobeying her parents. Most families wanted to gain something through the marriage of their daughter whether this be political advantage, land or rank and titles and this influenced their choice of partner for their daughters. A daughter could even be willed to a specific man or family in her father's will with the threat of losing her maintenance, inheritance and dowry if she did not comply with his and his executors wishes. Daughters marrying without the consent of their parents placed themselves at great risk for the future as there would unlikely be a dowry or jointure in place if she were to survive her husband.

For those who had been under a wardship, being free of their guardian at sixteen gave young females more freedom to have a say in their choice of partner. Most wards were wealthy heirs and heiresses and therefore young females would need to consider carefully how best to protect their interests and may instead choose to still seek the advice of their former guardian or male kin. It was always a possibility that the wardship of an heiress may be purchased with the aim to marry her to the guardians' own heir or less commonly to the guardian themselves when the ward came of age. Charles Brandon, Duke of Suffolk married his ward, the fourteen-year-old Katherine Willoughby. It is thought the wardship of Katherine was initially purchased with the possibility she may marry Brandon's heir.[16] Unlike parents, guardians could not withhold inheritance or dowries as it was not theirs to withhold and eventually the girl would come of age, the estate becoming hers to do with as she wished. They could however impose a fine on the estate if a young female did not consent to a proposed marriage. It is possible Katherine Willoughby felt she could not refuse the proposal of such a powerful man. Whatever Katherine felt towards Charles, the material gain for her in marrying him was impressive, she rose from a baroness to a duchess, married to a man high in the king's favour, a tempting proposal for any Tudor woman. Some aristocratic families chose to betroth the heir at an early age to ensure the choice was of their making as opposed to a guardian if anything were to happen to them. Marrying an heiress early also meant they could not become a ward of the Crown even if her father died. Instead, her family would retain control over her inheritance until she came of age and the marriage could be consummated.

Maids of honour and ladies-in-waiting to the queen, in addition to the usual formalities, would also require royal consent before they could marry. If consent was not sought, they could be banished from the royal court and shamed, thus bringing shame upon their family, reducing favour and possibly destroying further advancement of other family members. If they happened to be related to the king or queen and married without consent it was considered treason as the marriage of royalty was the prerogative of the monarch. It is doubtful many would refuse the request of a monarch to marry a partner of their choosing. Close relatives were highly restricted in their choice of marriage partner. Sisters or daughters to a monarch were at the mercy of them and were often used as pawns to secure alliances. Princesses did not have the freedom to decide who they married, the exception being Mary Tudor, younger sister of Henry VIII. In 1514 Mary married the ageing King Louis XII of France, becoming Queen of France. Mary had little choice and only agreed to the marriage on Henry's request, although part of her agreement was the bargain she struck that should she marry again, she could choose her next husband herself. The marriage only lasted ninety-two days, after which she married Charles Brandon without the consent of her brother. Although she chose Brandon herself, the king clearly expected to be consulted. The couple were very fortunate that Henry forgave them, although they were initially banished from court and fined a huge sum of money.

There were those who chose to break the rules and marry without the consent of their family. For those of humbler origin, this was not always an issue as there was little to discuss within the financial settlements beforehand. For the aristocracy it could be a disaster for the families involved, they lost the opportunity to advance their family, improve their finances and could at times face the wrath of the monarch. For the latter, the couple may even find themselves in the Tower or under house arrest like the sisters of Lady Jane Grey, Lady Katherine Grey and Lady Mary Grey. In 1560 Katherine married Edward Seymour, the eldest son of the deceased Edward Seymour, 1st Duke of Somerset and Lord Protector of England. According to the will of Henry VIII, the Grey sisters were in the line of succession to the throne, therefore Elizabeth I was understandably unhappy with the wedding. Elizabeth I had the marriage declared invalid and their child illegitimate, both parties initially being sent to the Tower, later followed by house arrest where Katherine died in 1568. Five years after Katherine's marriage, despite the consequences of her sister's actions, Mary married a man of minor gentry, Thomas Keyes. Unlike Katherine, Mary had more witnesses, likely in an effort to avoid the marriage being declared invalid. Thomas was committed to the Fleet jail where he was held in awful conditions. He was released in 1569 but sadly died a couple of years later having never seen Mary again. Mary was placed under house arrest under the supervision of various people including her step-grandmother, Katherine Willoughby. Mary was released from house arrest in 1572 but had insufficient income to support herself and had to rely on the goodwill of others for her maintenance. By 1573, Mary's circumstances had improved and she had been set up in her own household. She had also managed to regain the favour of Elizabeth I, becoming one of her maids of honour in 1577 before dying the following year in 1578. For those who did not face the wrath of the monarch as the Grey sisters had, they may perhaps still face criticism and banishment by their own family, particularly if one party was due to advance from a marriage and could no longer do so. It would be particularly dangerous for an eldest son to marry without consent as he could easily be replaced as the heir to the family fortune whilst younger sons had much less to lose.

The middling classes appear to have been the most problematic concerning possible clandestine marriages and seem to be the most common class of marrying without consent. This assumption is based on ecclesiastical court records. The courts are unlikely to have heard many cases relating to the poor as they were unable to pay for court proceedings and had little worth suing for. The lower classes also had much less at stake in terms of what could be gained through marriage and therefore commonly had more freedom in selecting their own marriage partner. Therefore, the records do not give an accurate reflection of the numbers of couples who married without consent. Those who married without consent likely did so as a result of a love match and perhaps believed one or both of their families would not approve of the match. The families may object on grounds of the differing social ranks or allege that there had been a pre-contract in place for another arrangement. This could result in an annulment if the family pressed their cause through the church courts. The discovery of a planned wedding could be halted with threats of disinheritance and banishment. Families could use their contacts and acquaintances to help persuade the parties to disband with their plans, for instance strong persuasive techniques from someone of a higher rank was likely to have an effect, particularly in cases where they could influence the man's livelihood. If neither party could be persuaded to abandon the match and there was no pre-contract or concerns around the prohibited degrees, there was little anyone could do other than continue with the threats. Many parents would not do this as they still of course cared for their children and did not wish to see them banished, destitute or lose the opportunity for a relationship with any future grandchildren. Another reason for a couple marrying without the consent of their parents or guardians was pregnancy. A couple might proceed quickly to marriage if a woman became pregnant as they did not wish their child to be born illegitimate. Some had also chosen to begin their lives as a married couple once contracts were agreed or they had been betrothed which meant they may be expecting by the time they came to marry. Those who married prior to the birth were not admonished but may be gossiped about within their community.

The planning of a wedding could take a long time, firstly with the reading of the banns or obtaining a licence if preferred. There were also those who required a dispensation to marry. Prior to the Reformation obtaining a dispensation could take months to acquire as it needed to be sought from Rome. As with planning a wedding today, there was much work to do. A venue or multiple venues were required for the ceremony and the celebration that would follow. The venues were most commonly the local parish church followed by the home of the parents or a close relative. Invites had to be delivered to guests, and with any correspondence having to be taken by messenger on horseback, this could also prove to be a lengthy process. If the family were inviting people from abroad, it could add weeks or even months to the planning to provide guests with ample opportunity to prepare for the wedding and make travel arrangements. Those living in the local parish did not necessarily require invites if the banns had been read as they would be aware of the upcoming celebrations. Wealthy hosts would have the additional obligation of ensuring they had suitable accommodation for any guests who would require it. This would include the bedding and furniture to furnish the chambers and communal rooms to make sure all guests would be comfortable and catered to, for the duration of their visit. Furniture may have to be transported from other properties or borrowed from obliging neighbours. It was rare, even for the rich, to have each of their properties fully furnished; many would transport some furniture when they moved between their estates. Many couples nowadays choose a favourite season to marry; for the Tudors they would select an appropriate time according to the church calendar. The Church forbade marriage on almost 150 days of the year due to them being holy days or religious festivals, such as during Lent and Advent. Couples would also have to consider their own availability according to their employment. Those residing in arable areas would have to avoid harvest time as there was too much work to be done to spend time organising and getting married. As a result, the months of October and November following the harvest were the most popular for weddings in arable areas. By this time of year the harvest had since been collected and many of those on annual employment contracts were free to move around in search of new employment. This could be the perfect time for them to search for a new contract, marry and set up their household. The months of April, May and June were popular in pastoral regions as the bulk of the work involving lambing and calving had been completed. Couples residing in urban towns had the most freedom in selecting a time for their wedding as they were not as restricted by seasonal work but did still have to honour the church calendar.

When the wedding day arrived, it was time for the final preparations. It was likely a nervous start to the day for first time brides as this was their leap into adulthood, their hopes would be centred on a happy, successful marriage. The majority of the population were superstitious to some extent and on her wedding day the bride and her family would look for signs that their marriage would be a happy one. The signs began with the weather, if the sun was shining on her wedding day, a bride could expect a happy marriage whilst bad weather foretold of unhappiness. A bride would dress in her finest clothing, though they rarely wore white as this was not the traditional colour worn by a bride until the nineteenth century. Instead, they would wear the brightest colours they could, keeping to the Sumptuary Laws, according to their rank. The gown may be new, created specifically for the occasion and if it could be afforded may well be an exquisite garment, embroidered with beautiful details and gems. The embroidery may be done by the hand of the bride herself or by another as a gift and could include plants and flowers that were favoured by the bride or symbolised good fortune. The patterns may perhaps also include symbols that were indicative of her and the groom's families. If a bride did not own a suitable gown, one may be borrowed, handed down by her mistress or provided through the charitable donations of the local parish. The bride's hair could be worn loose as a sign she was a maid if it was to be her first marriage and she may add flowers to her hair. Alternatively, a bride may choose to wear her hair gathered into a net, which could range from plain to exquisitely detailed, or covered with a beautiful headdress. Brides would commonly carry a posy of seasonal flowers and blend them with greenery and herbs or wear a garland of flowers. She would be accompanied to the church by her female friends, family and maids in a procession. The church would have been prepared with additional flower and herbal decorations, chosen both for their scent and symbolisation. These were often posies picked by the bride and her friends, then tied together with ribbons or could be expensive pieces collected for the wealthy by their own gardeners. Rosemary was a popular choice for the church and for the bride's own flowers for the scent. Once at the church door the couple would be asked to confirm the agreed dowry. With the banns being read one final time, the couple would then confirm their consent to marry. Assuming there were no last-minute objections, the bride's dowry should then be exchanged whilst the couple remained at the door of the church. Either an instalment or the full amount would be paid to the groom or his family as per the agreement between the families. Only after this could the service begin. Prior to the Reformation, humbler classes would remain at the door for the service whilst the aristocracy could proceed indoors at varying degrees according to rank. After the Reformation all classes were allowed to marry within the church.

Brides were given away by their father, closest male relative or guardian, and whilst today, for most people, it may seem a sweet gesture and nothing more, to the Tudors it symbolised passing the bride from parental authority to that of her new husband. It was the literal act of the father of the bride giving his consent to the marriage by 'giving' his daughter to the groom by the right hand. The vows and service changed with the Reformation, those of the *Sarum Missal* being replaced by those of the *Book of Common Prayer*. The *Sarum Missal* stated the bride should stand on the left of the groom as she was created from the rib on Adam's left side. The Protestant service does not make any statement on where the couple should stand but tradition meant the woman continued to stand on the left. Vows would follow with the groom speaking first, the Protestant version being: 'I (Name) take thee (Name) to my wedded wife, to have and to hold from this day forward, for better, for worse, for richer, for poorer, in sickness, and in health, to love and to cherish, till death us depart, according to God's holy ordinance: and thereto I plight thee my troth'. The couple would release hands briefly before joining them again for the bride to say her vows: 'I (Name) take thee (Name) to my wedded husband, to have and to hold from this day forward, for better, for worse, for richer, for poorer, in sickness, and in health, to love, cherish, and to obey, till death us depart, according to God's happy ordinance: and thereto I give thee my troth'.[17] Note the addition in the bride's vows of the word 'obey', though unlike the traditional vows, those within the *Book of Common Prayer* omit the requirement for the bride to promise to be 'bonair and buxom in bed and at board'. The service continued with the giving of a ring which was placed on the book of prayer, or a tray before being placed on the bride's fourth finger. Today we have a genre of wedding bands but the Tudors did not, the ring was dependent on the wealth and tastes of the family and could be plain or made with various gemstones. The change in this part of the service was the omission of the traditional blessing of the ring by the priest, it was then sprinkled with holy water before being placed on the bride's thumb, second finger, third finger, finally resting on her fourth finger. During this the groom repeated the words directed by the *Sarum Missal*. Protestants found this part of the ceremony unnecessary, instead the groom made a simple statement 'With this ring I thee wed: with my body I thee worship: and with all my worldly goods I thee endow'.[18] The bride would be endowed with the property agreed within the jointure during the ceremony, this gave the bride the additional protection of having witnesses present if the terms of her jointure were later disputed.

Prior to the Reformation, those of the humbler classes who would still be at the door of the church at this point in the ceremony, could now proceed inside to receive a blessing. Further prayers and psalms would follow with the priest proclaiming the marriage to the congregation. This was the point where the couple may kiss but the Protestant service makes no mention of it; again, tradition continued despite its omission. The proclamation was sometimes followed by a sermon, but if there was to be none this point marked the end of the Protestant service and the congregation could leave to begin the wedding celebrations. Traditionally, the Catholic service continued; if there was no sermon after prayers, a psalm would be read, encouraging the couple to take the advice of St Paul. The bride was advised to 'submit unto your own husbands as unto the Lord: for the husband is the wives head, even as Christ is the head of the Church… let the wives also be in subjection unto their own husbands in all things…Ye wives, submit yourselves unto your own husbands, as it is convenient in the Lord', the psalm continues with advice from St Peter 'Let wives be subject to their own husbands, so that if any obey not the word, they may be won without the word by the conversation of the wives, while they behold your chaste conversation coupled with fear: whose apparel let it not be outward, with braided hair and trimming about with gold, either in putting on of gorgeous apparel.'[19] The service makes it very apparent that the Church encourages the subordination and obedience of women to their husbands. Before the service finished the couple would receive the holy communion, and they were then welcome to leave the church for the revelries that followed. The couple would progress to the chosen venue for their wedding celebration; if they had ample space, this was usually the family home of the bride or groom. They may be led by a procession of music or dancing as the congregation made merry along the way.

The wedding celebration was known as the wedding feast. The term feast infers it is one meal, but like most things in the Tudor era, depending on the wealth of the families, the revels could last for hours or even days. The wedding guests and commonly the members of the local parish, including the priest who had conducted the wedding service, were invited to join the couple in their merriments. If the families did not have space at home for such a celebration, they might all visit a tavern to eat and drink in celebration of their marriage. Some feasts were more elegant affairs with rich foods served in abundance and dancing whilst others were drunken parties. For the extremely poor, local communities would hold bride-ales where members of the parish would bake, cook and brew for the couple as a gift towards their wedding celebration and they would celebrate together at the church. Communities could make and sell the produce in advance of the wedding to raise funds for the couple towards the wedding itself or the setting up their home together. The newly married couple would receive gifts from their guests but it was custom for guests to also receive a gift from the couple. Gifts for guests could be ribbons and trinkets but gloves were the most common. The gifts for the couple could vary widely, it may be an offering of food towards the feast, money, jewels, cloth, livestock, furniture to help them set up a home or anything a guest could reasonably afford to gift. Custom dictated the couple should be 'bedded', the ceremony of escorting the couple to their chamber and putting them to bed. The couple would be blessed, then the attendees would continue the festivities, leaving the couple alone to consummate the marriage. For some women, this was a mortifying experience and was omitted if the husband agreed; others eloped to escape the prospect. For royalty this was an important part of the ritual of marriage and was taken seriously. Following the wedding day a woman entered the next stage of her life as a wife. Numerous couples were required to initially live with the parents of one party of the couple until they could afford a home of their own or the estate passed to the husband.

The most common alternative to marriage was to enter a convent, although even this option was not as popular as the option of marriage. Amongst the nobility and even the royal family, where they had multiple daughters, they would commonly send one to enter a convent. It was a way for the family to show their piety and respect, by dedicating a child to the Church. Bridget of York, sister of Elizabeth of York, entered Dartford Priory when she was 10 years old. At the time it was known as a good place of learning for young girls, even those who were not intending to take their vows.[20] It is likely a blessing that Bridget died before her nephew, Henry VIII ordered the dissolution of the convents. Fathers with multiple daughters may choose to send one or more to convents as it was too costly to provide dowries for them all. By sending them to a convent, a father would be guaranteeing they received training and an education of varying degrees, depending on the convent. For families to whom the cost was not a concern, they would be unlikely to consider a convent if they only had a daughter or two as the marriage of the daughters could provide more opportunities for the family. If they had multiple daughters, they may agree that one could enter a convent either by her own choice or to appear as pious members of society by giving one of their own to the Church. Other women entered as it was their choice to follow a religious vocation and her family had the means to allow it without impacting the family estate.

There were 142 nunneries in 1534, housing approximately 1,900 nuns. The convents relied on donations for their maintenance, therefore even entering a convent was largely restricted to those who could afford to maintain their daughter or female relative whilst she was there. Families would continue to send money to the convent and nuns were frequently left bequests in the wills of family members.[21] Although they had little use of money or gifted jewels whilst there, they could use it for books or donate towards alms. When the convents were destroyed, they likely would have been grateful for any funds they had managed to save beforehand. Women who entered convents continued to be active members of their family. Nuns were able to visit and have visits from friends and family.

Although a large part of the convent's income came from donations made by the family members of nuns, there were some members of society who left charitable bequests to convents in their will and local communities who would donate when they could. If they had the capacity to do so, the convents may offer bed and board to women requiring it, charging a token payment or donation for the service. Like the monasteries, convents would be required to offer hospitality to pilgrims or those seeking shelter which could add to their income. The nuns were expected to observe the religious rules of their convent and would live modestly. Nuns were expected to organise their day around the seven offices of the day beginning with

Matins and Lauds at the very early hour of 2:00 am. After another few hours of sleep, Prime followed at 6:00 am and Tierce, Sext, None, Vespers and Compline throughout the remainder of the day. They would then spend time contributing to the work required for the maintenance of the convent including cooking, cleaning, and tending the gardens, which included the herbal garden. The ability to maintain a bountiful herbal garden enabled the nuns to concoct medicines to assist with caring for the sick who came to them for help. Most convents were self-sufficient to an extent, with many having the ability to brew their own ale and produce dairy products, both of which could be sold to gain income for the convent. Wealthier convents may also employ multiple servants to assist with more laborious tasks and to expand their ability to provide sustenance for the convent and if needed, the surrounding community, whilst also providing employment for local people. Surplus funds collected by the convents would be used for charitable purposes such as alms for the poor or to maintain any poor girls who were residing there but unable to contribute financially towards their upkeep. For those who wished for more solitude they could choose to live as an anchoress, someone who usually spent most of their time in seclusion in order to pray. The only company they had would be their servants, the number of whom would depend on the woman's wealth or gifts to her. Anchoresses would receive donations and support in return for prayers but like nuns, received no wage. The life of an anchoress could certainly be an isolated profession but offered great reward for those wishing to dedicate themselves to religious piety.

In 1536, Parliament ordered the closure of convents with an income of less than £200 per year. Many did not even receive half this amount, in fact in Yorkshire not a single convent earned an income over £100 per year. Therefore, due to the impact this would have on the number of closures at one time, nuns were given the opportunity to transfer to another convent. Two years later, after nuns had been asked to voluntarily leave, some prioresses tried their upmost to save their convents by raising funds to pay for exemption from dissolution. Those who succeeded in raising sufficient funds only extended their lifetime by a further year, following which all the remaining convents were dissolved and the residents pensioned. As an example, of the twenty-three convents in Yorkshire, nine were closed in 1536. The remaining fourteen managed to survive until 1539.[22] Following the Reformation and the dissolution of the convents, a religious vocation was still possible but to enter a convent meant travelling abroad which could prove just as costly as the provision of a dowry. Where the cost was not achievable or where the nuns had found themselves now homeless, the women could create small communities together, living in private homes and working alongside each other, continuing to live piously and charitably.

Other alternatives included remaining a spinster or residing as a dependent in a friend or relative's household. This was an option that was only available to the wealthy and the aristocracy. Women that chose not to marry, or for some reason could not marry, remained as daughters for life and were classed as dependents. They would often serve in another household as a gentlewoman rather than remaining at home. The homes they chose were usually that of kin or friends where they were treated well and often treated as companions as opposed to a servant. Unfortunately, other than those who served at the royal court, there are few records about the women who chose this path. We do know their parents or substitutes were responsible for their maintenance. The household they resided in may have been able to pay them a small wage, or provide other benefits of clothing, material, books and of course they gained much in terms of friendship and companionship. This may reduce the burden on the parents to pay for their maintenance. There were some females who were deemed 'unmarriageable' due to illness, disease or disability. Society at the time placed interest in looks above personality and ability. These women had little choice but to remain dependent on their family, unless they wished to find employment as a 'fool' to a wealthy family. Fools were sometimes those with a disability who would entertain their employer by acting silly and usually making jokes, sometimes to the point where they could insult people in a joking manner and get away with it where others most certainly would not.

Others remained single as their dowries had been used, either by parents in need or sometimes by a sibling who had inherited the estate and gone against the terms of their father's will. In these cases, the girls or their mother could sue or petition a member of the Privy Council but in some cases, there was little to be done if the funds had been used. Parents who remarried into families with additional children or went on to have more children sometimes focused on the new children. Daughters from previous marriages could be almost forgotten, until they were no longer of the ideal marriageable age. Some blended households had become so dependent on them being present that they did not wish them to marry and leave, particularly whilst incurring the cost of a dowry. Parents who believed their daughter would remain unmarried for life for whatever reason or were unmarried at the time of writing their will, would try to ensure she was taken care of, including after their own deaths. Many would bequeath a sum of money in their will which could be used for their dowry if she were to marry or used to pay for her own maintenance if she remained unmarried. They may also assign property and land to a daughter to give her an independent income and remove reliance on other family members, particularly an ungenerous heir. Regardless of the reason they did not marry, single daughters who chose to remain within their family household as opposed to serving another, were an asset to their family. If they received any inheritance or income from land, they could, if required make contributions towards their maintenance and would pay for their own servants if applicable. They would purchase their own gifts for people and give charitable alms from their own funds. Unmarried daughters could assist their mother, or other female kin with the management of the household. This was particularly beneficial where the family was to host visitors and they could be relied upon for their skills in hospitality. There was also the additional benefit of them having the experience and knowledge of the family if they needed to manage the household due to absence, whether this be illness, travel or the mistress going through labour. It would be a blessing to any man to have a female present who could pick up the reins of his wife whilst she was occupied with childbirth.

With the exception of heiresses, there was little expectation that women who chose not to marry would be able to keep a household by themselves. Even wealthy women were often unable to afford to maintain an estate according to their rank, if they remained single. For those who did not have the benefit of a wealthy family to rely upon, a placement within another household as a servant could provide them with a home, often for their lifetime. Wealthier women may be expected to reside with a family member, often within a male relative's household. Depending on their personal relationship and wealth, this could be a pleasant situation, or they may be treated as a servant. Most would expect to serve in some manner but the extent of service was at the discretion of the master of the household. Elizabeth Lisle, daughter of Lord Lisle, resided with her step-brother, John Dudley even whilst her father was alive. Lord Lisle, had moved to Calais and only took one of his daughters with them, although he did take four of his wife's daughters. Elizabeth remained behind in England, as did her sister Bridget initially. Bridget was placed in St Mary's convent in Winchester but later travelled to Calais in the company of her step-mother, Lady Lisle. The *Lisle Letters* offer a unique insight into how a blended family operated in the Tudor era. Lady Lisle does not appear to differentiate between her own daughters and those of her husband when making enquiries as to their welfare, paying for their maintenance and expenses, clothing and providing instructions for their care. Lady Lisle also maintained relationships with her step-daughters from her first marriage to Sir John Basset. When she moved to Calais with Lord Lisle, she allowed one of her step-daughters to remain residing in one of her properties, including the service of her staff and gave permission for some of the land to be used as pasture.[23] Unlike today, women would find it difficult to live in a patriarchal society without the security of a husband or male relative in their life, although elite women retained much more independence than their humbler counterparts.

## Chapter Four

## Lives of Wives

Following their wedding day, women faced the prospect of a new household. For some, this may be the first time they had been away from home. With regards to first marriage couples who belonged to the aristocracy and the wealthy ranks of society, it was the parents or substitutes who decided where the couple would live when they began their married life. Depending on their age, as previously noted, they may reside with one of the families. The parents of the bride and groom would discuss who was going to support the couple up until the groom received his inheritance or came of age to receive the income from his estates. In 1528, when Ellen Fitzwilliam married the 17-year-old Nicholas Lestrange, her new father-in-law, Sir Thomas Lestrange agreed to support the couple and any children the couple would have, until Nicholas reached the age of 21. This would be the age he could receive income from his lands and therefore be old enough to set up his own household. In 1545 when Sir Thomas died, Nicholas was in his 30s and the couple were still residing with him.[1] This may indicate that the family lived peacefully and resided together amicably. Alternatively, Nicholas may not have received sufficient income of his own to have been able to afford to set up a household of the same standards the couple were accustomed to and therefore, decided to wait for his inheritance as heir to his father. As her mother-in-law, Lady Anne, was still alive, we cannot be certain how much, if at all, Ellen's role within the household changed when her husband became head of the household. The records of the Lestrange family show Anne was a very competent wife. Prior to her husband's death, she kept accounts of income and expenditure for the household and the estates. She is known to have collected rent from tenants, paid the servants and suppliers, and ensured the properties on the estate were maintained. This suggests that Ellen did not easily step into the role of the mistress of the household but it is also possible that the two women worked together and continued to do so following the death of Sir Thomas.[2] If a couple did not require parental supervision, their marital home could still be decided by others and was likely to be one of the properties granted to the couple within the jointure. Those who marred at an older age, who were already in possession of their inheritance would have the option of deciding their main residence for themselves. The humbler classes may be able to afford to set up their own home but if not, they would also remain living with one of their parents or within their workplace.

Marriage changed a woman's role in society, she was no longer a maid and had progressed to the next important stage in her life. She had previously been a dutiful daughter but now her aim was to be an obedient wife, keep her husband happy and ensure her household was run efficiently. To complete the step into her new role she would need to understand her new position within her new marital family and society, beginning with her new home.

As a single woman she would have had a little more freedom in her behaviour including her expected attendance at church, but as a married woman she was held to a much higher standard of public behaviour and would sit in selected pews according to her status. Pews may be segregated by marital status or gender. A newly married woman may find herself welcomed to sit with other wives rather than in the pews reserved for unmarried women or be expected to join the pews of her new family if they were affluent enough to have pews reserved. She was also expected to attend church regularly, which although she should have been attending prior to getting married it was noted as an expectation for married couples.

> What the dutie of a wife is toward her husband.
> This duty is comprehended in these points;
> First, that she reuerence her husband.
> Secondly, that she submit herselfe, and be obedient vnto him.
> And lastly, that she do not weare gorgeous apparell, beyond her degree and place, but that her attire be comely and sober, according to her calling.
> The first point is proued by the Apostles, Peter and Paul; who set forth the wiues duties to their husbands, commanding them to be obedient vnto them, although they be prophane and irreligious, yea, that they ought to do it so much the more, that by their honest life and conuersation, they might winne them to the obedience of the Lord.

> Now for so much as the Apostle would haue Christian wiues, that are matched with vngodly husbands, and such as are not yet good.[3]

This was typical of the kind of advice given to wives during the Tudor era. Although wives were expected to be obedient to their husband, a husband in return owed a duty of protection to his wife, both physically and to her reputation. The bride became an extension of her husband. Though he was responsible for governing the household, she, as his spouse could give directions to the rest of the household and act on his behalf in his absence. The expectations of a woman within the community also changed upon her marriage.

> The properties due to a married wife are, that she haue grauitie when she walketh abroad: wisedome to gouerne her house, patience to suffer her husband, loue to breed and bring vp her children, courtesie towards her neighbours, diligence, to lay vp, and to saue such goods as are within her charge: that she be a friend of honest company, and a greater enemie of wanton and light toyed. So then, the principall dutie of the wife, is, first, to be subiect to her husband, Ephes. 5. 22. Colloss. 3. 18. 1. Pet. 3. 1. 2. To be chast and shamefast, modest and silent, godly and discreet. 3. To keepe her selfe at home for the good gouernment of her family, and not to stray abroad without iust cause.[4]

Advice such as this and the words of St Paul that a wife should be silent when in the company of her husband and his companions was expanded on during the Tudor era by religious writers like Thomas Becon. Becon believed that silence was the best 'accessory' for a woman, writing: 'doth so much commend, advance, set forth, adorn, deck, trim and garnish a maid as silence'.[5] Wives were not expected to be silent when alone with their husbands. The couple were encouraged to pray together and discuss spiritual difficulties, supporting one another through hardships. Although women were viewed as subordinate to men, they were expected to be respected within a marriage and conduct books for men urged them to treat their wives with kindness, they were not to beat them and were to discuss financial and property affairs even if they did not request their input in decisions. This was of particular importance when it came to discussing property which either the woman had brought with her to the marriage or those that directly affected her, such as those assigned to her jointure.

Prior to marriage women were known as *femme sole* (single woman), but once they married, they became *femme covert* (covered woman), meaning a woman under the protection of her husband. As a married woman, under the common law rule of *coverture*, all of the property a woman brought to the marriage came under the control of her husband. It was not until the later on in the sixteenth century that the Chancery courts took action to remedy women's property rights under coverture and began to enforce women's rights to property that was held in trust on her behalf.[6] Following this, property held in trust or that which formed part of a contract agreed prior to marriage, remained the property of the woman and was exempt from her husband's control. This was usually the property of heiresses. If a man married an heiress, he could use the income of the land and property and manage the estates but he had no rights to sell it, nor use it as equity against loans. This method was used to safeguard the estates of the aristocracy where there had been no male heir. The property would eventually be bequeathed to the heiresses' son if she were to have one. The property of an heiress included moveable goods such as jewels and plate, as well as land and properties, and even gifts she had received during the duration of her marriage. Prior to the changes in law, wealthy and aristocratic families would often include the specific property in any marriage settlement. This could result in a very lengthy agreement but was important to safeguard a woman's rights. If the husband then acted in a manner contrary to the agreement, although his wife could not sue him, her family surely would sue him on her behalf. An heiress was also likely to have friends in high places who may be able to apply a little influence where needed.

If a woman owned a property on a freehold basis, her husband would hold a life interest, with the property reverting back to her ownership upon his death. Husbands could not dispose of freehold property without the consent of his wife although often consent was given as women were taught to be submissive to their husbands. Leasehold property could be disposed of by the husband but if he retained the property, women could attempt to regain them if she survived her husband. The exception was the wife's dower or jointure, a husband could not dispose of these without his wife's express consent.

The concept of coverture did not just apply to the control of a woman's property, it also impacted her legal identity. Married women lost their individual legal identity when they married. They became an extension of their husband, rather than a separate individual and were subject to his will. They were unable to control and administer their own property or sign contracts. The exception of this was a specific contract which allowed females to trade as *femme sole*, more of which will be discussed in Chapter Six. Neither could they attempt to gain credit in their own name. Married women could not sue without her husband acting on her behalf, and if she herself was sued, her husband would have to be the person to act in proceedings. Whilst single, a woman could write a will but once married she would require her husband's explicit consent to do so. Parliament enforced that married women could not write wills in 1544 stating; 'Wills or testaments made of manors, tenaments, or other hereditaments, by any woman covert, by a person under twenty-one, by an idiot, or by any person not sane, shall not be good under law'.[7] Women who inherited property from their parents usually had to rely on their husband to assist them if their inheritance was challenged by a male relative. Katherine Willoughby faced the conflict of her uncle attempting to claim the whole of her inheritance when her father died. Luckily for Katherine, Charles Brandon assisted her and managed to retain the majority of her inheritance. Other women may not be so lucky if their husband was unwilling to assist them in legal matters.[8] All the financial aspects of life became the responsibility of her husband. Even those who worked and received a wage had no control over their income, their wage becoming the property of her husband.

If a couple could afford their own marital home, a wife could become mistress of her own household as soon as she married and all that she had trained for in her childhood and adolescence would now be needed. Newly married women who resided with their in-laws may have an amiable relationship with their mother-in-law and be able to manage the household between them, for others they may find themselves in a difficult situation if they could not exert any influence within the home. Once they were finally in their own home the majority of households were nuclear: the couple, their children and of course, their servants. Few families had other relatives residing with them unless they were a wealthy household who could afford the upkeep of relatives in need or could accommodate children of other families for their upbringing. A woman did not lose her importance to her natal family when she married, most remained close to their families, writing to them if they were literate or visiting if they resided close by. They also acted as intermediaries amongst the aristocracy, promoting the interests of their father or other male relatives to her marital family and friends.

Becoming the mistress of her own household gave a female authority over her domain, though it would be careless to claim that the experiences of wives could be generalised. The experience differed immensely, and was influenced by wealth, class and of course their spouse. Obviously, the larger the household, the more servants were employed. The man of the house could employ as many servants as he wished and could even appoint some in supervisory roles but the daily supervision of servants within the household generally fell within the remit of the wife. There were various writings on husbandry and Master Fitzherbert who had initially written the popular book of advice for husbands known as the *Boke of Husbandry* added a further book to his original volume, which he titled *The Boke of Huswifery*. *The Boke of Huswifery* advised how an ideal housewife should behave and the various tasks she should be completing. The text was largely aimed at farmers and their wives and as many of the poorer classes were illiterate, it was aimed at the middling class farmers, though much of the advice could be appropriate for all wives. Fitzherbert stated a farmer's wife should 'first in a morning when thou art waked and proposeth to rise, take up thy hand and bless thee and make the sign of the holy cross. In nominee patris, et filii et spiritus sancti Amen. In the name of the Father, the Son and the Holy Ghost. And if thou say a PaterNoster, an Ave and a Creed and remember thy Maker, thou shalt speed much the better'. Following the Reformation, Fitzherbert did amend his text to 'give thanks to God for thy night's rest and say the Lord's Prayer and other good prayers if thou canst'.[9]

Following the morning prayers, the daily housework could begin. The variety of work differed according to the status of the family. The aristocracy and wealthy merchants had large estates to be managed. The management of the estate was primarily the responsibility of the husband but wives would still assist and would commonly manage in his absence. Whilst her husband was at home, she may offer her counsel on decisions affecting the estate or merely offer companionship. Households of gentlemen and noblemen could be vast, employing over one hundred people in a variety of roles as well as housing other dependant family members, friends and children of others for the purpose of training.

Fitzherbert's *The Boke of Husbandry* states that one of the housewife's duties is to attend the market to both buy and sell goods which meant knowing how to barter for the best prices to both buy and sell. Markets stalls were set up early so for those intending to buy or sell they would need to be up, dressed and travelling to the market at sunrise as they were usually ready for closing by 8:00 am. Attending the market was one of many tasks expected of a wife, the variance depending on their status, wealth and occupation of their husband but the majority would be required to complete a range of tasks, either alone or with the assistance of servants and maids. Women of a high rank such as duchesses and royal women were not required to personally complete the majority of tasks, as their households employed large numbers of people completing the laborious tasks on their behalf. Gentlewomen, however, would assist their servants with tasks including cooking, even if they employed a woman specifically as a cook. A cook in a gentlewoman's home was a valuable part of the home, she worked closely with her mistress to organise the feeding of the household, including the servants. She would also assist the mistress in arranging for the purchase of goods for the kitchen and compiling menus when hospitality was required. Guests attending the homes of the middle and upper classes would expect a variety of dishes to be served with accompanying condiments. The housewife would be expected to know how to cook and serve all of these dishes herself even if she usually relied on a cook and kitchen help. Middle class housewives usually only employed a couple of servants, so although they may sometimes have assistance, she would generally have the sole responsibility for cooking within the household.

The most common tasks for women and her staff included collecting wood and making fires for cooking and keeping the home warm as well as for cooking purposes. Water also needed fetching from a well, stream or other water source. Water was vital for hygiene, cleaning and cooking, therefore, depending on the size of the household, fetching water could be an extremely arduous and time-consuming task. For this reason, some chose to complete tasks such as washing kitchenware and clothing at the water source. The housewife would also ensure the children were woken, dressed and fed, meals were prepared, the home was cleaned and servants were supervised in their tasks. Wives would also tackle the tasks of baking, brewing, sewing and spinning. Today we have the luxury of items such as hoovers, mops and specialised floor cleaners but for the Tudors, even cleaning their home was laborious. Humble homes had dirt floors that would need constant sweeping, they would become dusty in summer and if not swept regularly leave dust everywhere. Wealthier homes may have the benefit of flagged floors, making the sweeping much easier but if rushes were used, they would have to swept and replaced. Walls needed cleaning and sometimes windows, although the majority of the population had material or shutters covering the windows instead of glass. Cooking pots and dishes, whether wooden or pewter, all need scouring with sand or a plant known as horsetails as well as the fire requiring maintenance daily, ready for the day's cooking.[10]

The majority of the population ate what was available. For many, a popular meal was pottage – a broth with grain and whatever else could be added to flavour it, largely vegetables and herbs but if meat was available, it would also be added. The pottage could be left simmering over the hearth whilst the rest of the housework and chores were completed. The wealthy also ate pottage and it would be served as one of the many dishes on their heavily laden tables, but they also had plentiful access to meat produce whilst the humbler classes only ate meat occasionally, as it was expensive. The Tudors had to make the most of the food available to them; women would spend considerable time preserving fruit and veg, salting fish and meat and attempting to build up a store of surplus food ahead of the colder winter months. The Church ordered fasting days twice per week plus holy days. On these days meat could not be eaten, making fish a popular food source. The Tudors were more than capable of fishing in rivers, streams and the sea to provide food or as a pastime. Henry VIII and Edward VI both spent time fishing. The majority of those who needed to fish in order to feed their family, were often the same people who would spend long hours working and have very little time for fishing. Fish was therefore a popular commodity at markets, it could be bought fresh if you resided close enough to a water source or dried and salted from a merchant that had imported the fish. Fish was dried and salted so it could be kept longer and used to build up a food store, as well as reducing the weight so merchants could carry more cargo across the sea. Dried fish needed rehydrating before it could be eaten so would firstly need to be beaten, then soaked for a few hours, dissolving the salt but also replacing the much-needed fluid to make it edible. Grand households tended to have their own fishponds providing a constant source of fresh fish but this did not mean they avoided dried and salted fish. If you visit Hampton Court Palace, you will notice Fish Court, where all the fish for the court was stored, and this gives an idea of the huge quantities used to keep the court fed. Fish was a food source present in most households, even if the family only kept it to serve to servants or to add to pottage on fasting days.

Owning livestock was common but with the ownership of livestock came additional responsibilities and daily tasks. They had to feed and care for the livestock which could perhaps consist of poultry, cows, pigs and sheep, collect the eggs, milk the cows then prepare the milk. Some of the milk may then be used to make supplemental produce, such as cheese. Some tasks were expected to be completed at specific times of day. Milking was to be done early morning whilst it was thought cheese turned out best if made in the afternoon. Not all had the fortune of affording livestock but it was not uncommon for even poor families to own a pig. A single pig was kept for one reason – to provide the family with meat. A piglet would be reared on scraps or left to forage and before the cold winter months set in, the pig would be slaughtered. This avoided the family having to find scraps for the animal through the winter when food was already scarce, but also meant the family could preserve the meat to feed the family through winter.

Thomas Tusser, the sixteenth century author of *Five Hundred Points of Good Husbandry* and later *The Points of Housewifery*, targeted his advice to those with a simple estate in the country. His advice is similar to that of Fitzherbert but implies that those with a country estate were likely to have more staff to provide for and supervise. He advises housewives to wake early each morning and ensure her maids are also early risers. A stable breakfast of pottage containing a small amount of meat where possible, was to be served to the family and all of the servants. After breakfast a housewife, if required, would supervise the baking, cooking, dairy and laundering, pitching in to help the servants.

Laundry could be a laborious task and extremely hard work for Tudor women. Those residing close to a fresh water source could take their laundry to the source, rather than carrying water back and forth. The wealthy may well be able to afford to purchase soap for laundry and another variation for their personal washing and bathing. If it could not be afforded, some would make their own soap using lye, a strong alkaline solution with fat, whilst the poorest families would make do with water to clean. Larger items which were more difficult to manhandle could be washed using a large tub known as a 'buck tub'. These were particularly useful for washing bedding but could also be used to wash a whole bunch of linens at once. The tub was placed off the ground, with a tap near the bottom which could be opened to drain the water directly into another which could later be reused. As with most things, buck tubs could not be afforded by all, but it is possible some would share tubs with neighbours, and others may try to make their own versions by making a hole in any container large enough and plugging the spout when required. The garments or linens would be folded and placed in the tub, using wood to separate them and allow water to flow through the layers. Lye was then added to the tub and the garments left to soak. The items would be turned, more than once if required to ensure they were soaked well before the liquid was drained using the tap. The items could either then be removed and rinsed in a nearby water source or the tub filled with water repeatedly, leaving it to drain. Once complete, the laundry could be left to dry by draping the wet garments over bushes and fences and collected once dry.[11]

Some may think the Tudors were unclean but this is far from the truth. They took great care in keeping their clothes clean and would wear a linen smock as the first layer of clothing to wick away sweat and odour. This layer would be changed every day if they had spares. Those with plentiful smocks would change them more than once throughout the day. The majority of the population, including wealthy individuals, wore woollen clothing of differing quality. Wool was very difficult to wash and dry without the amenities we have today. Instead, woollen garments would be brushed regularly to remove dust and stored with herbs to keep away moths and vermin. They would not usually be washed, instead the linen smock would keep sweat and odour away from both the skin and the woollen garment. The more expensive fabrics like damasks and silks worn by the wealthier classes would be cared for through careful brushing and mending. Whilst it is true the majority of the population did not have plumbed water to bathe, they could use and fill barrels to bathe or bowls to wash from and would wash regularly.[12] Once the morning tasks had been completed it was time for dinner. At this time, a housewife was to ensure all of the servants were provided a stable meal before setting out the expectations of her servants for the remainder of the day. For women who had been employed as a servant themselves in another household prior to their marriage, these tasks were now work they were no longer paid for, and instead were part of their responsibility as a wife and mistress of the home.

Wives who found themselves as the mistress of larger households and estates would not have a dissimilar experience from those previously mentioned, although they likely had sufficient staff to be able to delegate the work rather than completing it themselves. A wife was expected to join her husband at mealtimes, providing companionship, and those with estates should have been prepared to spend time discussing the estate with her husband, particularly to receive instructions if he were to be away from home. In his absence, a wife may be expected to manage the estate, including property maintenance and the payment of bills, commonly with the assistance of a steward. Wives whose husbands were away from home regularly for periods of time would correspond with their husbands frequently. If he were a courtier, his wife would pay particular attention to any news which the royal court may need to be made aware of, or events that may directly affect her husband's interests. She could rely on the steward or bailiffs to collect rent from tenants on her behalf and the steward would also assist with the continuous management of farming operations. This could include the buying and selling of livestock and produce as well as the harvesting and planting of crops. Some estates were small enough that a wife may be able manage on her own with some guidance but for the larger estates or those with various land and property across the country, they would have relied on the assistance of staff to aid them. Women who were married for a long time expanded their knowledge in managing estates and if they married more than once would bring that knowledge and experience with them to each marriage. If a woman became widowed, she could be more than capable of managing estates and understanding the legalities and financial affairs relating to her land and its produce.

There were tasks which were largely seen as part of the wife's realm of responsibility, regardless of her wealth and whether her husband was home or absent. Wives with larger households often took on the responsibility of supervising the work relating to provisions, whether this be food and drink or the clothing and fabrics required for the household. Regarding produce, brewing, baking, cooking and the dairy all fell within the woman's remit of supervision as well as ensuring the food originating from the estate was collected and used effectively. This meant the selling of excess produce or arranging for grain to be taken to a mill, or even exchanging goods for others which the household may not produce themselves. Depending on the size of the premises, women with a dairy could make it a lucrative business. In order to make it profitable, the women and dairymaids would need to work hard, rising as early as 5:00 am to milk the cows and milk them again in the evening. Each product made in the dairy had its own allotted time, once the cows had been milked in the morning, butter was to be churned before dinner, and cheese was made in the afternoon. The most successful dairies did not make butter and cheese all through the year, instead they churned butter in the spring and made cheese in summer. This was due to the change in the grass during the months, making cheese more profitable in summer when milk was less creamy but higher in protein.[13] Some of the produce would be preserved for the winter months whilst any surplus could be sold at the local market or in the local village. Maintaining a dairy was extremely gruelling work. The premises and all of the equipment had to be kept spotlessly clean to avoid contaminating or souring the produce, but if it could be managed effectively the venture could be very profitable. A housewife and her dairymaids could spend most of the day making produce then cleaning the dairy ready for the next morning.

Ensuring her family was sufficiently clothed was also the responsibility of the housewife. Regardless of rank, all women would occupy themselves with the making and mending of clothing. For those with large families this would include carding and spinning wool, making smocks and other garments. Their skills in spinning were vital as almost all women wore wool. As noted, the quality was dependent on their wealth but irrespective of class it remained the most common material for clothing. Some women would ensure the clothing needs of the household were met by encouraging their female staff to contribute by sewing and mending clothes. Along with clothing her family, a woman also had the responsibility for ensuring her staff were provisioned with clothing and footwear. Clothing was usually provided twice a year ensuring they had suitable clothing for the seasons. The wealthiest households provided a uniform known as a livery, often reserved for men but female servants may be provided with matching gowns, aprons and such, signifying their role. A housewife may have to provide a lot of clothing depending on the number of servants. This task was eased by the fact that a mistress of such a household would have many females in her employ who would assist her in making the clothing. Alternatively, if required, they may be able to afford the services of seamstresses and tailors to make the clothing. Smaller households would often provide clothing of a lesser quality but designed to last longer, and female servants would be tasked with mending the clothing of staff and creating new clothing as required or for gifts at New Year. Female servants also had the chance of receiving additional clothing from their mistress or at least from the female next in line of their hierarchy in a large household. These gifts of clothing would become their best clothing rather than working clothes. Even those employed as maids or ladies-in-waiting may be gifted gowns down the hierarchy. These gifted garments could perhaps be worn daily depending on the gown, as the clothing in these settings was much more extravagant. Fabric was an alternative provision rather than readymade clothing. If male servants were gifted fabric their wife, female relative or another female servant would make the clothing on their behalf or they could pay for it to be made, although this could be a cost many could not afford.

Clothing was not the extent of women's needlework; all manner of things were created by women and their servants. Nowadays we would simply purchase bedding but the Tudors did not have that luxury for the most part. Of course, there were merchants who would sell coverlets, hangings and pillows but the majority of women either made them or were gifted them. Bed hangings were a luxury, as was a bed, but the hangings were designed to keep out the cold and afford its occupants a degree of privacy. Being a married couple in a household where servants may sleep on a truckle bed in their bedroom meant they had little privacy so it is not hard to imagine many women spending a vast amount of time working on bed hangings. The larger the household, the more linens were required, for the family but also for the servants. As a result, needlework was an essential task for wives and her servants to spend their time on. The more fortunate who could afford to purchase the majority of their clothes or have them made for them instead used their needlework skills for embroidering. Embroidery was a pastime or act of charitable work as they, along with their maids, would embroider beautiful items intended for the Church or would sew garments of clothing for those in need.

With all of this responsibility, it is no wonder Tudor women were rarely idle. But there were even more tasks to be done when it came to the health of the household, which was the woman's concern. Many women of sufficient means had a still room situated on their property. The still room was effectively a distillery room and the highlight was the still itself. A still was used to distil liquids by boiling then condensing the vapours whilst the contents cooled. A still room was used for preserving plants, herbs and flowers for use in food, medicine and cosmetics as well as cleaning products. It was a space for women to create medicines, tinctures and lozenges as well as recipes for soap, washing waters and the more elaborate tooth cleaning powders. These powders often incorporated cloves, both as a scent and for its pain-relieving properties.[14] Those without a specific room could still make most of these things, it was not essential to their creation, rather a beneficial addition for those with the means. All would pick their selected ingredients and dry them in bundles hanging from the ceiling. Most villages had a local wise woman who was unlikely to have a dedicated still room, but even without they were more than capable of creating medicines and everything else those with a still room could make.

Women took on the role of helping their family, household and any tenants with medical concerns. It was not just the men studying medicine who understood Galen's theories of four humours, all of society believed the body was made up these and when one was not in proportion with the other three it caused illness. The Tudors believed fire, earth, water and air made up everything within the universe, and each of these had their own qualities: fire – hot and dry; earth – cold and dry; water – cold and moist; air – hot and moist. The four humours which made up the human body were linked to these elements: red choler – hot and dry (fire); black choler – cold a dry (earth); phlegm – cold and moist (water); blood – hot and moist (air).[15] The symptoms of the person would indicate which of the humours was imbalanced and therefore how it should be treated. For instance, if someone was suffering with a fever, this may indicate their blood humour was out of balance, and they would be encouraged to take remedies consisting of 'cold' ingredients, and lots of fluid to quench the heat. Although it appears fairly complicated to us today, the Tudors used this theory to treat a huge variety of illnesses. Later in the sixteenth century other theories were developed and introduced but the majority of Tudor women, particularly the illiterate, continued using Galen's theories to treat themselves and their family.

Those with wealth could afford to spend the time and ingredients making medicines for the benefit of all within their local community, particularly their own household and their tenants. Lady Margaret Hoby, who kept a diary of her daily life, and Lady Grace Mildmay, were amongst the many women who were content to use their skills in herbs and medicine for the benefit of all. It became part of a housewife's duty to ensure her still room was fully stocked, whether this was through her own herbal garden which she may tend herself or by ordering ingredients through merchants and apothecaries. To use her still room efficiently, a woman had to understand which plants to sow and harvest according to the season, and how best to preserve them. Distilled waters were a popular way for those with a still room to preserve their concoctions. The waters could be kept throughout the year and could be mixed, used in the making of salves and lozenges, or for cosmetic purposes.

Thomas Tusser provides a wealth of information on what herbs and flowers were used throughout the period and their differing uses. Tusser recommends plants for all occasions and purposes, including the ideal time of year they should be planted. He makes particular reference to a variety of plants to be grown in a herbal garden for the use of medicine, including mandrake, valerian and poppies.[16] Others were recommended for their scent including rosemary, widely used for a variety of reasons. Women would need to spend considerable time creating remedies, either alone or with the assistance of her maids. It was wise to have some remedies ready to use in case of sudden illness. Poorer women were more than capable of making their own herbal remedies, and recipes were shared amongst families even by the illiterate. The local wise woman who had practised her skills could be relied upon to treat the community, particularly where an apothecary, barber surgeon or doctor could not be afforded. They may not have the resources of the rich but they could certainly make basic remedies with readily available ingredients. Freely picked herbs and flowers could also be used in cooking or dried out and spread over the floor, known as rushes, to keep it dry and smelling fresh and to keep away insects and vermin. Wormwood was recommended by Thomas Tusser for keeping away fleas and infection: 'While wormwood hath seed, get a handful or twaine, to save against March to make flea to refraine; Where chamber is sweeped, and wormwood is strowne, no flea for his life dare abide to be knowne'.[17] The wealthy also used floor rushes, as carpets were generally hung on walls as tapestries rather than laid on the floor. Rushes provided a scented floor covering which when stepped on released the scent. It also made it easy to sweep out anything spilled or dropped and dirt collected in the rushes.

Recipes for every possible scenario including dye for clothing, bedding and tapestries, repellents to keep away anything which may damage fabrics, perfumes and soaps were passed along the generations. Those who could afford to do so could also add to their own recipes by purchasing books such as that of Gervase Markham, *The English Housewife*. Women would spend time practising their skills and following recipes to keep their textiles in good condition. An extra supply of herbs was always useful for travelling chests to keep clothing smelling sweet and safe from pests. Mistresses of large households would also pass on their skills to their daughters, other female kin, and any girls who may be residing in their household; some of whom had been pauper children apprenticed to the household or entered into service by the parish. The passing down of this knowledge was not limited to herbal skills but often extended to a basic education as well as lessons in housewifery. Of course, whilst they were learning, the labour of these young females contributed towards the household. Women that took on poor young females either as apprentices or into their service had responsibilities for their upkeep and it served both the mistress and the young female well if both were committed to the experience. For the young female she could find a welcoming household, receive an education, gain valuable skills and possibly a lifetime position, whilst the mistress could mould a young female and teach her how to do things in a preferred manner as well as gain a loyal servant by the end of the term.

Gardens were not just a means of supplying herbs for those fortunate to have a stillroom. Anyone with a garden would make the best use of it, from planting and growing vegetables, orchards and herbs and flowers. Even the smallest of spaces could be used to plant some type of vegetable which would help families survive. Others had wonderful gardens separated into different areas: herbal, vegetable and of course the Elizabethan pleasure gardens where time could be spent admiring the flowers, plants and displays. Women of humble and middling ranks would often tend their gardens themselves, planting, cultivating and harvesting produce to provide for their household, with any surplus being sold to gain additional income or donated to those in need. If a household had staff specifically for the orchards and gardens, they would liaise directly with the kitchens regarding provisions to feed the family and staff as well as produce that could be preserved. The mistress would need to be aware of surplus produce so she may decide if it was to be sold, donated or sent as gifts to others. Where possible, the land fed the household including all the servants, this meant ensuring the gardens were maintained and run efficiently to maximise produce and reduce the need to purchase from elsewhere.

Wives who were fortunate enough to be the mistress of multiple properties had the additional responsibility of organising the movement of their household between properties. Families moved on occasion to allow the property to be cleansed properly, the rushes swept up, floor and walls cleansed, new rushes laid and all areas sanitised thoroughly. This operation was likely to be largely directed by a steward but the mistress of the house would be consulted throughout and would determine the items of furniture to make the journey with them, with beds often accompanying the wealthy along their travels.

In order to be effective as a mistress in supervising or completing these tasks, a female firstly had a lot to learn herself. Those who had grown up in a similar size property or estate would likely find marriage to be less intimidating as they will have learned skills in housewifery whilst growing up. Those who married up in wealth or rank may have found becoming the mistress of a larger household than they were accustomed to, to be an overwhelming experience. This is where a good experience with their mother-in-law was valued. If a young wife initially moved into a property with her in-laws, her new mother-in-law could immediately begin to teach her the intricacies of the household including giving information on what produce the estate supplied itself, what was ordered, details on the hiring of servants as well as their specific duties. If not already mastered, the art of keeping accounts as well as the ability of checking the accounts of the bailiff or steward would be a very beneficial skill to learn from their mother-in-law, particularly if they would one day be the mistress of the estate. A sound financial understanding of her household was vital for a wife to be able to manage especially in her husband's absence. Wives of merchants and men of rank would have experienced an absent husband on a regular basis when their husband was absent for trading or public duties. The wives of merchants and other successful traders would no doubt be responsible for their own household accounts, just as most housewives were, so it is likely their wives would often assist with their husband's accounts, or at least maintain them in his absence. Many men were content to leave their wife in charge of particular financial obligations, regardless of their whereabouts. Therefore, it was to a wife's advantage for her to learn to budget both produce and money so they could forecast harvests, wages, expenses as well as make charitable donations in the form of the giving of alms. Numerous households would distribute money to the poor, donate to the parish and share food left from their table with the poor in the local vicinity.

Women in an unhappy marriage found it extremely difficult to end a marriage. There were three methods of formally ending a marriage: separation, annulment and divorce. A formal separation could be obtained through the Church courts on grounds of cruel behaviour or adultery but the marriage remained valid. If granted a separation, neither party could remarry. When sanctioning a separation, in some cases the Church would order that the goods of the couple be separated, allowing a greater degree of independence for the wife. Alternatively, they may order that maintenance is paid by the husband to the value of up to a third of his annual income. An annulment meant the marriage was declared invalid, as if it had never occurred and any children of the marriage were declared 'bastards'. It could only be agreed by the Church, though as the Church favoured a couple remaining together, it was difficult but not impossible to achieve. Divorce was rare and frowned upon by the Church; it was possible but it was an expensive and lengthy process and did not automatically give a right to remarry. A private bill from Parliament was required to remarry as canon law forbade remarriage, therefore it was an option only available to those with enormous wealth and influence. William Parr, Marquis of Northampton was successful in obtaining a formal separation based on claims his wife, Anne Bourchier, had committed adultery. Anne was a heiress and Parr sought a bill in 1543 annulling the marriage and barring any future child she would bear from inheriting her wealth. Parr, who was the brother of Kateryn Parr, was in favour when he married Elizabeth Bray in 1547 but he was still ordered to separate from her. His first marriage to Anne was declared invalid, and his marriage to Elizabeth was recognised in 1552 but the bill was overturned in 1553 under the reign of Mary I. Despite how he had treated Anne, leaving her impoverished in exile and retaining a large portion of her lands in spite of the separation, it was Anne who pleaded successfully for his release when he was arrested for treason and placed in the Tower of London, condemned to die. The bill was overturned once more in 1558 and the second marriage declared valid. Anne, by this point had been granted an annuity and retired away from court but in much more comfort than she had been living when she had been left in exile.

The only grounds which could be used in requesting an annulment were pre-contract to another, non-consummation of the marriage or prohibited degrees of consanguinity or affinity. For a case which requested an annulment on the grounds of non-consummation, midwives or other ladies may be requested to examine a woman to determine if the wife remained a virgin. This was a highly unenviable task if the case had been disputed, as the result was bound to cause distress to one party or the other. If someone had the support of a powerful member of the nobility or the monarch, they may be able to obtain an annulment but it was a costly affair and as Henry VIII found, even then, it was not always guaranteed that the Church would agree to the request. Following the Reformation when the monarch became the Head of the Church of England, it was simpler for the monarch to demand an annulment if they wished, especially where they themselves did not agree with the marriage.

Those who could not successfully find a way of ending their marriage were faced with an extremely difficult situation as women had little control over finances. They could not save any funds for themselves to leave and even if they did manage to leave the marital home, their husband had every right to locate them and bring them home, take the children away, or withhold funds from their wife. A husband could take away his wife's wage and spend it how he saw fit, even if this meant his family went hungry, and there was little a wife could do to remedy the situation. Even desertion by a husband was not grounds for any method of formal separation. Therefore, most women would attempt to make the best of their situation and on occasion, a wife would even desert their husband. For some women, it was often a better situation if the husband was working away or living elsewhere with a mistress, as long as he provided funds to maintain his family and did not leave them destitute. Some did initiate an informal separation where they would reside separately, but this was frowned upon by the Church unless they had sanctioned it. If separated, neither could remarry or they would be committing bigamy and could face excommunication from the Church. Members of the aristocracy were fortunate enough to possess multiple properties so it was not difficult to live separate lives and only spend time together when required. Desertion amongst the humbler classes was usually the result of the financial burden of having a family. Men would leave their family to seek work elsewhere, others were deserted through a husband having to travel abroad for work or being imprisoned. Their wives were left with the responsibility of trying to support themselves and any children unless the parish intervened to provide assistance.

Marital rape was not a crime and women were advised to submit to their husband at all times.[18] In addition to this, wives, at the time were to tolerate their husbands' taking mistresses, something more common when a wife was pregnant. For women, adultery would result in the loss of her dower or jointure and the condemnation by society, but that was not their only punishment. After the Reformation the secular courts took over the administration of most cases concerning adultery. It was thought the Church courts had been too severe in their sentencing though they did continue to review claims of cohabitation. These cases were specifically concerned with unmarried couples living together, a sin in the eyes of the Church, unless they could mitigate the charge by proving they had been contracted or show an intent to marry. The secular courts issued a variety of sentences for the charge of adultery. Women could be sentenced to the stocks, have their hair cut off, be whipped and in some cases, imprisoned. For men, their only punishment for adultery was to pay maintenance if a child was born, so the child did not become a burden on society. One of the reasons for the difference in punishment was the fact that as a result of committing adultery, a child could be born, and for the woman it would call into question who the father of the child was. Husbands did not want to be forced into raising another man's child who was not their legitimate heir. Wealthy families generally faced no punishment as they had sufficient funds to maintain illegitimate children and mistresses if required.

Although the advice books of the time frowned upon men mistreating their wives, in reality, men were free to treat their wife as they wished, and some chose to treat their wives poorly. As a result, a London by-law was issued forbidding any man to beat his wife after nine in the evening so as to not disturb his neighbours.[19] The law also gave a husband the right to determine where his wife resided, who she communicated with and could restrict her to a particular place of residence, forbidding her to leave.[20] Physical violence could be grounds to seek a formal separation, but it was for a male judge to determine whether the violence was of such an extent that a separation could be granted. Men had the freedom to chastise their wife and violence was only to be the result of extreme provocation. Wives were meant to be obedient and if a wife were to disobey her husband, he could easily use that as an excuse to mistreat her, even physically, without much threat of recourse. If a wife were to kill her husband she could be convicted of petty treason as she was meant to obey her husband, for a husband who killed his wife his offence would be murder. A wife would face burning to death whilst a husband would not commonly receive a death sentence.

Marriage was an important stage in a Tudor woman's life. It led to restrictions in some areas of her life but presented opportunities to socialise with other married women in ways she had probably been unable to do so beforehand. Once married, a woman could attend another's confinement or labour. This is where a woman could really begin to learn about the experience of childbirth and observe it first-hand. For those with many children it could become an enjoyable social aspect of life to attend. For the newly married, it was likely to be a frightening experience at first if they had never witnessed childbirth, and they would need to take advantage of the knowledge and experience of those around them, in preparation for their own pregnancies that may come in the future.

## Chapter Five

# Motherhood

For those women who were already pregnant when they married, the wedding proceeded in order to ensure the child was legitimate. For those who were not already pregnant, following their marriage, the birth of children was the next aim for the majority of Tudor women, particularly those married for the first time. Although all pregnancies were seen as a blessing, the first was of particular importance as it signalled the couple were fertile. For those of aristocratic and royal birth it was extremely important to produce children, preferably males to continue the line of succession. With most women marrying in their twenties, and a lower life expectancy than today, women would have around a decade or more of childbearing years. On average, women of the humbler classes gave birth every couple of years, whilst the wealthy experienced pregnancy almost every year. Much of this was a result of the wealthier classes marrying earlier and therefore having more time to bear children. The wealthy were much more likely to acquire the services of a wet nurse, as such they could return to the marital bed before their less-wealthy counterparts, who would not resume sexual relations until they had ceased breastfeeding.

The experience of motherhood would differ depending on wealth, status and whether the household included maids or servants, but the protocols surrounding pregnancy and childbirth were known by all women irrespective of class and wealth. There were no pregnancy tests or scans available to confirm pregnancy. Vomiting and cravings were a sign to Tudor women that they may be expecting. Women had to rely on understanding their bodily functions, if their courses ceased and a bump began to appear, this was a more prominent sign. With experience, women recognised the signs that they may be pregnant. A pregnancy was usually confirmed when the baby began to move, an occasion referred to as the 'quickening' of the child at around the third or fourth month. At this point a woman may seek the skills of a midwife to confirm her pregnancy. Being superstitious, many expectant Tudor parents and their families would look for signs of the sex of the expected child. Those who followed the humoral theories of Galen believed that expectant mothers features could indicate the baby's gender. A ruddy complexion or her right eye being bright, for example, was said to indicate a boy, whilst if she was pale it was thought she was expecting a girl. Others turned to astrology for an indication not only of the sex, but also to predict the date of birth and signs of what the future held for the child.[1]

Many women, particularly those of the working classes, would continue as normal for the majority of their pregnancy. Expectant mothers who were literate may introduce specific reading into their day. There were conduct books providing a wealth of advice on the care of expecting mothers, and they would rely on the guidance and support of female friends and kin, particularly their mothers. Many women would also include additional prayers for the safe delivery of the baby and their own survival and before many pilgrimage sites were destroyed during the Reformation, some would travel to sites such as Our Lady of Walsingham to make an offering and pray. Certain saints were associated with childbirth and even those who could not go on a pilgrimage would pray to one or more of these, such as the Virgin Mary or St Bridget. There was little in terms of pre-natal care for expectant mothers. Some may begin consuming herbal remedies that they believed would nurture the child whilst in the womb and strengthen the mother in preparation for childbirth. Expectant mothers could also cease fasting on holy days, and they were permitted by the Church to continue eating meat throughout the term of their pregnancy. They would avoid anything of an unattractive or frightening nature as they believed experiencing fright could result in harm to the unborn child. Maternity clothing was non-existent for Tudor women so they had to make do with what they had. Fortunately, many of their clothes used lacing so could be loosened at the sides, back or front. If required, a piece of material known as a stomacher could be added to the front of a gown to disguise where the laces had been loosened. Once a woman believed herself to be pregnant, she could begin making clothes and other necessities for her expected arrival, including the swaddling bands. Mothers-to-be with female servants and maids would find much help from her ladies producing a variety of baby clothes either under her supervision or gifted to her.

There were also preparations to be made for the setting where a woman intended to give birth. Women that were appointed at the royal court would begin to make arrangements to return to their own home. It was rare for such women to remain at court to deliver their child. For those with the financial means to do so, custom dictated that women should enter what was known as her confinement for the last four weeks of their pregnancy. Women of rank and wealth were usually accompanied by a group of women known as 'gossips' whose presence was to keep the woman in good spirits, provide companionship and pray with and for her. Pregnancy was much more dangerous then than now and therefore a safe environment for the birth was vital. For those with the resources, confinement took place in a separate room or set of rooms and they likely attempted to emulate the proceedings of the royal court. The rooms would need to be prepared ahead of time, and all but one window would be closed and covered with tapestries or materials. The remaining window was to allow in a little light. The walls would be hung with arras to help keep the room warm and cosy. The purpose was supposedly to symbolise the womb to comfort the child once born. Clean bedding, furniture and supplies would need to be brought in and ready for the arrival of the company of women who would join the expectant mother. If it were possible women would often arrange for a small area within her rooms for prayer or have a prie-dieu brought to the rooms. Others made arrangements for a priest to be able to visit, without the women being visible to him; a curtain could be used to section off an area where the priest could enter, without having to join the company of the women. Around four weeks before the expected birth, the expectant mother would enter her rooms with her ladies and would not emerge until after the birth. The doors would even perhaps be guarded against unwanted visitors. From then on, the room was kept very warm, and all meals, drink and other necessities would be brought to the room for the duration of her confinement.

The confinement of an expectant queen was dictated by the royal household ordinances. According to the royal ordinances, when the queen wished to begin her confinement, she would attend the chapel alongside the nobility. After prayers, she would proceed to the great chamber to partake in a cup of wine with added spices. Two men of noble birth would then escort the queen to her chambers, where the walls and windows were all covered with beautiful tapestries, often of a religious or morality theme, and the floor would be carpeted. There would be a pallet bed and the royal bed, both with all the required sheets and coverlets, ready for the queen.

and they then to take their leave of the Queene. Then all the ladies and gentlewomen to goe in with her; and after that noe man to come into the chamber where shee shall bee delivered, save woemen, and they to bee made all manner of officers, as buttlers, panters, sewers, kervers, cupbearers; and all manner of officers shall bring to them all manner of things to the great chamber doore, and all the woemen officers for to receave it in the chamber: a traverse of damaske, the bed arrayed with sheetes of fine lawne or fine raynes, great pillows with a head sheete according too the sheetes; a pane of ermines embrothered with riche cloth of gould, the ells breadth of the cloth, and headsheete of ermine and cloth of gould of the same suite; a pallett by the bed arrayed according to the bed, with sheetes and paine; except the cloth of gould on the paine to bee of another collour than that of the great bed; and over the pallett a large sperner of crimson sattin, with a bowle of gould or silver and guilt; and above the openinge of the same sperner to bee embrothered the King's and Queen's arms, and the residue of with crownes of gould: and that such estates both spirituall and temporall as it shall like the Kinge to assigne to be gossippes, to bee neere the place where the Queene shall bee delivered, to the intent anon after they bee ready that the child may soone bee christened.[2]

The ordinances were evidently very precise in what is expected of those who escorted the queen to her confinement and the ladies who would be chosen to spend confinement with her. They continue to discuss in detail how the royal bed and pallet should be arranged, down to the minute detail of how many pillows should be provided and the materials used to dress the bed. Elizabeth of York would have certainly followed this protocol in her many pregnancies and it is likely the Tudor queens who followed her into confinement, including Mary I, would have done the same.

Confinement was a woman's world; no men were allowed entry into the chambers, and there were various rules within confinement. Confinement was a time of piety, reflection and the contemplation of death through childbirth. Some women chose to spend this time writing letters to their unborn child, spouse and family. The women wanted to ensure their wishes regarding the upbringing of the child were known if she did not survive the ordeal, and she may even provide advice for the child if it were born a female for when she grew older. The working classes could rarely afford to take a month away from work and did not commonly have the means to have a separate chamber to provide for confinement. Being without the means to have a separate confinement room did not mean a lack of preparation, women of all classes prepared for childbirth in some manner. All would ensure there was a white linen sheet to cover the bed; those less fortunate may need to borrow clothing and bedding to assist them during their labour and afterwards until they could resume their own laundry duties. Whilst confinement may not be as lengthy for working class women, they would still have the company of 'gossips' with them when their time was near. Amongst the humbler classes, the gossips likely undertook more laborious tasks and kept the household running than those attending royalty or aristocratic women who would fundamentally provide companionship and care for the expecting mother.

When the labour pains began, various women could be called upon to attend the expecting mother if they were not already with her in confinement. Poorer women may not be able to afford the services of a midwife and may be reliant on family, friends or the local wise woman and her assistant to support with the birth of her child. If there was an estate nearby, the mistress may be asked to attend and assist with the birth as well as bringing with her remedies for the labouring woman. Those who could afford to would seek the services of a recommended midwife who would be called for with the onset of labour and would remain throughout.

> 'the Mydwyfe muste instruct and comfort the partie, not onlye refreshing her with goode meate and drinke, but also with sweete wordes, geuyng her good hope of a speedfull deliueraunce, encouraging and enstomackyng her to pacience and tolleraunce, byddyng her to holde in her breath to muche as she may, also strokyng gently with her hands her belly above the navell, for that helpeth to depresse the byrth downewarde.'[3]

Mothers of expectant women often played a large role in their daughter's confinement and labour, passing on her knowledge and experience, providing comfort, and ensuring her daughter was provided with food, drink and herbal cordials. Some women would choose to travel to their parents' homes for their birth, typically if it were her first child. This option gave an expectant mother the comfort of her own mother being present and not having to worry about her own household, here she was ensured of the care and rest she needed. The midwife would likely arrive with herbal remedies she had created beforehand. If not, she and the other ladies would spend time concocting remedies using ingredients which were believed to speed up the delivery of childbirth and ease pain, some of the most common being lilies and rose. Pain relief was limited to wine and herbal remedies, although one recipe did contain opium, but was likely to only be affordable to those with wealth.

Prior to the Reformation, and no doubt covertly afterwards, much faith was placed in holy relics such as girdles which were associated with specific saints. Women also believed that certain charms and stones could provide relief and aid in ensuring a safe delivery. Eagle stones were a popular choice and had been referred to as early as the seventh century. An eagle stone was a hollow stone with another stone or alternative within so it would make a noise when shaken.[4] The stone was meant to symbolise the child inside the womb and was believed to assist with the pain of childbirth as well as prevent miscarriage. The Tudors believed the stone acted as a lure to the unborn child, therefore by wearing the stone as an amulet it kept the baby from miscarrying. Once labour began it would be moved to the lower abdomen, encouraging the baby to move lower, resulting in the birth.[5] Protestant reformers sought to suppress many of the traditions and midwives were instructed to avoid incantations and were to report any others who continued to do so. The *Sarum Missal*, the most popular pre-Reformation collection of prayers contained masses for expectant mothers.

> Almighty God, be present with our supplications, and grant unto Thine handmaid the gift of thy bountiful protection; and when the time of her labour is at hand, she may receive the protection of thy grace; and that the child she may have borne be brought to the laver of salvation, and increase and grow in grace.[6]

There was no prescribed method or position for women to give birth, some lay on their own bed, others would have a pallet bed brought in to avoid their own being soiled. Pillows could be used to support the woman's back or she may prefer to brace herself against a piece of furniture or the wall. Birthing stools were popular but could not be afforded by all, and some women chose to crouch and be held up by the women assisting them.

Mary I.

Dress hook.

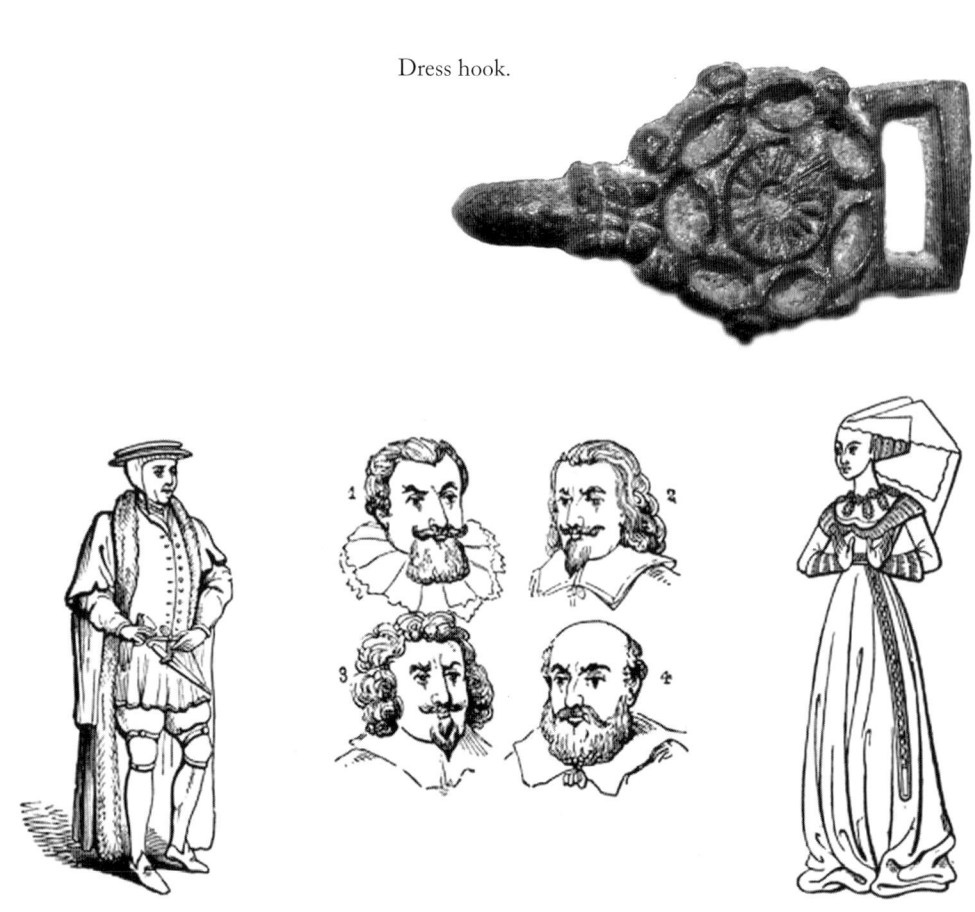

Fashions of the era.

Music book and instrument owned by Elizabeth I.

Clothing comparison between peasants and the queen.

Lady Jane Grey.

Sir Thomas More with his daughter Margaret More-Roper.

Lawn Bowling.

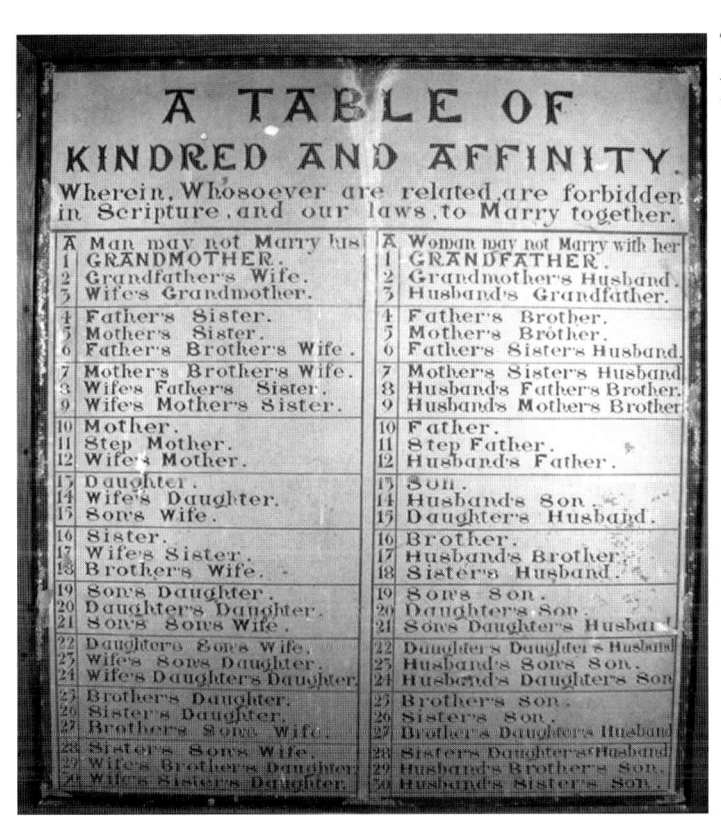

Table of Kindred and Affinity in relation to marriage.

Wedding procession.

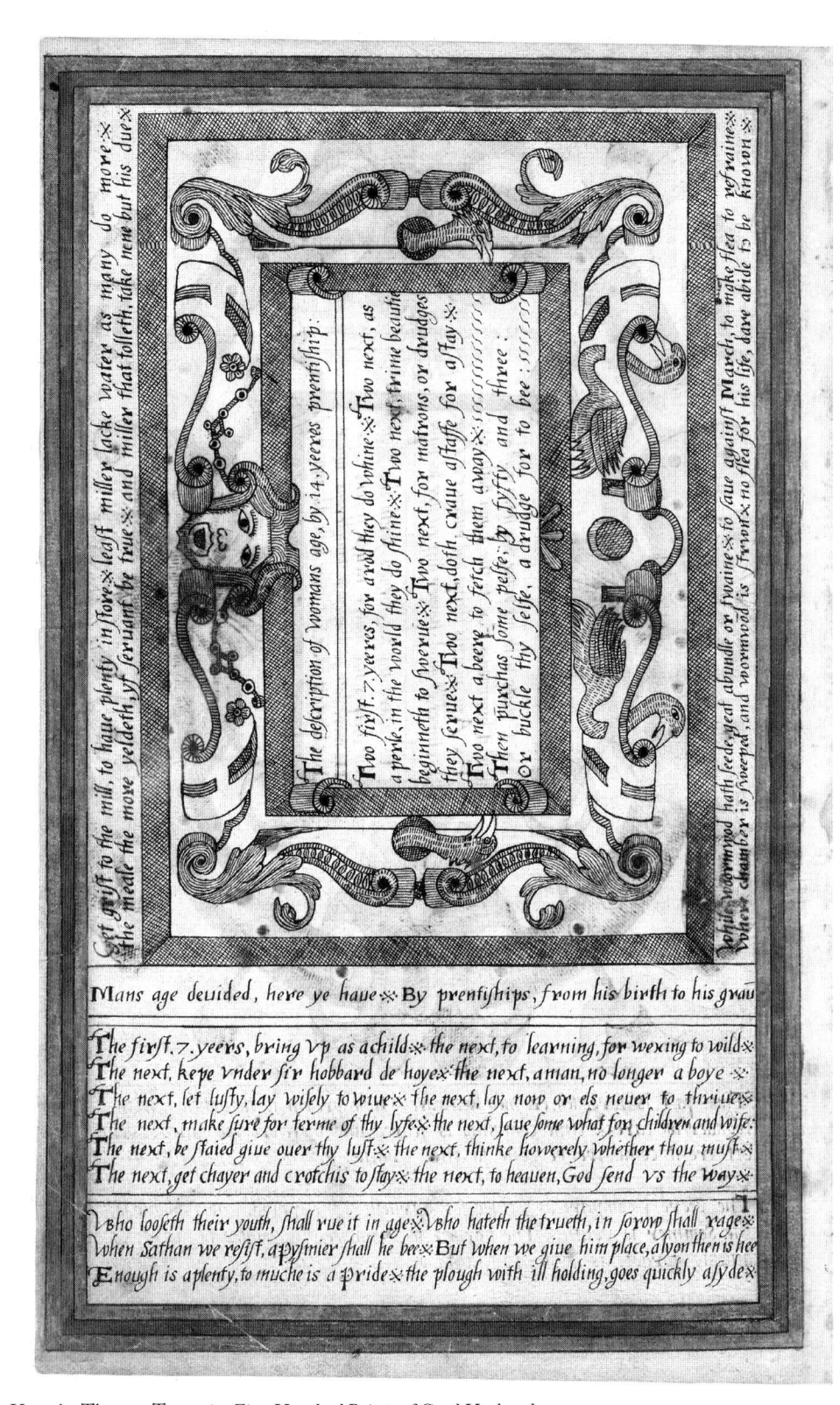

The description of womans age, by 14 yeeres prentiship.

Two first 7. yeeres, for aroif they do whine: Two next, as
a perle, in the world they do shine: Two next, twine beautie
beginneth to swerue: Two next, for matrons, or drudges
they serue: Two next, doth, craue a staffe for a stay:
Two next a beery, to fetch them away:
Then purchas some pelfe, by fyftý, and three:
Or buckle thy selfe, a drudge for to bee:

Mans age deuided, here ye haue: By prentiships, from his birth to his graue.

The first, 7. yeers, bring vp as a child: the next, to learning, for wexing to wild:
The next, kepe vnder sir hobbard de hoye: the next, a man, no longer a boye:
The next, let lusty, lay wisely to wiue: the next, lay now, or els neuer to thriue:
The next, make sure for terme of thy lyfe: the next, saue some what for children and wife:
The next, be staied giue ouer thy lust: the next, thinke howerely whether thou must:
The next, get chayer and crotchis to stay: the next, to heauen, God send vs the way.

Who looseth their youth, shall rue it in age: Who hateth the trueth, in sorow shall rage:
When Sathan we resist, a pysmier shall he bee: But when we giue him place, a lyon then is hee:
Enough is a plenty, to muche is a pride: the plough with ill holding, goes quickly asyde.

Verse by Thomas Tusser in *Five Hundred Points of Good Husbandry*.

A Lord and Lady.

A sixteenth-century room.

Birthing scene.

Chap.1. *The expert Midwife.* 79

ring woman to her Stoole, which ought to be prepared in this fashion.

The forme or fashion of the stoole.

Let the Stoole be made compasse-wise, underpropped with foure feet, the stay of it behind bending backeward, hollow in the midst, covered with a blacke cloth underneath, hanging downe to the ground, by that meanes that the labouring

Obstetrical chair, also known as a birthing stool.

A mother and her children.

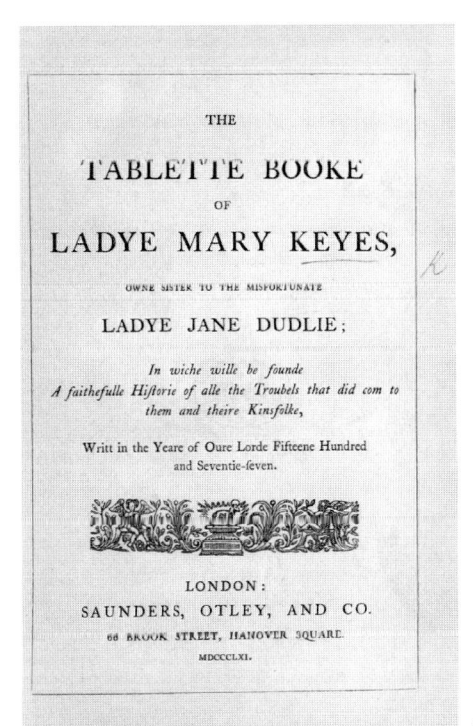

Tablet book belonging to Lady Mary Keyes.

THE
HERBALL
OR. GENERALL
Historie of
Plantes.

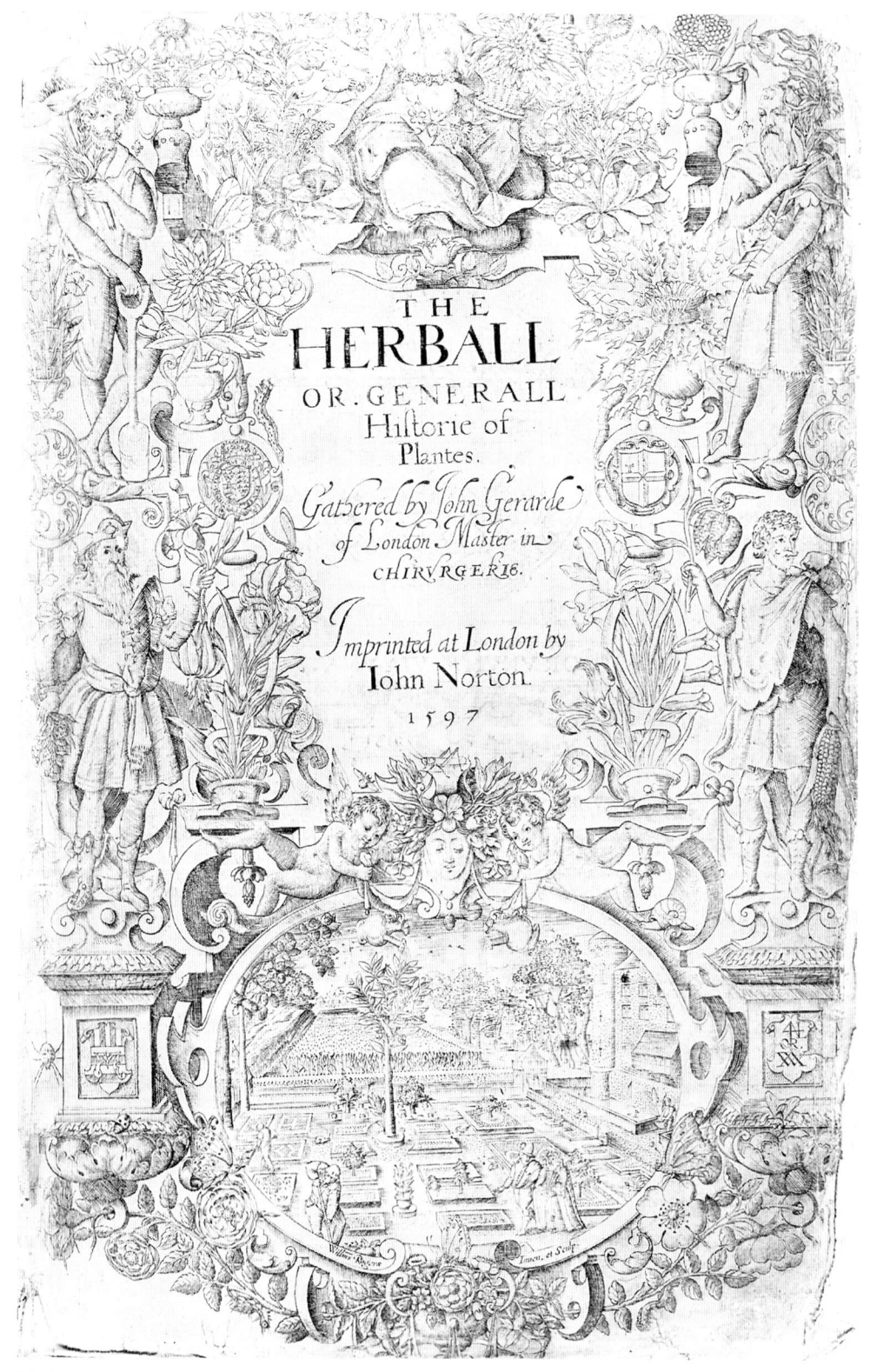

Gathered by John Gerarde
of London Master in
CHIRVRGERIE.

Imprinted at London by
Iohn Norton.
1597

Herbal book.

Woman using a spinning wheel.

A Tudor hospital.

Midwife assisting a woman in labour.

Caesarean section.

Woman spinning.

HEAD-DRESSES, SIXTEENTH CENTURY.

Headdresses.

Female Costume, 1600.   Ladies' Head-dresses, 16th Century.   Ordinary Costume, Time of Henry VIII.

Fashions.

Elizabeth I

Monumental brasses of Sir John Bassett (1462–1529) of Umberleigh, with his two wives: (right) first wife Ann Denys; (left) second wife Honor Grenville. Monochrome negative image, detail from top slab of his chest-tomb, Atherington Church, Devon.

Once the baby was born, the midwife remained in charge of the chamber. She would have the responsibility of cutting the umbilical cord and checking there were no obstructions to the breathing of the baby. Midwives had a knife reserved specifically for the cutting of the umbilical cord; the knife became the emblem of midwives. The midwifes main concern was ensuring the umbilical cord was severed and tied efficiently and that the navel was then cleaned, sometimes using an astringent powder of frankincense. The other women in the birthing chamber who may be of a superstitious nature, may try to have a peek at the navel to try and determine if the new mother would have more children in the future. It was thought if the baby's navel had wrinkles, then more children would follow. To help the baby's breathing the midwife or her assistant would clear its nostrils, checking for obstructions and could then, if she were comfortable doing so, pass the child to another to be bathed and swaddled. When swaddling, the limbs of the baby would be massaged before being tightly wrapped in bands of linen. Swaddling was thought to encourage physical development and keep limbs straight whilst growing. Most mothers would have prepared more than one set of swaddling bands as they would need to be changed and laundered. If swaddled incorrectly it could damage the child and restrict blood flow, therefore many midwives chose to complete this task themselves on the first occasion. She would then administer to the mother, assisting with the passing of the afterbirth and dispensing with it. During these tasks she would be directing the other women to clear away soiled materials, provide the mother with restorative drinks and if she wished, cleaning her with a bowl of water, before placing her in bed if she had given birth away from her main bed. If the new mother required any dressings or poultices, the midwife would administer these, at least initially.[7] Once the baby and the mother had been tended to and were clean, the midwife would allow a period of bonding between mother and child but this would be brief if there was an impatient father waiting to see his child or a wet nurse standing by ready to feed the child. If there were concerns surrounding the health of the baby, the midwife would christen the child. Midwives were sanctioned by the Church to perform this where there was an urgent requirement to do so for fear of a child dying prior to being christened. Women were at risk of puerperal fever, therefore, if the health of the newly delivered mother became a concern the midwife would remain, attempting to restore her with herbal remedies, making sure the placenta had been delivered in full and keeping a watchful eye on the mother. The ministrations of the midwives and even doctors when consulted, were not always successful; mothers died from childbirth including Elizabeth of York and Jane Seymour, showing that wealth and rank could not protect them during this vulnerable time.

During this time there were ongoing debates about the benefits of mothers breastfeeding and those of using a wet nurse. It was believed nursing passed on qualities to a child through the milk, therefore many argued mothers should feed their own children. Some mothers did not produce enough milk and had little choice but to use the services of a wet nurse. Usually, the wealthier or higher-ranking the mother, the more likely she was to employ a wet nurse rather than feed her baby herself. Breastfeeding was thought to halt conception, and the aristocracy and royalty were keen to conceive again quickly so, even if she wished to feed her child herself, a new mother could be overruled by a husband wishing to begin trying for another child. Others chose to secure the services of a wet nurse in an effort to appear fashionable by acting as the aristocracy did. A wet nurse would be chosen with care:

'First, that she be of good colour and complexion, and that her bulke and brest be of good largenesse. Secondly, that it be not to sone ne to long after her labour, so that it be two monethes after her labour at the leaste, and that (yf it may be) such one which had a man child. Thyrdly, that she be of meane and measurable lykyng, neyther to fat ne to leane. Fourthly, that she be good and honest of conversation, neyther over hasty or irefull, ne to sadde or solome, nytherto fearefull or timorous: for these affections and qualities bee pernycious and hurtfull to the mylke, corruptyng it, and passe foorth through the mylke into the chylde, makynge the chylde of lyke condicion and manners. Also that they be not overlight and wanton of behaviour'.[8]

Wet nurses employed by wealthy families would either take the baby to their own home or would reside with the family until the baby was weaned. Some chose to send their baby in the company of the wet nurse away to their country home if they had not already travelled there for the birth. If they resided in a busy town or city they may lease or borrow somewhere in the country, as it was thought the air in the countryside would be more beneficial for the baby. If they had chosen to have the child nursed in their country home, they could of course visit, or the mother would also go and stay for a while whilst the husband remained in town and visited in between obligations. Mothers with duties at court had to prioritise their role, her duties at court taking precedence and she would have to be content with visits to the child around her obligations. No child would be sent away until it had been christened, therefore, regardless of obligations or her husband's wishes, a mother would at least get a few days with her new baby before the nurse travelled away.

Where there was no urgency for the child to be christened, the baby would be taken to church on a Sunday or another holy day soon after the birth for the ceremony. Even where there was no urgent requirement for the child to be christened, it was still a ceremony that occurred usually within days due to the high mortality rate of children at the time. Mothers would customarily not attend the christening as it was often too soon after the birth for a mother to be out of confinement; most would still be resting at this point. Fathers also played little part in the christening of their children, instead the godparents were the key players of the day. The midwife would usually carry the child, though in aristocratic and royal ceremonies, one of the godparents was given the honour. Tradition required that boys were to have two godfathers and one godmother whilst girls would have two godmothers and one godfather. The selection of godparents was very important to the Tudors; as with marriage it could provide opportunities for the family as godparents were expected to play an active role in the child's life. By selecting influential godparents, it not only meant the child would benefit from their involvement early in life but they may have opportunities later in life that were perhaps not possible without the assistance of their godparents. The nobility, courtiers and the royal family were often asked to be godparents to children. This would of course mean an expensive gift for the child, provided they accepted the role, but also required an interest in the child's upbringing and education. The christening ceremony would usually begin at the end of the usual service, when the godparents would approach the font whilst other guests arrived or waited for the ceremony to begin. The service began with prayers and the Gospel of Saint Mark. The godparents would then actively take part in the next part of the ceremony.

Dost thou forsake the devil and all his works, the vain pomp, and glory of the world, with all covetous desires of the same, the carnal desires of the flesh, so that thou wilt not follow, nor be led by them?
Godparents: I forsake them all.
Dost thou believe in God the father Almighty maker of heaven and earth? And in Jesus Christ his only begotten Son our Lord, and that he was conceived by the Holy Ghost, born of the virgin Mary: that he suffered under Pontius Pilate, was crucified dead and buried, that he went down into hell, and also did rise again the third day: that he ascended into heaven, and sitteth at the right hand of God the Father Almighty, and from thence shall come again at the end of the world, to judge the quick and the dead?
And dost thou believe in the Holy ghost, the holy Catholic Church, the Communion of saints, the remission of sins, the resurrection of the flesh, and everlasting life after death?
Godparents: All this I stedfastly believe.
Wilt thou be baptised in this faith?
Godparents: That is my desire.[9]

After further prayers the child is immersed into the water and baptised. If the child is not in good health the water would instead be poured on to the child. A cross is made on the baby's head before further prayers are recited by all. Before the ceremony ends the godparents are commanded to bring the child to church for confirmation once they have learned the Lord's Prayer, ten commandments and the articles of faith. Prior to the Reformation the baby would be wrapped in a chrisom cloth during the ceremony which the mother was to return to the church at her churching ceremony. Baptisms or christenings were an occasion for gifting. As expected, the child would be given gifts, many of which they were too young to have any use for, for instance gold cups, but they were not the only ones to receive gifts. The godparents, friends and family of the parents would also give gifts to the midwife and any nurses that were present. This was surplus to any fee they may receive and was a gift of appreciation for the delivery and care of mother and child. Gifts from the wealthy could perhaps be extremely valuable and if gifted something from the royal court, they would perhaps save it as a keepsake as well as a focal point for gossip amongst friends.

The period following the birth of a child was known as the woman's month or lying-in and ended with a service known as 'churching' or 'purification'. The majority of women could not afford to remain in any kind of lying-in for a month following the birth and would have to work almost immediately to ensure she could provide for her family and avoid the baby being taken by the parish. If a woman could work at home, then she could keep her child with her but otherwise taking the child to work with her would be subject to approval from her master or mistress. Alternatively if there were older children within the household, a grandmother staying after the birth, or relatives living nearby, they could assist with childcare whilst the mother went out to work or resumed her daily chores once more. Mothers of a middling status could perhaps spend some time lying-in though perhaps not the full month like their wealthier counterparts. These households were more likely to have more domestic help than humbler homes and could share the mother's duties amongst them for a short period. The man of the house may even take some responsibility for resources and finances, though it is unlikely they would be involved in organising the cooking and cleaning.

Although a woman could use bowls of water and a cloth to clean herself whilst abed, after a period of time ranging between three days to two weeks, if there were no concerns for her health, she could then fully bathe. At this time her bedding would be changed so she could return to a clean, fresh bed after bathing. This was known as her 'upsitting'. Although this was the usual practice, most of those who had the resources available to do so, likely changed their bedding before this time whilst lying-in, particularly if it were to become soiled. After this stage, the mother was not confined to her bed, she could move around her chambers but remained within them for the remainder of the lying-in period. For the working classes they did not have this option and needed to return to work, in which case they would only spend up to three days in bed before their upsitting, then health permitting, would return to work. A woman's upsitting was a social event and a further step in her recovery. It signalled that she was on her way towards a full recovery, and it was a time when more people could visit, and gifts would be brought for the mother and child by well-wishers. Those who had accompanied the woman throughout her confinement and labour would be treated to a feast and entertainment as a sign of appreciation from the new mother. Subsequently, when guests had been welcomed and thanks given, a woman could leave her chambers but would remain within her household until the end of her lying-in period, sometimes another ten to fourteen days following her upsitting. Society expected a woman to be 'churched' before she resumed her role within society.

Wives of wealthy merchants, gentlewomen and aristocracy would most often participate in a long period of lying-in for up to four weeks, and so her upsitting would signal the halfway mark. Aristocratic wives would be expected to rest and recover so they could begin trying for another child as soon as possible. Being wealthy did not necessarily mean the family would pay for additional domestic service during this time. There was often more than enough help from family and friends who had come to stay with the woman for her confinement. Other women of rank who were attending, would of course bring their own ladies, maids and servants with them, therefore there was an abundance of staff to keep the household running efficiently even whilst their mistresses were indisposed. Female relatives or friends would take on the supervisory role of the new mother temporarily, directing the servants, maintaining the household and supporting the mother to regain her strength through rest and herbal remedies. During her lying-in not all the women who had accompanied the woman to her childbed would remain but many would return regularly to provide company and gossip. It was seen as an honour to attend a birthing mother during her confinement and lying-in and some travelled considerable distances to be there for family and friends.

Prior to the Reformation the service of churching was considered as the purification of the woman following childbirth. While it was not a formal requirement, traditionally some recently delivered women would arrive at the church for their churching carrying a lit candle and wearing a white veil, accompanied by two married women. Afterwards, those with Protestant leanings regarded the purification element as superstitious and offensive to assume that women were unclean following childbirth. During the reign of Edward VI, although the ceremony did continue and the 1549 edition of the *Book of Common Prayer* referred to the ceremony as *The Order of the Purification of Women*, this was amended in the 1552 edition to *The Thanksgiving of Women after Childbirth*. Churching became a thanksgiving ceremony; veils, candles and blessings that included the use of holy water were removed from the service. All women who had given birth would attend a churching ceremony regardless of whether she had experienced lying-in for a month or not, and all would be expected to make an offering to the church. The offering may be the return of the chrisom cloth or a sum of money and in some cases, both. For those with little money the return of the chrisom cloth, sometimes a communal one, was the most suitable option. The woman, her female servants, friends and family, and the midwife, all in their best clothes attended church for the service which in comparison to other services at the time, was short. On occasion the woman's husband would attend but it was largely a female gathering to give thanks for a safe delivery and welcome the new mother back to society.

Prior to the Reformation, similar to weddings, the service took place at the door of the church, not inside. It began with Psalms 121 and 128 and concluded when the woman was blessed and sprinkled with holy water. According the *Sarum Missal* as the holy water was being sprinkled, together, the woman and the priest would say: 'Thou shall purge me, O Lord, with hyssop'. Only after this 'purging' could the woman enter the church.[10] After the Reformation and the removal of the 'purification' elements of service, the new mother would enter the church and kneel whilst the priest began the service, in accordance with the *Book of Common Prayer*:

> Forasmuch as it hath pleased almighty God of his goodness to give you safe deliverance, and hath preserved you in the great danger of childbirth: ye shall therefore give hearty thanks unto God and pray.[11]

The service differed from the catholic rites and continued with Psalms 116 and 127, followed by prayers, and ended with:

> O Almighty God, which hast delivered this woman thy servant from the great pain and peril of child birth: Grant we beseech thee (most merciful father) that she, through thy help, may both faithfully live and walk in her vocation, according to thy will, in this life present; and also may be partaker of everlasting glory in the life to come: through Jesus Christ our Lord. Amen.[12]

Those who had lost their child during the labour would also attend a churching ceremony. The Tudors believed it was God's decision as to whether a child and the mother survived the birth leading some to wonder if they had somehow displeased God if the baby did not survive. The service for those who had lost their child would focus on the survival of the mother and that God had chosen their baby to go to heaven rather than survive. In these cases the chrisom cloth may be used as a winding sheet for the burial of the child and therefore could not be returned. The ceremony of churching could be a commemorative event for women, celebrations may follow where women would join together after the ceremony to enjoy the occasion. For others who had lost their child it would have been a more solemn affair shadowed by grief. The extent of the celebrations varied according to wealth but where the mother and child had both survived the ordeal, it was certain to be a joyous affair. Even the humblest of households would partake in food and drink to celebrate the survival of the mother and her return to society.

The care of a baby was the remit of the mother, or if a child was unfortunate to lose their mother in childbirth, then a female relative, if possible. Alternatively, if the family were impoverished, the parish could take on caring responsibilities. The parish could place a new born with another mother to feed and maintain the child, at the cost of the parish, or may pay a wet nurse on behalf of the family. For the Tudors, in theory, being a good mother was supposed to be 'natural' but there was little definition of what this meant in reality. Some argued it meant mothers should breastfeed their own children and maintain a very involved position in the lives of their children whilst others believed it meant ensuring they had all they needed to succeed in their ranks. This could be employing the best nurses, governesses, tutors, securing them a place in another household, and taking an active role in arranging their marriages when the time came. Wealthy and aristocratic mothers generally took a more supervisory role in caring for their young children, delegating the bathing, swaddling, feeding and even the rocking of the cradle to nursemaids and servants. Royal courtiers would have little option but to return to their duties at court, therefore they had little alternative than to recruit women to care for their children. If they did wish for a longer period of time at home with their baby, they would need the permission of their mistress to either remain at home for an extended period of time of time or bring the child to court with them when they returned to their duties.

Babies were usually swaddled for approximately nine months, after which their arms would be left unrestricted. It was, therefore, imperative that the mother and those involved in the care of the child were taught how to swaddle correctly and not to bind too tightly, which could cause harm to the child. Mothers were the dominant figure in a child's life for the first six years, responsible for their care, religion and education. Up to this point young boys and girls were largely treated the same and even dressed the same. At the age of around 6, boys may then enter the male world whilst young girls would begin to learn decorum and the virtues expected of them as they matured. Mothers were responsible for ensuring their daughters understood their status in society, how to recognise another's status and the method of greeting different social ranks.

It was a mother's purpose to begin the education of their children. For daughters this also meant installing an understanding of their duty to be pious, charitable to the poor, and obedient and faithful wives. They were also instructed in the necessity of raising their own children to be good Christians and behave in a manner befitting their station. For most this began with mothers teaching their daughters prayers, by rote if they were illiterate or through the use of books if they were able. Lower classes were largely restricted to learning prayers, other religious quotes, poems and quips from their mother, whereas middling classes had the benefit of more literate mothers who may be able to expand on their education, possibly teaching them basic arithmetic, spelling and writing. Wealthy mothers were those who had the least direct involvement in their daughter's education, particularly if their daughters were raised in another household, but they maintained a supervisory role, instructing what they should learn and who should teach them. Mothers also took on the duty of providing an education and training to other children; those of relatives or those seeking a placement where their daughter could be trained in a household that could provide her with opportunities to improve her status and marriage prospects. Though she did not conceive any children of her own, Lady Margaret Hoby offered places in her home for other children, providing them with an education and training suitable for their station. Having spent some of her youth in the household of the Countess of Huntingdon, Lady Hoby likely wished to continue the goodwill by welcoming others into her own household.

As there was contemporary advice for husbands and wives there was of course also advice for parents;

Such parents therefore as be Christians must know, that their children are also the children of God, and partakers of those blessings that are promised to them in Christ Iesus their Sauiour: and therefore they shall do great iniurie to God himselfe whose children they are, if they shall not see them carefully brought vp in his feare: and much more, if they, as before time many haue done, bequeath them, & in a manner, consecrate & sacrifice them to the seruice of men, by thrusting thē into Abbeyes, Munkeries, Fryeries, Nunneries, and Seminaries, there to be brought vp, and remaine in perpetuall bondage of ignorance, in and idolatrie.

The second point is, that fathers and mothers do nourish and traine vp their children in shamefastnesse, hatred of vice, and loue of all vertue.

They be charged by the fift Commandement, to feede, to nourish, and to bring vp their children, to teach them the principles and seede of Christian religion, to see they learne the Catechisme, to teach them to praise God before and after meales: as also to teach them by little and little, and by often repetitions, to vnderstand wherefore the Sacraments were instituted: to teach them manners how to behaue themselues decently in their going, in their speaking, and gesture of their bodies: how to order themselues reuerently in the Church, how abroad in all places, and towards all men in all honest companies; and so to begin some conscience in them. For it were better for children to be vnborne then vntaught.[13]

There were often instances of childbirth outside of marriage; it is estimated one in forty births were outside of marriage.[14] Some women thought it was acceptable to consummate their marriage once betrothed, even if there had been no wedding. For some, this was the wrong decision as not all men upheld their promises to marry, particularly when learning their intended was now pregnant. Other men were coerced to leave the relationship, perhaps as a result of threats of disinheritance, or the offer of a more influential match. Women working in service could find themselves the object of attention of other servants or sometimes even their master. If she succumbed to advances and found herself pregnant, the consequences for the woman could be tragic. If her master was her admirer, and married she would almost certainly lose her job and be banished from the household.

She may be extremely lucky and have a caring generous master who would ensure she received maintenance for herself and the child or be asked to keep his name a secret so she could remain in employment. If the father were another servant, the master may insist they marry or both may be dismissed from service or at least receive a punishment such as whipping.

Whether the conception was the result of an accident or rape, it was the mother who faced social shunning. Women faced the prospect of losing their job, banishment from their parish and her child bearing the title of 'bastard'. Some parishes went as far as physical punishment including the mother being carted through the parish before being whipped in a public act for all to witness and as a deterrent to others. Those without the financial means to protect themselves could be subject to humiliation and punishment by the parish authorities in an effort to force the mother to divulge the name of the father. In these cases the midwife would often act on behalf of the authorities in trying to convince the mother to divulge the name. If the name was given, the parish could then force the father to pay for the upkeep of the child instead of the baby becoming a burden on the parish.[15] Those who refused to divulge the name would find themselves in receipt of a more severe punishment; they may be whipped in public or have to face a public form of humiliation and penance. The financial implications may be too much for some mothers who may lose their child to the parish. Those who were known as a 'bastard bearer' would find it extremely difficult to secure work following the birth of a child. Society believed these women were untrustworthy. Due to the implications, some may have chosen to attempt abortion rather than face the humiliation of giving birth outside of wedlock. As with contraception in the Tudor era, abortion was disapproved of by society but also the Church. That did not mean it did not happen and there were methods of using herbal remedies in an effort to abort a child. For some this may be the means of keeping their job, avoiding humiliation or becoming destitute. The more fortunate women who had conceived by a man of wealth, could be kept in sumptuous conditions, whether the baby was acknowledged by the father or not. Mistresses may be disapproved of morally but the mistresses of the nobility likely lived a life of luxury protected from any such ostracism by her lover's wealth.

Regardless of whether she be married or not, it was rare for a woman to face her labour alone. Friends, family and neighbours would assist and wealth could pay for the services of the best midwives, none of whom would object to assisting an unmarried woman through her labour. Single women who were forced or chose to leave her parish for another where she was unknown, would usually find assistance from other women when her labour pangs began. A new parish where a woman was unknown could mean she was not shunned. It may be wrong to lie but it is difficult to find fault with a woman who may lie about the father of her child if it meant she would be accepted into the parish, for instance, if she were to say he had died in battle.

For couples who could not conceive, it was seen as the fault of the woman, sometimes being perceived as God being displeased with her. Commonplace books usually provided alleged remedies for barrenness, none of which have any evidence of effectiveness. Giving birth was not the only way to become a mother, women who married a widower, in effect became a mother to his children and would be referred to as such, rather than step-mother. Despite taking on the role of a step-mother, women who did not conceive their own children could face a negative attitude from their husband, resulting in an unhappy home. Men who had children from a previous marriage were perhaps not as disappointed as those who remained childless.

As children grew up and began to leave the nest, a portion of the poorer mothers would miss out on a close relationship with their children due to them having to possibly move away to secure an income. The poorest, being largely illiterate, could not correspond with their children unless they were acquaintances with someone who could write on their behalf and may also need assistance in reading any responses received. Wealthy children of course also moved away but as they were literate so could maintain the close bond with their mother. Those who were poor but managed to remain in the area likely had the closest relationship with their mother as they could visit often, even daily, and the mother could then provide support when the time came for her to become a grandmother.

The marriages of her own children were one area where women could exert their influence and authority, particularly amongst the aristocratic ranks. Mothers were actively involved in selecting suitors and would sometimes approach the parents of a potential suitor before even consulting their son or daughter about the possibility. Mothers did not seek to only find suitors for their children in order to improve status or wealth, they cared about their children's happiness. Katherine Willoughby, who had been married to Charles Brandon, Duke of Suffolk was a widow when she was negotiating a possible marriage for her son to the daughter of the Duke of Somerset. Katherine wrote to William Cecil that she wanted the duke's daughter to be agreeable to the wedding of her own accord rather than be persuaded by friends and wished for the couple to 'begin their loves of themselves, without our forcing'.[16] William Cecil, who would later become 1st Baron Burghley and one of Elizabeth I's most trusted advisers, was Secretary of State in 1550, so may have been tasked with some of the settlement negotiations on behalf of the Crown; the couple would not have been allowed to marry without royal consent due to their rank. Katherine herself was only 14 years old when she married her first husband, Charles Brandon, Duke of Suffolk. Charles had held her wardship following the death of her father. It is possible that due to her youth and lack of supportive male kin, she perhaps felt she had little choice in the match and later wanted to ensure her proposed daughter-in-law did feel like she had a choice in the matter.

Mothers would be engrossed in negotiating marriage portions and of course the arrangement of the wedding itself. It would also be the mother's responsibility to ensure her daughters were aware of what was expected of them on their wedding day and the celebrations which would follow along with providing advice on how to keep their husband happy.

# Chapter Six

# Working Women

The majority of the female population earned a wage, or at least contributed to their maintenance, sometimes from a very young age. Their income was mainly comprised of wages earned through employment or making and selling their own produce. This was in addition to the work they completed on a daily basis within their own homes, whether as a mistress or servant. Amongst the majority of the population, the man of the household did not earn enough to maintain his whole family, therefore women and often children had little choice but to supplement the family income. For young females who had been placed in a household by the parish, few earned an actual wage and instead received clothing, bed and board. Parishes would charge the master or mistress a sum for the placement of a young female. These fees contributed towards the parish whilst the household received cheap labour until the girl came of age. The sum varied according to the age of the female, if she were very young, the sum would be higher as the family would benefit from the labour for a longer period.[1] Young girls of humble families could also be apprenticed by the parish. Parish apprentices tended to begin their tenure much earlier than other apprentices, sometimes as young as 4 years old. Apprentices in these cases could be bound until the age of 18, unless they married prior to that age, though their master would have to consent to any marriage, as it was not usually allowed during an apprenticeship. Alternatively, the term could be shorter with the expectation that the young female would move onto a standard apprenticeship or enter into service at the usual age of around 14 years old. In exchange for taking on the apprentice the parish would recompense the master with a small fee and funds for the clothing and footwear of the child. Apprenticeships were not limited to poor children and the parish; parents could pay a premium to a master or mistress with the specific aim of their daughter being taught a trade which she could later rely upon to earn an income. The term of an apprenticeship was usually a minimum of seven years during which her mistress would be expected to care for, clothe, and where possible, educate her.

For the lower classes, the type of work they could secure largely depended on their geographical location, for instance, East Anglia and some other areas were largely dependent on the cloth trade, especially when demand for English wool increased from abroad. Those working in agriculture or other outdoor occupations had to make the most of the daylight hours, and so usually started their working day around 5:00 am, breaking their fast around 8:00 am before continuing to work until midday. The midday meal for poorer people was simpler than their wealthier counterparts and labouring people may take the opportunity of the break to have a nap. At 2:00 pm they would return to work until around 5:00 pm, or as late as 6:00 pm in the summer. The humbler classes had their main meal soon after they finished work for the day, and following their evening prayers, were in bed by 8:00 pm. For the wealthy, the day would start a little later and for those in attendance at the royal court it would certainly end later with the evening's entertainments beginning around the same time that the lower class were heading to bed and could last until way past midnight.

Although many occupations were barred to females there were roles available, some of which were predominantly undertaken by women. Women were recruited for nursing and were sought after in times of disease and plague to care for the sick, observe and confirm if someone had signs of plague, and even visit the dead to determine if they had died of plague. They could also find work washing and wrapping the dead. It was usually poor women who were recruited to tend to those with plague or infectious illnesses, whether alive or dead, as it was a dangerous occupation. These women were risking their own lives as well as others as they travelled from home to home and even back to their own family. There were less dangerous duties such as cleaning, as well as jobs they shared with their male counterparts for instance, seasonal agricultural labour. Women would not commonly undertake the labour-intensive tasks like ploughing or those involving heavy machinery, but it was not unheard of and women were certainly paid for working during the harvesting, planting crops and haymaking. The inequality in wages is made apparent by a royal proclamation in 1595 which stated that during the harvest women would be paid 2d with food and drink or 4d without refreshments whilst men would earn fifty per cent more at 3d and 6d respectively.[2]

For women today it is difficult to imagine working in the fields wearing an ankle length dress but women could not wear hose. Women who were required to be out in the fields or standing on a riverbank washing clothes, would therefore sometimes wear their dresses a little shorter, just above the ankle to avoid their clothing becoming wet, dirty or entangled in crops. Showing of the arms was not as socially frowned upon as showing legs so they were allowed to roll up their sleeves whilst working or laundering, and they would wear an apron over the front of their gown. For the upper classes the showing of ankles or arms remained immodest, meaning the poorer classes were those to be found working in the fields, or harvesting and laundering clothes in tubs of water, streams or at the river side.

Women could also earn a living as *hucksters*; selling food, drink, or seasonal produce. The occupation of huckster meant the selling of something and comprised of women in roles such as fishwives, alewives and bakers. We have so many options today for what we refer to as fast food, and this is something that was also present during the Tudor era. In towns and cities there were a number of food outlets serving ready to eat hot food such as pies. This was a reasonably priced option for those who spent long days at work or needed a break from cooking for the family and created another opportunity for women to use their skills to earn an income. The occupation of *victualling* was very similar to that of the huckster, but was associated with widows, who would support themselves by boosting their income through the sale of various food items or ale. Those who walked the streets or visited markets with a basket of oysters, bread, fruit, cold pies and other consumables, selling their goods, were also classed as victuallers.[3] Fortunate women may be able to build up a small customer base and could earn a little extra by delivering goods directly to the homes of their customers. This saved people attending stores or travelling to markets but it was hard work for the seller, particularly if they did not own a horse or mule, or even a cart with wheels to help them transport goods. It was not uncommon for poor women to take produce to the homes of the wealthy in the hope they would purchase the goods. Princess Mary, the future Mary I, regularly rewarded poor women for bringing produce, including apples, to her household.[4]

Alewifery was meant to be a licensed practice, though those selling their surplus ale to neighbours would not have been licensed and it was therefore practised by many on a small scale. Licenses were often issued to poor women and widows who had no alternative way of securing an income to support themselves. They would hold this licence in their own right but if a woman was married, the licence was usually held by her husband whilst she did all the work. The process of brewing during the Tudor era was little different than today, just without all the modern equipment. Brewing was simple and could be done by housewives over their hearth, without requiring any expensive equipment. Ale was usually made using barley which firstly had to be malted before being mashed, though many would buy malt already dried and ground. Hot water is added to the ground malt and after a time the liquid, known as wort, is drained and left to cool. Yeast is added to the cooled wort and left to ferment. The liquid could then be filtered and was ready to drink. Beer was introduced when hops became available in England in the late fifteenth century. Hops were added to the wort and boiled for a couple of hours before being cooled ready for the yeast to be added. Hops preserved the drink for longer, making it easier to brew larger amounts without the risk of it going bad. The Tudors, keen to avoid waste, would use the malt repeatedly, the ale becoming weaker each time until it was of no use; it could then be used to feed animals. They also reused the yeast, which was drained off the liquid, and could then be used in baking. In consequence, brewing and baking were often entwined in the duties of a Tudor woman.[5] Alewifery was not always a respectable occupation as those with alehouses or inns may also succumb to the temptation of an additional income from boarding prostitutes.

For some females who were not fortunate enough to secure an income from any other avenue, they might turn to prostitution. Some were also forced into prostitution as a result of debt, whether the debt was their own or their families. There were brothels and tippling houses, often run by women, which perhaps added a layer of security for these women and provided a roof over their heads. Others had no option other than to remain on the streets. Unlike today, there was no protection against sexually transmitted disease or pregnancy, so it was a high-risk occupation but often some women, especially those in towns and cities, had few other options if they wished to feed themselves, their family and have a home. Prostitutes could be prosecuted for the offence by the Church courts and faced fines and penance. It was a cycle which was difficult to break; prostitutes would be fined but the fines could not be paid if they did not continue with prostitution. The brothels of London were ordered to be closed in 1549 by Henry VIII but it did not stop the trade and before long the brothels were back in business.

A career in domestic service provided many opportunities for females of varying ages and classes, the majority beginning their career in adolescence or earlier in some cases. There were traditionally three kinds of service: the previously mentioned apprenticeship, a contract in husbandry and a contract in domestic service. The lines between the latter two were blurred, and the work largely depended on the wealth of the household and the number of servants employed. The contracts in husbandry and domestic service were usually annual contracts. The contract usually stipulated that the servants would be paid on a quarterly basis, with the pay being determined by the Justices of Peace. As with the wages for harvesting, the annual wage for servants was lower for women, but increased with age. Late in the sixteenth century, women aged 24 or over would be paid a wage of 20s plus an additional 6s 8d for clothing. Those under 24 years old would receive a wage of 16s and 5s for clothing. This is the equivalent of approximately £300 and £225 today respectively.[6] Their male counterparts aged 20 to 24 years old would receive a wage of 26s 8d which is the total received by women over the age of 24, including their clothing allowance. Men in wealthy and aristocratic households would often be provided with a livery rather than a clothing allowance, or an additional 5s if no livery was provided. Males aged 16 to 20 would receive 20s, again almost the same as females but note the difference in the age brackets between the genders. The wage of servants takes into consideration the fact that the majority received lodgings and food, therefore in theory they could save almost all of their wage. It still appears low for work involving long hours, especially when compared to a dairymaid who could earn more than four times the amount of a female servant. The work of a dairymaid was highly skilled and therefore sought by employers who were willing to pay more for their experience.[7] A dairymaid that could manage the dairy without instruction from her mistress could negotiate for a higher wage. This allowed her mistress more time for other tasks and gave the dairymaid the opportunity to gain an excellent reputation which she could then use to move to a more influential household or negotiate her wage once more. Depending on the number of cows, the dairymaid may require the assistance of under maids. Each dairymaid usually looked after up to six cows, any more than that and they would struggle to complete all tasks and care for the animals effectively. Younger girls or those wishing to learn may be willing to accept a lower wage than knowledgeable under maids if they were certain to be taught by a successful dairymaid.

The kind of work women were expected to undertake whilst in service was determined by geography and the type of service they had entered; those in husbandry would usually be employed to take on more laborious work such as farm chores whilst those in domestic service were responsible for the day to day running of the household, ensuring food preparation was complete, clothes were washed and mended and any other ad-hoc tasks as directed by the mistress of the house. Those employed for any personal tasks would have to be up early, well before their master or mistress to ensure the fire was lit, clothes were warmed and everything they required was ready upon them waking.

Single or childless widowed women generally found opportunities where they could reside within the household of their employer. By securing a live-in contract they were not only securing bed and board for a year at a time, but also earning a small wage they could save towards marriage or retirement. It would take longer for women to save for marriage as they were paid less than their male counterparts. Married women, widows with young children and those with a property could find more casual roles in domestic service which did not require them to agree to a yearly contract or to reside in the house of their employer. Instead, they could attend the household on a daily basis or whenever their services were required, which enabled them to maintain their own household whilst supplementing their income through work. Widows with dependent children could find the working situation particularly difficult when trying to earn sufficient wages for her family but not being able to take on a live-in contract. The disadvantages of the more casual work were the disapproval of the parishes and lack of secure income. Women who provided daily or casual assistance were known as *charmaids* and were called upon for general housework as well as ad-hoc duties, perhaps to cover for someone who was sick or during times when a household required additional help. Large households would often recruit women as casual labourers for seasonal work such as weeding the garden, assisting with the collection of produce, flowers and herbs for the mistress to preserve or help with cleaning if a large party was expected. The authorities were conscious that these women could become a burden on society if work became irregular or ceased altogether.[8] For this reason, women were encouraged to find more permanent roles whether in domestic service or an alternative occupation. Under the reign of Elizabeth I, the Justices of the Peace were empowered by the *Statute of Artificers* to order any single female aged between 12 and 40 to undertake a period of service; the period ranging from a day to a year. This was in an effort to reduce the reliance on parish alms and those who refused could find themselves imprisoned until they agreed to a position within a household, chosen by the authorities.[9] Around 1570, a census of the population in Norwich found that of the women over the age of 21, 86 per cent were employed.[10] All women with the required resources could increase their income through making additional produce during the course of making their own. This could include ale, cheese, butter, pies and if they were fortunate enough to own poultry, the sale of surplus eggs.

The work involved in domestic service varied greatly as did the pay. Households with the means to employ a single female servant meant her duties would be vast and laborious, whilst those households with multiple servants could provide opportunities for more specialised roles in varying areas of the household including dairymaids and launderesses. Some of the aristocracy maintained over 150 people within their households, consisting of the family, visitors, servants and labourers. The estates of the aristocracy therefore provided employment for large numbers of people. Not all of the servants moved around with the family as they travelled between estates, some had roles requiring them to remain within a specific household but others would have the opportunity to travel with them. The grander households rarely employed women for laborious tasks, other than launderesses. Avis Woode was employed as launderess to Henry VIII's daughter, Princess Mary, when the princess was less than a year old.[11] Anne Harris was employed as a launderess at the court of Henry VIII for £10 per year, later £20, equivalent of over £7,000 and £15,000 today, and similar to the amount paid to skilled tradesmen at the time. Although a generous salary for a launderess, particularly considering the wages of servants discussed earlier, her tasks were extensive and she also had to provide the soap and herbs to keep the laundry smelling fresh.

> The said Anne shall weekly wash 7 long Breakfast clothes, 7 short ones, 8 Towells, 3 douzen of Napkins, and Pieces as need shall require; and of the same shall dayly deliver as much to the said Officers as shall be necessary to serve the King's Majesty withall; and the said residue

of the said Diaper to remaine still in the hands of the said Anne shall not faile dayly, upon deliverie of the said cleane stuff, to take with her the stuff which was occupied the day before, to wash again, discreetly perusing and viewing the stuff how it hath been used and ordered; and in case the shall finde and thinke it hath not very well ordered or used, that then immediately she shall bring the same to some of the Officers of the Compting-house to see the same, that remedy may be for the amendment thereof.[12]

It is apparent that although there was a lot of work to be done by Anne, there is not as much as one may think for the laundry of a king. That would be because Henry's clothes were not cleaned in the same way. Henry's and the rest of the royal court's clothing consisted of opulent, expensive fabrics that could be ruined if washed in the same way as linen smocks, napkins or towels. These expensive clothes, made up of furs, velvets, silk and cloth of gold and silver had to be cleaned and maintained much more carefully. The garments would be brushed regularly removing any dirt. Repairs would be done when needed and they would be stored with herbs to keep them smelling fresh. Henry would have had an abundance of servants to brush and care for his clothes, all under the supervision of the Keeper of the Wardrobe. Courtiers would bring their own servants with them to court to care for their clothing. The royal household, like the aristocracy, would move between residences on a regular basis to enable them to be deep cleaned. The rushes would all be swept and replaced, walls washed, tapestries, carpets and wall hangings removed, beaten and brushed to remove dust before being rehung ready for the family's return.

The majority of the work in grand households was undertaken by men, though Henry VIII did also employ a woman in his kitchen as a confectioner.[13] The wealthiest households such as those of the aristocracy could also employ ladies-in-waiting, maidservants and kitchen maids. Irrespective of the household all maidservants and ladies-in-waiting would perform some sort of needlework, working with the mistress of the household to spin, sew, or embroider garments. Whilst those in humble households would also have the responsibility of the more laborious tasks including assisting with cooking, brewing and helping in the fields during times of harvest, wealthier households would have specific servants for these tasks. This made the role of the maidservant in wealthier households less laborious but that does not mean they did not work just as hard; the demands of a mistress could be burdensome and time-consuming. The wives of courtiers who did not reside at the royal court were no doubt formidable women, and were perfectly capable of managing their estates whilst their husband spent much time away from home, in service to the monarch. Their wives would shoulder the responsibility of managing servants, tenants and the household accounts. If a husband had given permission, she could even make and negotiate contracts and leases on his behalf in his absence. This applied to any wife but was largely used by the aristocracy and wealthy traders due to their frequent absence. Upon the husband's return he would need to formally approve any actions taken on his behalf but this was largely a formality.

As expected, the most prestigious place of work was the royal court. The royal household staff were separated in to two types; *Domus Regie Magnificencie* and *Domus Providencie*. The first were the courtiers, those of privilege and often ranked individuals, whilst the latter were the servants.[14] With regards to the first group, there were a variety of roles for women including gentlewomen of the privy chamber, maid of honour, and lady-in-waiting.[15] The second group encompassed all the other, more laborious and less esteemed positions, though no less sought-after. The role of a maid, not a maid of honour, was a little blurred, they could be kitchen maids and therefore classed in the second group of staff or could be a young maid appointed to serve the rooms of the ladies of the court; a more prestigious position, also known as a chamberer. Gentlewomen of the privy chamber became more common under the reign of Elizabeth I. Some had remained unmarried through choice and were therefore given the title in recognition of their service, despite the fact the title was usually reserved for married women. The household of the queen was separated into three sets of chambers: watching chamber, presence chamber and privy chamber. Each led into the other and with each advancement to the next chamber, admittance was reduced. The watching chamber was where people could petition the queen. The presence chamber was where the queen would eat publicly, meet and entertain visitors as well as the king. Lastly, the privy chamber was where the queen spent most of her time, here, she could eat privately, had her bed chamber, privy and wardrobes. Only her ladies that had been specifically granted permission to enter were admitted to the privy chamber, as well as the king and his companions. Those holding positions within the queen's household would be expected to know the household regulations, abide by them and were required to take an oath of loyalty and obedience upon joining. They could easily be dismissed in disgrace if their conduct was not impeccable. Although the queen was not required to give an oath in return, she did owe her ladies a duty of care and would try to ensure they retained a good reputation.

Some women were offered places at court in their own right, due to the rank and influence of her family. Others were offered a position following their marriage to an influential courtier and therefore, would be faced with a steep learning curve of how to behave at the royal court. No learning would prepare a young lady who had not been expecting it from an early age, for the life they were about to experience. There were books available to guide those both aiming for the role and those who gained a position as a result of marriage but most would learn on the job. The most popular piece of literature was *The Courtier* written by Baldassare Castiglione. *The Courtier* consists of a series of conversational dialogues which provide advice on how to be the perfect courtier. The advice of Castiglione and others suggest women should be chaste, obedient and never view themselves as equal to men.

The women appointed to the queen's household were expected to introduce a new queen to the workings of the English royal court including the household regulations. A new queen may bring some of her own ladies, particularly if they were moving from abroad but many would remain in situ from the previous queen. The most obvious examples would be the wives of Henry VIII. Katharine of Aragon and Anne of Cleves both travelled from abroad. Katharine had plenty of time to understand the court before she married Henry VIII, not that she needed it. Katharine had been brought up at the court of her parents King Ferdinand and Queen Isabella, was experienced in the ways of a royal court and extremely well educated. For Anne of Cleves, it was an entirely new environment, one she would need assistance in navigating. In this situation, her women would be a valuable asset in teaching her about the formalities of the court, events and of course, the English language. All queens would appoint a few of her ladies herself, usually her closest family and kin but others were appointed due to their rank in society and connections to the monarch. The queen would have less involvement in appointing women to the positions of maids; those that would undertake the more laborious tasks than the maids of honour.

The maids were not as close in proximity to the queen and were usually appointed through the patronage of the aristocratic women at court, and may be their family, friends or distant kin.

One of the most sought-after positions was that of a Lady of the Bedchamber. It was the equivalent to the role of Groom of the Stool to the king. The position of Groom of the Stool was not recorded for a queen until the late sixteenth century, though it is unlikely she would visit the close stool alone.[16] It is likely a Lady of the Bedchamber would provide companionship to the queen but would also attend her when she visited the privy. The position offered close proximity to the queen and was therefore the perfect role to whisper any requests for favour, out of earshot of the rest of the court. The Mistress of the Robes would hold responsibility for the queen's wardrobe, ensuring her clothing and jewels were ready to be worn, and returned afterwards as well as supervising all those responsible for cleaning, mending and updating her clothing.

The Tudors had an expectancy of beauty in women appointed at court, it was common for those hoping for an appointment to be 'viewed' to see if they fit in with the standard expectancy of beauty. The ideal of 'beauty' was blonde and blue-eyed. Maids of honour were usually appointed after they had turned 16 years old but on occasion were appointed younger. The young ladies had to be beautiful, unmarried at the time of their appointment, and very accomplished in the societal skills expected of them, for instance music and dancing. Maids of honour were responsible for attending the queen in public as well as entertaining her with singing, dancing and music. The maids of honour came under the supervision of the mother of maids, who was responsible for ensuring their behaviour was impeccable, they were fulfilling their roles and were not behaving in a way which could be detrimental to their position or reputation, or that of their families. Ladies-in-waiting had the responsibility of more intimate tasks such as washing and dressing the queen and keeping her company in her chambers. They were women of rank, usually older than the maids of honour, more experienced and married; their marriage on occasion, being the reason for their appointment. Some had been promoted from a maid of honour upon their marriage, others were appointed due to the position of their husband. The queen would take on a protective role towards her maids of honour and nurture their skills at court. For the young lady and her family, not only was it an honour to serve the royal family, but it also provided an excellent opportunity to secure an advantageous marriage to another courtier. If a woman was a lady-in-waiting and therefore already married, she could use her position to influence the prospects of her husband, children and wider family. Maids of honour who had made an impression on the royal family could be fortunate enough to receive the gift of a dowry in part or full from the monarch. It was a high honour for courtiers if the monarch chose to attend their wedding or that of their children and would indicate to others that the family were high in royal favour. A dowry paid by the monarch was an extremely enticing opportunity for the men of Tudor England. It was usually paid in land belonging to the Crown, making it particularly lucrative. Katharine of Aragon paid the dowry of her lady, Maria de Salinas. Maria had travelled from Spain with Katharine years earlier and had remained with her ever since. Maria was to marry William, Lord Willoughby and would later give birth to Katherine Willoughby. The queen gave Maria a substantial dowry of 1,100 marks which was then supplemented by Henry VIII with a reversion gift of four properties. Lord Willoughby, in exchange, settled on Maria a jointure of 500 marks, way more than the custom ten per cent of the dowry which shows how lucrative it could be to have a dowry supported by the monarch.[17]

During the reigns of Mary I and Elizabeth I, positions in their household would have been particularly rewarding with much competition for a role. As queen regnant there would be an increased number of positions within their households. Wages in the royal household were not large but the perquisites were extremely enticing. Not only did they receive their bed and board, they had opportunities to receive patronage for themselves and their family and could influence the monarch to become a patron to the causes they supported. There was also the additional grant of a royal pension when the time came to retire from service. The first Tudor queen, Elizabeth of York, paid her sister Kateryne a pension, and paid wages to twenty-seven women in 1503. Some were her ladies but her privy purse expenses also include nursery staff and her launderess, Agnes Dean.[18] Henry VIII continued to value the staff of his mother, granting Anne Hubberd an annuity of 5l in 1511. Anne had been in service to both Elizabeth of York and before that her mother, Queen Elizabeth Woodville. She was 80 years old when granted the annuity in consideration of her service.[19]

The queen was not the only woman at court to provide employment. Women of the aristocracy appointed to serve the queen also had their own ladies and maids serving them. The number of servants a lady could bring with her was usually agreed at the time of her appointment as their lodgings and food were paid for by the Crown. Serving one of the queen's ladies offered opportunities to make a good impression and be within the company of the king and queen almost daily. By making a good impression a young lady could be appointed in time to the queen's household. The household of the queen was not the only royal household during the Tudor era. If a role could not be secured within the household of the queen, families sought to place their daughters and female kin in the households of the relatives of the monarch including the princesses Mary and Elizabeth and Mary Tudor, Queen of France. Some may even have preferred a position in one of these households. Alternatively, there was the option to serve in the household of one of the great ladies such as a duchess or dowager duchess. These women did not serve at the royal court as they had vast households and wealth of their own to manage. They also did not require wages and did not need to be present at the court each day but they would attend for celebrations or when required to attend for events like confinement, feasts or religious events. Serving one of these women also brought opportunity to visit the royal court on occasion and promote oneself.

Pay varied not only by household but also by role and rank. A woman of lower rank would receive a lesser wage than one of higher rank for the same role. The wages of a female in service could be made up of bed and board, a monetary salary, gifts, clothing, jewels and other perquisites agreed upon before she began work. All households employing live-in servants, regardless of rank, would provide food and drink to their staff. Households would attempt to organise and budget the provision of food and drink within their available resources. The most organised was the royal household, which became even more organised in 1540 with the *Eltham Ordinances*. The ordinances recorded the daily allowances, known as *bouche of court*, for all servants including those appointed to the queen's household. The women's allowances were organised by rank in a similar manner to the number of servants they could have attending them and horses they could stable at the cost of the monarch. The allowances are extremely detailed including the volume of wine and ale, amount of bread, and number of candles a woman was entitled to.[20] Main food dishes are not mentioned as this would be far too difficult to organise and supervise, but bread and drink were fairly simple as the court would have specific numbers of loaves to bake and gallons of ale to brew.

Women employed in households with sufficient resources, including aristocratic and royal houses, would be given a type of livery. It was not quite the same as a uniformed livery worn by the men of some households, but something of quality which denoted their position. Outside the royal household women dressed according to rank but within they dressed according to their position within the household. A lady appointed to the queen would be granted much more sumptuous fabrics for her clothing than a lady serving another high ranking woman regardless of the rankings of the two servants. They may also be issued with a gown or materials to make a gown for Sundays which could be worn to attend church. These fabrics and clothing could be worth a fortune to women. Although they may be issued gowns, they were much more likely to be given the fabrics to either make, or have made, gowns for themselves in the latest fashion. Those with a generous mistress may be the beneficiary of further clothes and gifts passed down from her mistress or those in a higher ranked role, some of which could be valued at more than her annual salary. In addition to regular clothing, those appointed to the queen's household had the additional benefit of being able to borrow materials from the Great Wardrobe during celebrations.[21] Women in service, including those on apprenticeships, could receive the gift of a dowry from her master or mistress and were frequently bequeathed gifts in the wills of their mistress, showing some formed a close bond akin to friendship. Katharine of Aragon in her last letter to Henry VIII requested he pay her servants a year's wage for their good service to her. Another perquisite was that women employed at the home of the wealthy, nobility and royal family could often expect the benefit of being cared for when sick. There was no sick pay but those with the resources to do so often ensured their servants were well looked after, receiving the medical attention they required, helping care for them and maintaining their pay through the payment of board wages.

Domestic service held the risk of women being subject to abuse. There was no protection for maids and servants against being beaten by their master as long as it wasn't fatal. Unmarried female servants were also at an increased risk of sexual abuse, forced into a situation where to report it would mean the loss of her employment and she was likely to face disbelief regardless. Some victims found themselves dismissed if they conceived a child by their master or a male servant within the household.

Teaching, though not a formal occupation, was habitually the role of many women. Those who employed young servants, whether as their own or through their husband's trade, were responsible for providing them with an education, usually in religion. All mothers were responsible for the education of their own children whilst they were under her care, and extended that education to others in their care, if they accepted children into their household from other families. Formally there were only a few women who taught as an occupation. Dame schools usually had a female teaching practical skills, and generous women may open their homes to local school children to teach them, but this was an informal situation and they were not licensed as schoolmasters ought to be. Some grateful parents may of course donate to the dame school but it was not a requirement. The women who were employed as governesses would commonly undertake at least the early education of her charges. The girls under their care may become pupils of professional tutors later in their childhood.

Spinning was a very popular occupation amongst Tudor women as it could provide a steady income and could be done within the home as most women owned a drop spindle or a spinning wheel. Before the wool could be spun it had to be sheared and combed. Sheep shearing took place in May and was men's work but once it was sheared, women and children took up the task of combing and carding the wool; removing dirt and debris by hand. This could provide supplemental income to families as it required many hands. Once the wool had been combed it was ready for spinning. Spinning could also fit into the lifestyle demands of most women as they could accept piece rates meaning they would be paid for each piece completed and could therefore work on their own schedule, as much or as little as they needed. They may even take advantage of varying prices and make excess to sell when prices rose. Those who took up spinning or other occupations such as making buttons and knitting tended to originate from the poor population although some may also teach children alongside completing their own pieces. Spinning, even if done daily, was unlikely to earn sufficient wages to maintain a woman and her family and was therefore mainly supplemental for those with a family. It became associated as predominantly work for unmarried women, perhaps why the term spinster remains in use today for single women. A woman would be paid a little more if she were able to provide her own wool and the occupation allowed women to work around other responsibilities. For those wishing to merely supplement the household income, they may take on tasks such as laundering for others, or taking small spinning, knitting and lace-making commissions. Those who could afford to do so would usually pay a woman to wash clothes and bedding as it was such a time consuming and laborious task. Weaving however, was considered men's work as it required more strength than spinning, each weaver needing multiple spinners to keep his loom at capacity.[22] That is not to say some women did not take on the task which may have been a factor in 1511 when the Norwich Worsted weavers forbade women to undertake any work connected to them.[23]

Young women had the option of becoming a wet nurse where required. Wet nurses were highly regarded within the higher levels of society and the women would be expected to be of good reputation.[24] Wet nurses may possibly be able to take a child into their own household to nurse whilst others employed in aristocratic or royal households may be expected to reside within the household of the parents until the child was weaned. Some children were breastfed for up to two years which could provide income for a wet nurse for the whole period the child required breastfeeding. The majority of children were breastfed for a year before being weaned on to pottage. Some wet nurses were fortunate enough to become nursemaids and governesses to the child they had nursed and eventually, if the child was female, they could become a maid or lady-in-waiting when she reached adulthood or alternatively the nursemaid to the next generation of children. There are occasions where nursemaids have remained an important part of a family even when the children are grown. Elizabeth Denton, who had been the lady mistress of a young Henry and his sister Margaret, was later employed to supervise the nursery of his daughter, the future Mary I.[25] Kat Ashley found employment within the household of a young Elizabeth Tudor and became an adored member of Elizabeth's household and one of her closest confidantes, for the remainder of her life. In more humble conditions, young women may be asked by the parish to be a wet nurse for a child whose mother had passed following childbirth or who could not breastfeed herself. They may receive a token payment for this service but it was unlikely to be sufficient to maintain themselves and their own children and they would therefore supplement this income with additional work in childcare, housework, laundering for others or spinning whilst caring for children.

Just as we change jobs today, so did Tudor women. They would have to change their work according to their circumstances and location, if they moved from the country to a town for instance, they may have to search for new work in a different occupation. Or if they married, their role may change according to their spouse's trade. Men with a trade may request their wife works with them, depending on the trade. Men whose trades were labour-intensive and required the use of equipment or machinery would often use assistants or apprentices rather than their wife, but those in trades which required skill could often call upon the assistance of their spouse. Merchants may install their wives in a shop to sell goods or even leave their wives in charge of the business along with an apprentice whilst they were away on business ventures on the understanding the wife would regularly communicate with her husband and provide any important updates whilst he was abroad. To take on this role, a merchant's wife, if she had not already been taught, would benefit from learning to write so she could keep records, and keep her husband informed about his business whilst he was travelling. Those involved in trades requiring needlework of some description could certainly use the skills of their wife in their creations. The extent of work required by the wife would also be influenced by the wealth of the husband. For an affluent tradesman he may be able to afford employees and apprentices and therefore not require additional labour, but for those less financially stable, the labour of the wife could be vital to ensuring orders could be met and income secured.

Women who remained single were known as a *femme sole* and unlike wives, had the benefit of independent legal rights similar to men. Although their marital status may be frowned upon by society it did mean that under the common law they could trade as an independent woman. Authorities in some areas attempted to push single women towards either a career in domestic service or marriage by restricting them from selling bread and ale or working at trades.[26] Regardless of the authorities, a single woman could set herself up with a trade, obtain credit, sue and be sued. Local custom in some areas allowed married women to apply for *femme sole* status in order to run a business, providing she had the consent of her husband. This meant wives could pursue a different trade to that of her husband which may be advantageous in increasing income for her family, particularly if the trades complimented each other in some way. If granted, the status only applied to her business, all other restrictions regarding property remained in situ. Many widows would also continue their husbands trade after his death. The most famous and successful tradeswomen were the silk women. These women worked from their own shops or homes, transforming raw silk into thread. The silk women had their largest presence in London where the wealthy would do most of their shopping but there were smaller groups of silk women in towns and cities all over the country. They were skilled enough to create very small items with exquisite detail such as ribbons and fringes which were purchased by a range of customers including royalty. The most renowned skill of the silk women was the finger loop braid followed by plaited braids, bringing together multiple threads into a braid. The silk women did not work on large pieces of silk to create garments such as gowns but the thread they weaved could also be sold to merchants to be used in creating larger garments. Silk was expensive; some silk women were married to merchants making the material they required more accessible and affordable than to those who had no beneficial trade contracts.

Being a business owner opened opportunities for women to join a trade guild, which existed for many trades. Although a few restricted membership of women, the majority allowed it either independently or through marriage to a member which could continue if she were widowed, though was lost if she remarried to a member of a different guild. The guilds may restrict the actions a woman could take as a member such as the right to employ apprentices or trade as an unmarried woman.[27] The guilds also provided an active social life for members which may have been a comfort to widowed women. Guild halls usually provided a room where women could meet and socialise whether they were members themselves or attending as the wife of a member and while away a few hours in the company of other women. The silk women were the closest to being an all-female guild but there were no formal guilds specifically for women, during the Tudor era. As a group the silk women acted almost like a guild, employing and training apprentices, of both genders, ensuring their skills were passed on to the next generation. Their apprenticeships were little different to those of the formal trades; there was a fee to be paid by the apprentice's family and there was a term of seven years to complete. The apprentice would be treated like any other; taught manners, fed, clothed, given lodgings and taught his or her skill. They would not only be taught the skills of the silk women but given the training required to set up their own business on completion of the apprenticeship. Skills taught would more than likely have to include literacy and numeracy if they had not already learned those and of course, the keeping of accounts. In return the apprentice was to behave respectfully, care for their employers' goods and trade and perform to the best of their ability.[28] As one of the few apprenticeships available to girls, a position was likely much sought after. Although the opportunity to apprentice in this trade had no gender restrictions, it was not a common choice for boys who instead had a much wider variety of apprenticeships available to them. Despite their skill and being respected as traders the significance of the silk women lessened towards the end of the era, which in turn reduced the opportunities of apprenticeships for girls.

Roles in the legal system, courts and other esteemed professions were all closed to women. It was believed that women did not hold the required intellectual capacity to undertake such roles. Despite the limitations on the occupations of women many had exceptional business acumen. Wives of merchants were often responsible for their husband's trade whilst he was away, taking responsibility for stock, accounts and employees. Others may find themselves in the unfortunate position of having an imprisoned spouse and would continue his business in his absence. The largest responsibility was that taken on by Katharine of Aragon and Kateryn Parr who both acted as regent in Henry VIII's absence.

Possibly the most respected of occupations for women was the role of midwives. The majority of midwives were respectable, middle class, married or widowed women with a wealth of experience from their own labours and that of others. Almost every town and village had at least one woman acting as a midwife. These women were supposed to be licensed by the Church but in reality, they were perhaps just helping their fellow women through the ordeal of childbirth. Many had no licence, or training, and simply worked from experience. Others were fortunate to have some elementary training from surgeons and may be initially supervised but there was no formal training or qualifications to practice. Some would have the benefit of practising under an experienced midwife until they were competent enough to work on their own. The first printed book especially for midwives was *Der Rosengarten* (The Rose Garden), written by the German physician Eucharius Rösslin in 1513. The book was translated and printed in English as *The Birth of Mankynde: Otherwyse named the Woman's*

*Booke* in 1540. Rösslin was concerned about the number of stillborn babies and felt midwives were neglectful, he therefore sought to advise them using his medical knowledge.

> 'And when the tyme of laboure is come, in the same stoole ought to be put many clothes or cloutes in the backe of it, the which the Midwife may remove from one side to another according as necessitie shall require. The Midwife herselfe shall sit before the labouryng woman, and shall diligentlye observe and wayte, howe much, and after what meanes the chyld styrreth itself, also shall with her hands fyrst annoynted with Oyle of Allmondes, or the Oyle of whyte Lillies, rule and direct every thyng as shall seeme best.'[29]

Churchwardens had the responsibility of reporting unlicensed midwives to the bishops' courts, but in a society where few could afford the service of a licensed midwife, most parishes simply requested they restrict their practice to their own parish or those in need from humble origins.[30] Efforts were made to regulate the practice of baptisms by midwives during the reign of Henry VIII. The *Injunctions for the Diocese of Salisbury (1538)* advised:

> That every curate instruct his parishioners, and especially the midwives, the essential manner and form how to christen a child in time of need; commanding them women, when the time of birth draweth near, to have a vessel of clean water ready for the same purpose; charging also the said midwives, to beware that they cause not the woman, being in travail, to make any foolish vow to go in pilgrimage to this image or that image after her deliverance, but only to call on God for help. Nor to use any girdles, purses, measures of our Lady, or such superstitious things, to be occupied about the woman while she laboureth, to make her believe to have the better speed of it.[31]

Midwives were also respected within the courts, particularly those who were licensed to practice. They could be called upon to examine women and testify as to whether they remained a virgin, were currently pregnant or had recently given birth, and provide knowledge that may prove useful in cases relating to rape, infanticide or non-consummation of a marriage. They may also act on behalf of the courts to determine whether a woman was pregnant if she had 'pleaded the belly'. Part of the reason that midwives were so respected by both the general public and the courts was because not only did they have valuable experience, but many had taken an oath which was part of the process of obtaining a licence. Those who sought to obtain a licence would have to prove their observance of religion, particularly in relation to baptism in case of urgent requirements, demonstrate they were of a good reputation and pay a fee. The matter of the fee would have restricted many from applying for a licence, particularly for a role without a guaranteed income. The oath was to ensure she would use the correct words and would avoid superstition but would also avoid anything harmful to the child, or to the labouring mother. Whilst the oath would vary, that given by Eleanor Pead in 1567 does give an indication of the concerns around practices noted by society and Rösslin.

> I will be ready to help and aid as well poor as rich women being in labour and travail of a child, and will always be ready both to poor and rich, and in exercising and executing of my said office. Also I will not permit or suffer that any woman being in labour or travail shall name any other to be the father of her child, than only he who is the right and true father thereof: and that I will not suffer any other body's child to be set, brought or laid before any woman delivered of child in the place of her natural child, so far forth as I can know and understand. Also, I will not use any kind of sorcery or incantation in the time of the travail of any woman: and that I will not destroy the child born of any woman, nor cut, nor pull off the head thereof, or otherwise dismember or hurt the same, or suffer it to be so hurt or dismembered by any manner of ways or means.[32]

The fact that a midwife had to take an oath not to dismember or pull off the head of a baby is truly terrifying in today's standards. The oath also highlights the role of midwives in encouraging mothers to provide the father's name in cases where the baby was born outside of wedlock.

The role of midwives did not secure a sufficient wage to live off, unless of course they were fortunate enough to be employed within an aristocratic or royal household where they may receive a substantial payment for a safe delivery. Those who impressed their aristocratic master and mistress may be offered further employment within the nursery and perhaps later, a pension in their old age. Midwives who had assisted an aristocratic woman in her labours could benefit from further requests for their attendance to other households following recommendations from their clients. All expecting parents were keen to secure the very best they could afford to ensure a safe delivery for both mother and child. Tudor midwives did not earn a set wage but were instead rewarded. Rewards could of course be in monetary terms but many received goods as payment for their service including livestock and plate. The fee paid was ultimately dependent on the resources of the household of the labouring woman. The majority of midwives would have to supplement their income with additional work, this could be childcare or ad-hoc work like spinning. There were a few women who were also licensed by the bishops to practice surgery. Isabel Warwike was one such female who was permitted to practice and Lady Margaret Hoby also performed surgery though it is not known if she were licensed to do so.[33] Ladies like this would certainly have made use of the increasing amount of medical literature that was becoming available at that time. Those who did practice any form of medical care whilst unlicensed, were liable for prosecution by the College of Physicians. The college remained steadfast in their stance against medical literature being published for a general audience. In reality, though there was little they could do about it or the increasing number of herbal books published in English.

Though hospitals existed there were no nurses as we would expect today, instead, women learnt their healing skills through experience and recipes for remedies passed from mother to daughter. St Bartholomew Hospital employed women to cook, launder, supervise and nurse, although at the time they were referred to as sisters. Hospital matrons were required to be married or widows and were responsible for overseeing the care of women and children by supervising the nurses, launderesses and cooks. At St Bartholomew Hospital the cook was paid more than the matron but it is likely the matron received additional benefits to mitigate the difference in salary. Nurses were paid by salary along with clothing, bed and board.[34] Elderly women of all classes, even those with no substantial skills, were expected to tend to the sick and were called upon within their communities to tend local parishioners, for which they may receive a token payment. Even the poorest who relied on alms for their maintenance or resided in alms-houses would tend to the sick as a method of paying their way and contributing to the house. The local wise women who were skilled in healing often also acted as the local midwife and were respected within their communities. Many could not afford the medical care of professionals and therefore were wholly reliant on the local wise woman. Those needing the services of a wise woman would usually give a token payment but were not obliged. Payment could be money, food, material or anything else of value the family could afford. They may also offer a service in return, for instance, they would take the woman's grain to the miller, brew ale for her, or collect her bread from the baker for a period of time in thanks. For the wise women, they likely did not earn enough from their services to maintain themselves so would have had to supplement their income with another occupation. Wealthy women with their own stillrooms who tended to the sick did not often accept payment but were likely recipients of gifts of thanks, sent to their home when the sick could afford something.

Though women could not enter legal or other professional occupations there were some ladies that were elected as churchwardens. This was not a common occurrence and the duties were extensive for no tangible reward. The position was an elected one and those who elected these women clearly did not agree that women did not have the intellectual capacity to undertake such roles. The churchwardens were responsible for arranging and supervising repairs, the retail of produce, and planning events to generate income for the church including church ales and feasts, amongst other significant tasks.[35] Though it has been noted that nuns and anchoresses did not receive a wage, it was a respected vocation prior to the Reformation. The dissolution of convents affected the workforce of the country by leaving the nuns and all those who had been dependent on them searching for work. The nuns and anchoresses were meant to receive a pension from the Crown for the remainder of their lives, though in reality not all did. Those who received it were able to use it to try and sustain themselves and dependent on the amount possibly retire into private life or set up a home. For the majority the pension awarded was £1 per year and was insufficient to fully sustain an individual so the majority still had to find work whether they received it or not. Anchoresses and prioresses would have been awarded a pension much more than £1 and would have been made a priority, and much more likely to receive it than some of the others. Some chose to share a home with their fellow sisters or like-minded women and would remain chaste, working in the community together at tasks such as gardening, brewing and spinning. Others were wealthy themselves and had the funds to take in their sisters and could continue living a life of charity and piety though they were no longer to profess themselves as nuns. Elizabeth Lord, who had been allocated a pension of £5 per year, purchased the site of Wilberfoss priory where she had been the last prioress before the dissolution. The purchase, which was made directly from the Crown in 1553, cost Elizabeth £615. This is a huge amount for someone with a pension, therefore it is likely Elizabeth had resources of her own or her family to assist her.[36] The alternatives to working were to either return to their family, which could be the most appealing option for some, or others chose to marry, especially once clerical marriage became legal, allowing them to marry a man of God. They could travel abroad to a convent, which some did choose to do, but the travel was costly and therefore only a viable option for those who could pay for themselves or were fortunate to have a wealthy family willing to assist them in meeting the costs.

Sundays, in theory, were to be a day of rest for all, with church attendance being mandatory. Those who worked in the fields, trades, and shops could take the day as rest. Those in service were not afforded such a privilege, at least not on a weekly basis. A household could not function if all staff took the day off and so although all would attend church, it was not in fact a day of rest for all workers. Those who failed to attend church or used the incorrect service book may be fined, which for workers was not a risk they could take. Therefore, those who failed to attend church on Sundays were either sick, infirm or, following the Reformation, Catholics who did not wish to attend Protestant services and chose instead to pay the fine.

During this period there was no state benefit system, pension service, and no formal retirement but taxes did exist. The women who earned their wages through labouring or other humble occupations were unlikely to earn enough to pay taxes, but may still be expected to contribute when able to parish funds. The wealthy would be taxed but also contributed separately to charitable causes. Those who served the crown or aristocracy may be granted a pension but as with parish alms for the elderly, this was not guaranteed. Therefore, anyone wishing to retire from work would need to have either support, adequate capital or income to maintain themselves. Old age was reached around 50 years old, which seems young to us nowadays but life expectancy was much shorter for the Tudors. Men with an adequate income, whether from an estate generating income or savings from a lifetime of work, could of course retire from work. Women, though they may have a reduction in work if their husband retired and they had been assisting him, would still have to manage their household. For some managing the household remained a huge task of its own, especially for those with servants, livestock and larger estates with tenants.

## Chapter Seven

# Recreation

Daily life was not all about work, women had social lives in the Tudor era. They would often visit neighbours, congregating in each other's homes to gossip, eat, drink and assist those who may need it such as the sick, infirm or labouring women. This was also a good way for women of parishes and villages to share childcare and have company whilst they worked. They could sit gossiping whilst spinning or sewing and their children could play together. Other public spaces such as the local riverbank, village well and establishments frequented by all such as the bakery, also acted as meeting points for women to gather and gossip, largely whilst completing their household chores of laundering, or collecting food and drink. Men mostly left these areas to women, which was not difficult for them to avoid as the running of the household was a female domain. It was here that women could share advice on medical ailments, remedies they had taken that helped, recipes for items such as soap, lozenges and tinctures as well as general conversation around life, children, marriage and village events. For those that spent much of their week working, Sundays were the day of rest, after attending church of course. Markets and fairs could also be an enjoyable time for women, particularly those who attended with the aim of taking pleasure in shopping or watching the entertainments as opposed to those having to work. It was not unusual for married couples to attend entertainments together. Taverns, festivals and other entertainments were common and provided an opportunity for families to spend quality time together outside of the home. Markets were a regular occurrence where a variety of goods could be purchased; they usually opened early and were closed before modern day lunch time. Fairs were more infrequent; in some areas they only occurred annually. Fairs would be much larger, and open for longer periods of time featuring more entertainments and a wider range of merchants including those selling the most fashionable textiles and goldsmiths. These events were an opportunity for women to spend a day with their spouse, friends and family. They could catch up on the latest fashions, watch the entertainments of jugglers and acrobats or if they were single, possibly make the acquaintance of their future spouse.

Mistresses of larger estates would also visit neighbours, although they were unlikely to be within walking distance and may take a little more planning than arriving unannounced. Despite the distances, women would still visit to chat, read together and spend time on embroidery pieces. Hospitality was expected during the time and the responsibility fell to females for the most part. For poorer women this perhaps just meant sharing their food and drink if they were able, or each visitor may bring a single dish to share the burden of providing food for everyone. For those with grand estates offering hospitality could be an extravagant affair, especially if their home was to be visited by royalty or an aristocrat of a higher rank. The aim was always to impress, so a flurry of activity was needed, all supervised by the mistress of the household to ensure the house was ready for its visitors. Food and drink would need to be ordered, menus agreed, rooms cleaned and ready for occupants, and entertainments arranged. The costs could be extortionate for funding a royal visit. The expense drove some to the verge of bankruptcy after having to board and feed the royal household and the staff who travelled with it. They also had the expense of guaranteeing the room for stabling, which could mean having additional stables built. Then there was the upkeep of the horses and dogs belonging to guests, especially if there was to be a hunting party during the visit. Females would participate in hunts as well as spending time playing bowls, dancing, playing musical instruments, reading and hawking.

Hunting was a popular sport amongst males and females, especially the aristocracy. Margaret Tudor was an accomplished hunter, killing a deer on her way to Scotland to take up her role as queen consort, following her marriage to James IV. Based on their skill in hunting it could be assumed that some women, at least those of the aristocracy, may have enjoyed practising at the butts. Archery was predominantly a male sport, which was not only a recreational activity but also acted as preparation and maintenance of their skills for war. This does not mean women did not practice but was perhaps only enjoyed by those who also enjoyed hunting. For the aristocracy, the kills from a hunt would provide food for the household, and could be sent as gifts to others, sometimes in an effort to secure favour. For the humbler classes, hunting was possibly more of a matter of survival; hunting purely for the purpose of providing food and for the coats of animals to fashion warmer clothing. They also had to be careful where they hunted as it was illegal to hunt in a royal park. Hawking was a more preferable pastime than hunting for gentlewomen. It was an expensive pastime and therefore restricted to those who could afford the costs involved in purchasing and maintaining a bird for this purpose. Those visiting others for the purpose of a recreational weekend or hunting party may take their birds with them, or alternatively may borrow a bird belonging to their hosts. Those who owned birds often employed a falconer to care for their birds. The most popular breed for women was a Merlin, a small bird that was skilled in catching small prey, whilst men would use larger breeds like Gyrfalcons and Peregrines, dependent on their rank. Those who partook in some form of hunting for recreation and even those who observed could use the event as an opportunity to place bets on who would be most successful.

Today, casinos are full of card and dice games and although casinos did not exist at the time, all classes, both men and women, partook in gambling. The Tudors played a variety of card and dice games. Princess Mary, daughter of Henry VIII, was given money on a regular basis to play cards, sometimes multiple times per month.[1] Some games such as cards were banned in certain households other than at Christmas, when servants could play under the supervision of those ranked above them. Card and board games were popular amongst all, and those without the means to purchase a specific board could make do with making one or marking a surface to play on. Some of the board games played by the Tudors are similar to those we would recognise today. They played chess, backgammon (though it was known as tables), the Philosophers game which used a double chessboard and today's snakes and ladders is similar to a game of goose in the Tudor era. Games like bowling, shuttlecock and tennis could be played by all and were also sports which spectators could place bets on. The lower classes would use whatever materials they could find to make the required pieces of equipment, using their hands to play tennis, playing with marbles, or visiting the purpose-built bowling alleys that were beginning to appear in towns. The wealthy were beginning to have bowling alleys and tennis courts installed in their homes. Henry VIII was an avid tennis player, being complimented by ambassadors for his skills in the game.[2] Henry was likely a favourite amongst the betting courtiers.

The differing classes shared some recreational activities whilst others were reserved for the royal court and its courtiers. Tournaments were one of those largely reserved for the upper classes. These occasions were a huge show of pageantry with multiple events, usually ending with a joust. For women this was spectator pastime, but one which was enjoyed nonetheless, though the frequency of including martial elements decreased under the female Tudor monarchs. Attendance to observe was open to those who were not courtiers but at a cost for admittance, restricting attendance to those with the means to pay. Tournaments usually began with a large procession making them an event for all, at least initially. The general public could watch the nobility arriving in their finest clothes and costumes, a sight that would no doubt be very exciting. They were often the pinnacle feature of large celebrations such as weddings or religious celebrations. There were other forms of entertainment between shows of martial sportsmanship including puppet shows, dancing and short plays to entertain the masses while they awaited the main event.

Also drawing crowds were the bloodier events and sports. A public execution was a popular spectator sport, especially amongst the poorer classes. Although it was meant to act as a deterrent, the public would congregate at the execution site and spend the time with friends gossiping and drinking, which in turn gave the opportunity for victuallers and nearby taverns to have a profitable day. Crowds could also be found at cockfighting, bear and bullbaiting events which again gave the opportunity to gamble. Cockfighting was perhaps the most accessible to all classes as they were the cheapest of the animals used for fighting and the event provided food for the family of the winning individuals. A cock would be partially buried and attendees would throw stones, the winner being the person to hurl the fatal stone. As their prize they received the bird to take home. Bears were expensive as they had to be imported and were therefore more costly to gamble on. Bearbaiting took place in pits as did bullbaiting. Dogs would be set upon the animals and bets placed on the winning dog or the number of dogs that would survive.[3]

As religion formed a central part of Tudor life, it also provided the basis for much of the public entertainment. Church events were based on the liturgical year. Celebrations were not consistent across the country as many parishes had their own way of celebrating festivals and marking important days. Due to the changes in religion during the Tudor era there were modifications to the number of events and how these were celebrated, but the events that survived remained an integral part of entertainment for all classes. The events were a valuable method for churches to hold fundraising events, which in turn, would help support those in need within the parish. Christmas was not the gift-giving celebration we know today, instead gifts were exchanged at New Year. All would try and gift to those around them including servants gifting their master and mistress, even if a very humble offering. In return they would of course, receive a gift, if they were lucky, and it would likely be more valuable than that they had gifted. As part of the Christmas celebrations, wassailing was participated in by all classes. Wassailing was a communal activity that involved participants passing around and drinking from the same vessel whilst singing. Epiphany marked the end of the Christmas festivities, and all would attend Mass after which further celebrations involving singing and dancing commenced. Other days or events that were celebrated within communities included Candlemas in February, where parishioners would all proceed to church carrying a lit taper, then followed Lent and Holy Week. Shrovetide marked the beginning of Lent and was seen as the last opportunity for fun before the fasting and religious observances began. It was celebrated amongst communities with various entertainments including plays, music and dancing. Within the royal household there would also be elaborate masques and entertainers. Celebrations for Easter and Whitsun could comprise of processions, singing, dancing and more flamboyant entertainments at the royal court. Not all of these survived the Reformation and the services and events that did survive were usually less extravagant. Corpus Christi did not survive the Reformation but had been a popular celebration with pageants and processions featuring plays which parishioners could watch as floats passed them by.

Some events which we may not think would have been celebrated by the Tudors as they are perceived as commercial today, include Valentine's Day which was celebrated with a 'Valentine' being chosen and tokens exchanged. Many households would participate and some were lucky enough to receive a token from their master which would be valuable to a humble servant. Warmer weather in summer allowed for bigger outdoor celebrations. This would have benefitted the humbler classes who did not have the indoor space of the wealthy to hold events. They were restricted to using the church, if it were allowed, making the summer a welcome season for those wishing to participate in events. May Day and Midsummer were celebrated throughout parishes with dancing and fun amongst the local populations. May Day did involve a maypole but not as we would think. Instead of ribbons it was decorated with greenery that people would gather as part of the celebrations, although they did dance around it.[4] Midsummer was an important time of year for the Tudors and was celebrated in varying degrees across the country. As the name suggests, the celebrations marked the middle of summer and was celebrated with feasts, singing, and dancing. In some places a cartwheel of hay was set alight and rolled down a hill; if it stayed alight until it reached the bottom, it was believed to indicate a good harvest that year. Larger towns would have pageants, processions and players performing for the local inhabitants.

Regardless of class, all would participate in activities involving music, playing instruments, dancing and singing. Dancing, in particular, was instrumental to participating in most social events. Admittedly, the quality of instruments and level of skill may vary, but music remained a consistent aspect of entertainment for all classes throughout the period, as well as being linked to religious services. The Tudors had a wide range of musical instruments, and wealthy households used different types for differing occasions. More intimate events such as family dinners called for softer instruments like the lute, whilst more lively events and celebrations would call for louder sounding instruments, intended to be heard amongst a greater number of attendees. Humbler classes were mostly self-taught players or learned through practising with another player. The wealthier classes had access to tutors as well as literature that gave instruction on how to play, and printed music to improve their skills. Wealthier households would play to entertain themselves and employ minstrels to regale them. Minstrels were talented in music, singing and sometimes skilled in acrobatics, giving them a wide range of skills. They could play during intimate dinners or at large events. The Tudor monarchs all loved music, were accomplished players and had minstrels play frequently. Even the children, Mary, Elizabeth and Edward, had minstrels in their households.[5]

New songs and dances would filter down from the royal court and homes of the nobility to public taverns and the homes of the humbler classes. Elizabeth I is well known for her love of dancing, and she continued to dance into old age. There were a range of dances with varying numbers of dancers required, suitable for a diverse range of events. Elizabeth's favourite dance was reportedly the Galliard, an extremely lively dance which required the female to be lifted into the air by her partner. The lower classes may not have spent their time performing extrinsic Galliards or Pavanes but could all participate in the Branles, which was easy to learn and did not require a partner as it could be danced by many. Dancing was not only a form of entertainment but also gave people opportunities to meet prospective partners. Couples who were courting could respectfully spend time together dancing in the company of others, therefore not requiring a chaperone. Skill in dancing was a respected accomplishment, particularly amongst the aristocracy. A skilled dancer could attract the attention of suitors, and therefore, was one of the reasons wealthy families were willing to incur the costs of dance masters and dedicate time for practice. They also had the ability to procure literature providing instruction on the steps of the latest dances, although often there was no recommended accompanying music to consider against the steps shown in books. Music and dancing were a common occurrence in most social settings. Taverns and inns would have a player entertaining other guests, or perhaps a talented customer would play. Women were able to attend alehouses, taverns and inns; some would only attend for a few minutes to collect a jug of ale for their home and have a gossip whilst there. Others would spend an afternoon or evening there in the company of family and friends, socialising just as people do today in bars and pubs.

Just as music and its accompanying activities were popular amongst all classes, so was drama. Drama was a form of entertainment which, although varied greatly in quality and materials available for costumes and such, was a pastime that could be enjoyed by almost all. Productions were largely focused on tales of chivalry, morality or the scriptures. Performances were customarily enacted by two groups of people; 'mystery' plays were those performed by members of trade guilds whilst 'miracle' performances were those featuring actors. Mumming was also a form of theatre, usually a performance by masked actors performing the actions of a hero, which for the English would often be St George slaying the dragon. Most drama, whether at a venue or a parade through a town, took on the theme of a religious or moral nature. Throughout the period, more secular themes began to emerge through the works of men such as William Shakespeare, who had twenty-four of his productions performed by the end of the Tudor era. Only males could participate in theatre, even the characters of females were played by young males. The humbler classes did not miss out on opportunities to view theatrical performances. Attending a theatre was becoming popular during the Tudor era as new venues opened in London, beginning with the first permanent stage at the Red Lion in 1567 and followed by theatres including the Globe and the Amphitheatre. Venues changed their productions often and entry could be reasonable, particularly if attendees were willing to stand, making the theatre a popular choice for a day out. There were also bands of actors who travelled the country to perform in villages or at the homes of the aristocracy. The plays staged by travelling actors were technically not approved of by authorities as they tended to include more humorous topics or less favourable characters, but they did little harm and provided entertainment to local parishes. As well as the bands of travelling actors, inhabitants of towns and villages would perform a series of short plays as an element of a pageant throughout the year, usually in connection with religious festivals. Within the royal court there would be entertainments in the form of masques which were like plays, usually with a moral or chivalric theme alongside dancing. The entertainments required elaborate costumes which the ladies of the court would assist in creating, providing them with additional needlework tasks to keep them occupied. These entertainments took considerable time to arrange and practice and provided young ladies of the court with an opportunity, not only for fun but also to show off their skills and possibly catch the attention of a prospective suitor. At the end of the performance, the guests could then join the fun and dance with those who had participated in the entertainment.

Along with the minstrels, and bands of actors and acrobats that were paid to entertain the wealthy, some households employed a jester or 'fool'. Their role was to entertain their audience through acting silly, sometimes at the expense of their host, but they were maintained in their employer's household in some comfort. Henry VIII is thought to have been fond of his jester Will Somers and Princess Mary ensured 'Jane the Fool' was maintained effectively. It was rare for a female to be employed in this role, possibly due to the nature of having to act silly when society expected women to behave modestly. Mary paid for Jane's lodgings, food, clothing and the stabling of her horse. Jane apparently shaved her head, possibly to wear wigs to entertain her mistress, and received medical care for her eye, which Mary also paid for.[6]

A pastime which generally related to the wealthier classes was reading. This was due to the lower classes either being illiterate, or because of the unaffordable costs of purchasing books. As the Tudor era progressed, books did become much more affordable, with the increase of available material as a result of the improvements in printing presses. Reading was the perfect pastime for all weathers, females could read indoors during the colder months or outdoors when the weather warmed. Reading was a solo and group activity as women could spend time with friends reading passages to one another out loud or entertain themselves when alone. Many books were initially printed in Latin but throughout the period an increased number of volumes were translated and printed in English. The ancient Roman and Greek authors such as Aristotle and Cicero were extremely popular as were advice and conduct books. *Miroir des Dames* was written for aristocratic women as a guide to moral instruction, and members of the Tudor family owned copies which perhaps encouraged other women to obtain a copy.[7] Vives' *De Institutione Feminae Christianae* written in 1523 for Henry VIII's daughter, the future Mary I, was translated into English in 1529 by Richard Hyrde with the title *Instruction of a Christian Woman*. It became the standard book for educating aristocratic females. William Caxton aimed to publish books specifically for females including an English version of Geoffrey de la Tour Landry's *Book of the Knight of the Tower*, a book of moral stories and *The Book of Good Manners*, a compilation of texts based on the scriptures. Well educated women would often spend time translating texts themselves. Margaret More-Roper is known to have translated *Devout Treatise upon the Pater Noster*, written by Erasmus. The 12-year-old future Elizabeth I, translated *Prayers and Mediations* into French, Italian and Latin as a gift for Kateryn Parr, and she was still spending time translating works at the end of the sixteenth century. Kateryn Parr was the author of *Prayers and Mediations*, published in 1545; she was the first English queen to publish work in her own name and went on to publish *Lamentation of a Sinner* in 1547, following the death of Henry VIII.

Fictional works were available such a *La Morte D'Arthur*, but unsurprisingly, there were no female authors of fictional work. Even nonfiction topics of a feminine nature were mostly written by male authors, although Anne Wheathill was amongst the few females who did publish under their own name. Wheathill wrote *A Handfull of Holesome (though Homelie) Hearbs* in 1584; it contained a number of prayers for varying situations. Books for females at that time aimed to provide advice on and improve the skills which society deemed useful for them. There was a variety of literature on sewing, lacemaking, embroidery, music and housekeeping. Recipe books were also popular amongst the wealthier classes. They were not restricted to food recipes but contained advice and recipes for using herbs for medicinal purposes, cleaning and washing waters. Many women kept their own book of recipes which they added to throughout their lives before leaving to their daughter or female relative upon their death. Reading was not completely restricted to wealthy people, the humbler classes could purchase literature on a variety of subjects, including those more fun by nature, including joke and riddle books, as well as more serious educational subjects. Pedlars would travel the country selling books, pamphlets and sheets that the lower classes could purchase for their reading material. Poetry was a popular pastime, particularly amongst the aristocracy. At the royal court, poetry was used in the game of courtly love; a game of exchanging poems and tokens of affection without (in most cases) any serious intentions. Courtiers were well aware of boundaries within the game but it provided the opportunity for them to show off their skills in composing verse and ditties and catch the attention of potential patrons.

As noted, women of all classes spent time in needlework and this was not always for the purpose of wages. Young females would practice on samplers, although these could result in beautiful pieces themselves. More accomplished women would embroider magnificent pieces of work, or incredibly detailed embellishments on garments. A wide range of literature was available providing needlework patterns for practice or to copy the latest fashions. The humble classes would spend time creating clothing and textiles for their family, home and gifting. Needlework was an activity that could be done indoors during the winter months or outside when warm. It always had an end result making it a valuable pastime for all women, regardless of their aim.

Some recreational sports were inappropriate for women, they did not play football, joust, run at the tilt or wrestle, or at least there are no records of them doing so. This did not stop them from attending as spectators and gambling on events. Hunting and hawking were the most active pastimes for women, whilst needlework is likely the most common as all classes and ages partook in spinning, sewing and embroidery. The degree to which women could participate in drama was extremely limited as women were not allowed to join acting groups and they couldn't be cast as any characters. The women of the royal court could participate in masques which were a form of drama. The roles they played were modest, pious women, awaiting valiant knights, usually Henry VIII and friends, to rescue them from some kind of threat. The ability to play music was dependent on circumstances, not all could procure an instrument and those who did had varying methods of learning to play. Dancing was an activity for the masses. Dancing took place in religious events, social celebrations and the more extravagant courtly events. One of the benefits of dancing was that marital status, wealth and rank did not matter. Single, married, widowed, poor, rich, nobility, they could all dance. Whilst it could be a talent used to attract a spouse it was predominantly a form of entertainment enjoyed by all classes and ages, providing an acceptable method of socialising for those who otherwise should not be in close proximity to the opposite sex; women such as maidens and widows.

# Chapter Eight

# Woes of Widowhood

As with infancy, childhood, marriage and motherhood, Tudor women viewed widowhood as a life-stage. For women, losing a spouse usually had a much larger impact on their lives than a man losing his wife, due to the dependency of women on men as a result of the patriarchal society they lived in. Women conformed to the culture of being subordinate to men, therefore to lose the man who oversaw her whole life was a huge blow. Upon the death of her husband, a woman's life changed drastically. A widow became an individual in her own right. Unlike when she was a maid, she had no duty to be obedient to anyone. She was no longer the responsibility of her father or husband and could take life into her own hands, at least theoretically.

It was principally men who executed a last will and testament. Although men of the lower classes did not generally have much to bequeath, they did sometimes create a will. But wills were more common amongst the wealthier classes and the aristocracy. Of the men who did make a will, it was often their widows who were trusted to be the sole executrix. If the estate was complex, a man's widow may be selected to act alongside others. Sir Anthony Denny, whose will was mentioned earlier in Chapter Three, appointed his wife alongside another as his executors, under the supervision of other influential men.[1] Henry VII, having already lost his wife, Elizabeth of York, chose his mother, Margaret Beaufort to be one of his executors.[2] Over seventy per cent of the nobility selected their wife to act as the sole executor of their will, perhaps indicating that there were many successful marriages amongst this class, or that they trusted their wife to act in accordance to their wishes and for the best interests of their children.[3] As a sole executor a widow also had the responsibility of organising and paying for her husband's funeral, which for the nobility could be a grand affair. However, it was not uncommon for another member of the family or the nobility to request the opportunity to pay for the funeral as a way of showing their respects and endearment for the deceased. Henry VIII paid for the funeral of his best friend, Charles Brandon, Duke of Suffolk, and had him buried in St George's Chapel, Windsor, where he wished to be buried himself when his time came, remaining together in death as they had been in life. Along with arranging and paying for a funeral there was also the construction of a tomb and the distribution of alms for the widow to undertake. Some men would design and pay for their tombs long before their death so this could be as simple as informing the stonemasons he had now died. Alms were a different matter; some men had simple requests such as distributing alms to the poor who attended his funeral and paying the servants who were no longer required. Other men left their wives numerous instructions which could include the endowment of schools, hospitals or other charitable institutes, distributing differing amounts of alms to different groups of individuals or, prior to the Reformation, establishing a chantry chapel in his honour. In 1511, Joan Bradburye, was granted a licence to found a perpetual chantry for one chaplain in the church of St Stephen, London. The licence granted the chaplain the right to pray for the souls of her two deceased husbands: Thomas Bradburye, mayor of London, and Thomas Bodley.[4]

Executors, depending on the complexity of the estate, may have to attend court a year after the death to file probate. During the proceedings the executor would be required to provide an inventory of the deceased's goods, his will and show that they had taken on the responsibility for the man's debts. This could be a huge undertaking for someone of wealth. A widow was not expected to travel all over the country, visiting each property her husband had owned. They would use the services of servants or lawyers to travel amongst them, recording inventories at each one or if each had a steward present, he could take on the responsibility and the burden of creating the inventories. A woman could also decline to act as an executor. A widow was under no obligation to agree to the role. Widows could perhaps decline if they were aware that their husband was in debt when he died, as they did not wish to accept the responsibility of acknowledging the debts and taking them on. Widows whose husbands' debts exceeded the value of his estate were protected to some extent but it remained a very difficult situation if others were attempting to claim against the estate.

If a man died intestate, his widow had the legal right to administer his estate. If there was no jointure, the right of dower would apply for the purposes of the widow's inheritance. Her rights were determined by where she and her husband resided. Traditionally the widow would be entitled to a third of her husband's estate, but only for her lifetime at which point the rights to her share would transfer in full to the heir (or were bequeathed as per the rest of the estate if there were no sons). This remained the position across most of England and Wales. Local custom did allow for variances as independent dioceses could impose their own rules. For instance, in Canterbury if a man died intestate, the widow's inheritance was decided on the basis of whether there were children or not. If they had children, she was entitled to the traditional third of his estate, if there were no children this increased to half. Residing in Canterbury also enabled men to will their property however they saw fit. This could cause further issues as widows could only claim specific legacies. If the will was not specific, she may lose something which was intended for her. For example, a man could bequeath his wife's gowns, furniture and bed hangings to her to ensure she would keep them and avoid disagreements with other benefactors.

Widows of craftsmen, tradesmen and merchants were often bequeathed their husband's business and depending on the trade, could continue to trade as before. Most widows would have to rely upon her husband's employees or apprentice to assist her. Widows of merchants would undoubtedly require assistance to continue as it was extremely doubtful that a widow would go off travelling overseas as a merchant, particularly as she would be unlikely to be taken seriously when arriving at foreign ports. If she wished to retain the business, she would require a current employee such as her husband's apprentice, to take on the majority of the travelling work or hire a new employee. Some towns such as Oxford, did not allow women to trade as *femme sole*. The exception was that they did allow widows to continue the trade of her deceased husband on the basis she would abide by the regulations of his guild and continue to make the relevant guild payments. Widows receiving a business in other trades could decide whether to sell it or continue the business on behalf of her family. If the woman had a son who was currently undertaking an apprenticeship in the same trade, she may decide to keep it running on his behalf until he completed his apprenticeship term. Dependent on the term he may also be required to complete a term as a journeyman too. This was a period when he was qualified but would work for his master for a period of time before he could open his own business. The Stationer's Company who regulated the guild of the printing industry had such a clause in their apprenticeship agreements.[5] Its aim was ensure masters got a period of skilled work from their apprentice after the effort they had put into teaching them but also avoided flooding the market with business owners. Once a widow's son was able to take over the running of the business, she could, if she wished or was required to, continue working within the business for her son until he either married or she was no longer able to work. Alternatively, she may choose to sell the business, and often an apprentice could be approached with a view to him purchasing the business. Other men left their business or tools of the trade to their apprentice but this did not mean the widow was completely cut out. As with those who chose to sell, a widow could often continue to assist the new master. There were also cases of widows marrying the man who had previously been her husband's apprentice. For some couples where tools and property had been bequeathed separately, it meant the business could continue to trade as it was. Perhaps some of these cases were a husband's way of ensuring his wife would be secure. By bequeathing a business to his wife and his tools to his apprentice, it was likely the pair would continue to work together, providing some security for his widow (although presumably they never thought their widow would marry their apprentice).

Although land or property was the most common bequest from men to their wives, there were alternatives and even the gift of a property could be restricted. It was not uncommon for a man to stipulate that his widow could only have the rights to a property for a specific term. The term could be as long or as short as he wished, for example until a dependent child came of age, the youngest daughter married or until his widow's death. Men intending to bequeath the main residency or estate to his heir or other benefactor, may choose to add a maintenance or dwelling clause to his will. Maintenance and dwelling arrangements safeguarded a widow by providing her with a specific amount of maintenance for the rest of her life, or at least whilst she remained unmarried. A man may request his widow be entitled to remain living in the main residence until death or remarriage. If the chosen residence was the family home, it was probable she would have to reside with the heir and his family. If they had a good relationship this could be a pleasant arrangement for a widow, providing company and support. Some women would perhaps have discussed the arrangement with their husband when he was preparing his will and specified a preference in property; some may have been happy with any of the properties they owned. Therefore, the clause may be as simple as stating a dwelling for her purpose. A dwelling agreement was much more beneficial for a widow than a bequest of moveable goods as it removed the need for her to find a new home, even if the dwelling was not the one she wished for. A maintenance clause gave reassurance to widows who may have been concerned for their future. It also meant she would not receive the bulk of her inheritance at once and be at risk of becoming a target to another man because of her wealth. Or, if she were an irrational spender, running out of funds and becoming a burden on family or society. Although these types of clauses provided greater security it did limit the independence of a widow. If she wished to move to another area, perhaps to be closer to family, she would be unable to do so unless a further agreement could be made regarding the dwelling. A further clause could be added that maintenance would cease if she were to remarry. This could be the deciding factor for a widow when she was considering remarriage, especially in instances where the maintenance grant was generous. As with all bequests within a will, if the executor or heir chose not to, or could not, honour the clause the widow could sue to obtain her rights.

Some women were left financially comfortable, mostly those of the aristocracy and widows of successful tradesmen. Of these women, some were savvy enough to continue their lives with the assistance of servants. Other widows would often seek the support of a male relative to help her understand her new obligations. The aristocracy managed huge estates, and many women had the responsibility of managing the household. Despite this, those without previous experience would likely find the management of the whole estate to be overwhelming to begin with. One of the widow's first concerns would be to ensure the estate continued to generate an income. The majority of the aristocracy had rent-paying tenants and farmers living and working on their land. If a widow had previously formed a relationship with the estate tenants, maintaining the rental income would perhaps be an easier task than for someone who was a stranger to them. She would need to learn the payment schedule of rents, how to collect them, when rental reviews were due as well as the obligations she now owed to her tenants, including negotiating lease agreements and encouraging new tenants to settle when required. There was also the farmland to consider. Farming could be a complex business and the majority of widows would require assistance to manage this land unless it was all rented to tenant farmers.

Estates would certainly have their own dairy, bakehouse and perhaps a mill but a housewife would probably already have experience in managing these areas.

Although women generally had experience of managing the household monetary accounts, as a widow she was now responsible for the accounts of the whole estate. This would include rent, maintenance, wages, household expenditure and any other income such as the farm and market goods. It was also not as simple as learning one more account. If there were a large number of properties across the country, each would have different rent values, agricultural produce and costs and there would be an abundance of details for a widow to learn. The most common resolution was to appoint a steward or bailiff to run the estate on her behalf whilst she managed the financial aspects. He would be responsible for finding new tenants, collecting rents, and recruitment within the estate. A widow would also keep herself abreast of recruitment and would usually maintain control over the appointment of household staff. The majority of widows would certainly require male assistance where legal matters were concerned but they were not obliged to defer to a man if they felt capable of undertaking the tasks themselves. Alternatively, a widow may decide to lease out parcels of land or whole properties to other wealthy and aristocratic families, sometimes members of her own family. By leasing out the property, the widow no longer had the responsibility for maintaining the land and property, managing the tenants and farming, and all other obligations that went with that particular manor or property. This could also create additional income for a woman when she had no use for a particular property in the foreseeable future. It could also be a beneficial method of managing any property a widow was holding for dependent children until they came of age.

The extent of change to a widow's life in terms of her financial security largely depended on the settlement arranged when she initially married, namely her dower and jointure but also her husband's last will and testament. For all classes of women, the death of her husband could mean the loss of her home, or in some cases her primary residence. Women who had experienced an unhappy marriage could find themselves out of favour when their husband died, leaving her with little other than her dower or jointure, if one had been agreed at the outset. Husbands were within their rights to dispose of their goods as they wished and could leave his wife out of his will completely. For the most part, those who had a jointure or dower agreement upon their marriage could take possession of their property without any legal interference, and executors would not have to undertake much work on this aspect of the deceased's estate.

Another priority for widows was to ensure she and her family were provided for. The ability to accomplish this varied according to social and economic status, as well as the widow's own training and experience. If there were no children born of the union, a widow may find herself in a difficult legal battle. It is doubtful the man's male relatives would allow her to inherit his estate, and she would have to fight to maintain control of any land and properties. She was of course entitled to her jointure but if there was a dispute regarding her claim, a widow would need the approval of the crown or chancery courts to finalise her rights. If a widow was claiming dower rights, she required a petition to the Crown to obtain a writ of right of dower before she could take possession. Widows could not claim both jointure and dower. The aristocracy were keen to keep their estates together and sometimes resented the life-long claim widows held to certain properties, despite the fact a substantial dowry had been paid by the bride's family in exchange for this right. If her husband had male children from a previous marriage, this would be the point which evidenced their opinion of the widow as a stepmother. He (or they if there was more than one son) could work against her in attempting to reduce her inheritance, or they could help her and come to an amicable agreement, perhaps with a stipulation that all goods and property reverted to them upon her death. Surprisingly, it was not just stepsons that chose to sometimes work against a widow. A woman's own sons and in-laws may also debate her inheritance if they thought they were being wronged in some way or were just plain greedy. Fortunately they could do little about the dower or jointure agreements and would most likely lose any legal battle, though that did not stop families from attempting to reduce or negate the jointure settlement.

Due to the custom of primogeniture passing the bulk of the estate to the heir, men could only provide for their other children in the form of alternative bequests, dowries, jointures and annuities. This would mean the heir would not receive the full estate as a sibling may have a lifetime right to reside in a property, or receive income from specified land. An heir may find this to be disagreeable, forcing a widow to fight for the inheritance of her other children. Not all widows had a negative experience and some would negotiate with the heir of the estate. In some cases, widows may wish to reduce the spread of her jointure lands and exchange some for property closer to her place of residence. This would make managing her affairs more efficient and result in less travel. Of course, the opposite may be the case and a widow may wish for a specific property, for instance, away from her main residence but close to family or friends that she liked to visit, so may make an agreement for obtaining that property. Alternatively, if the heir wished to retain a specific property, agreements could be made to exchange the property for income from alternative lands. Not all heirs disputed a widow's right to her dower or jointure and in many cases worked with them to make an arrangement agreeable to both parties.

In some cases the husband or his family had never actually formalised the jointure leaving a widow in a very uncertain position. Prior to the death of a husband, due to the custom of coverture, a wife could not take legal action against her husband or his family for failure to settle her jointure. If a wife wished to sue for her jointure to be settled, she would require a male from her own family to act on her behalf. Widows, unlike their married counterparts, were well within their rights to sue her husband's family for the settlement and many did so.[6] There were also the families that only had daughters. Due to the practice of primogeniture, daughters did not necessarily inherit estates if there was a male relative. Upon the death of her husband, an aristocratic widow would likely be the target of the male relatives pressing their claim to the estate, aiming to disinherit her daughters. Widows would be responsible for protecting the inheritance of their daughters where male relatives were attempting to make a claim. The outcome of this would be determined by the man's will and the courts. It was possible for a daughter to inherit, the main problem came where there were multiple daughters. They could inherit jointly which often meant the estate was torn apart. The best-case scenario for keeping the estate together was for one of the daughters' sons to inherit and add an agreement that the widow could remain living where she chose until her remarriage or death.

As a widow, a woman largely regained all of her rights that she lost when she married, and those widows with the means to do so enjoyed a level of freedom which included financial independence. Widows reverted to the status of *femme sole*. Unlike married women, widows held full legal and financial capacity for their possessions and property. She could dispose of and procure property and land, agree contracts and sue on her own behalf within the courts. Like single women, widows could create a will without permission from anyone. For the majority of the female population, this did not alter their lives much as they did not have the wealth for it to have a large impact. As noted, widows could dispose of their property how they saw fit, the exception being their dower. Widows were usually entitled to her dower, usually a third of her husband's property, for life if she survived her husband. This right was supported by common law. The dower could vary as some local customs allowed more than a third but it was for the widow to prove her case if her claim was contested. In the sixteenth century, if a married woman held any land, it had usually been granted through the jointure aspect of the marriage settlement. Upon the death of a man, as the surviving tenant, his widow gained the rights to the property until her own death. This at least secured her a home, even if an heir did not approve of the arrangement. The dower system provided much more disparity than jointures but was protected and enforced by the common law and the Church. The problem with relying on a marriage settlement which could have been agreed many years prior to the death of her husband, was that during her marriage, the wife may have been persuaded to part with some of her rights through agreeing to the sale of a property which formed part of her dower. For most, an alternative property would be used to ensure a widow was not left homeless but if there was a male heir, a widow could find herself at the mercy of her own son or stepson to provide an adequate property, which on occasion was not forthcoming.

The rights of a widower in comparison were very different. If there were children, the widower was entitled to a life interest in all of his wife's real estate, a custom known as 'by curtesy of England'. This was also the case even where there were no surviving children at the time of the wife's death. But if there were no children at all from the marriage, the woman's property reverted to her heirs, usually parents, siblings or children from a previous marriage.

The majority of titled women earned their title through marriage; few held a title in their own right. As a result, when they became widowed their husband's title was usually passed to their son. The widow may be referred to as dowager, or their title may even continue to be used but it was used only as a courtesy. The exception were the widows of knights. Whilst their husband was alive the wife of a knight was known as 'Lady' but on his death, his widow became 'Dame'. Knighthood was not a hereditary title and therefore, the title died with the husband. Women who did hold a title in their own right had the ability to transmit their title to their son, with the monarch's consent. This could ensure the son held a title in the event of a mishap with his father.

A proportion of men left their wives much more than what had been agreed in their marriage settlement. During the Tudor era, sixteen per cent of aristocratic men left their widow more than the initial settlement.[7] Though a fairly small number, it should be considered that the aristocracy were contending with the rule of primogeniture – that the eldest son would inherit the bulk of the estate. It should also be considered that a marriage settlement amongst the aristocracy is likely to have been substantial and generous; anything additional could be inferred as genuine affection from those with the resources to do so. Those who did not increase bequests to their wives should not be harshly thought of. Their finances could change quickly; someone who was in favour one week may be banished from court the next, influencing their income and what they could leave behind for the family at the time of death. Hosting the royal family during one of their progresses could leave a man almost bankrupt so it is understandable that not all were able to bequeath more, though there are likely a number who made a specific decision not to. Other men would make further bequests on their deathbed of land, goods and property to their wife or others. Widows could face difficulties in claiming these unless there were witnesses or the bequests were supported by the last will and testament. Even then, this did not stop male heirs from disputing claims and attempting to retain as much of the estate as possible intact.

Wealthy widows, chiefly those of the aristocracy, not only lost their husband but faced the prospect of losing their children to wardship. They could petition the monarch to purchase the wardship of their own children, but if they were heirs or heiresses to a large amount of wealth, the widow may find others were able and willing to pay more than they could afford for the wardship. It was possible the monarch would grant the wardship to the mother with no costs incurred but there was a risk she would have to attempt to purchase the right to raise her own children. Margaret Ramsey was granted the wardship of her son Thomas, in 1511.[8] Thomas had been the heir of his father, also named Thomas. The loss of a woman's children could result in a reduction in income as the guardian would be entitled to the income from the heirs' lands and estates until the child came of age.

The guardian may determine the child could reside with their mother, but overall they would be responsible for decisions affecting the upbringing of the child. A guardian did have a duty to ensure the children were brought up in accordance with their rank, so whilst their mother may lose income, theoretically the child should have everything provided for them. Widows who retained custody of dependent children not only had to manage her own estates but also those she was holding on their behalf until they came of age. A widow was able to make use of any income from the property intended for the children but was also responsible for ensuring the children were cared for, and provided with everything they required, in accordance with their status. Being separated from their children was not just applicable to wealthy widows, it also extended to the poor, who were at risk of losing their children to the parish if they could not afford to maintain them without becoming a burden on the parish.

The majority of widows were women of humble origin. They were not left large estates to manage or businesses to run and instead each day could be a struggle. If a widow with young children found it difficult to both work and care for her children, they may be removed from her care and placed within another household or apprenticed within the parish. The widow could then continue to work and support herself, whilst the children would from then on, contribute towards their upkeep as servants or apprentices. Others managed to keep their children by having them work from a young age, either alongside them or within the local vicinity. Whilst their mother worked, children may take on the role of providing childcare for younger siblings or local children earning a little for their troubles, though not necessarily money. They may be paid with food or alternative goods which would still be a benefit to their family. A widow could take on multiple jobs in order to make ends meet without losing her children and, dependent on her parish, may receive alms to assist her if it were apparent she was trying to manage without becoming a burden. Of course, those who already had employment prior to their husband's death would have the experience and training to rely upon to be able to continue in their role or seek new employment. Work could also be done at home as noted in Chapter 6. Spinning work could be done at home giving a woman the ability to earn a living whilst caring for her children. If she was already spinning for a living, she could consider working longer hours or increasing the number of pieces she completed, therefore increasing her income. Another option was to begin teaching her daughters to spin. The family could then take turns on the spinning wheel to allow additional time for other household chores and the care of younger children.

Widows with sufficient wealth to support themselves and any dependent children, but not having the wealth to attract the interest of those seeking wardships of their children, were the only widows who were not at risk of having their children removed from them. This could of course change with circumstances, especially if she were unable to manage the estates effectively, resulting in a loss of wealth. Those at the very bottom of the scale who could not secure sufficient income resulting in debt could find themselves residents of a debtors' prison. If condemned to prison, a widow could lose her children, her home and was subject to the conditions of jail. During the Tudor era, those in prison or their friends and family could make payments to improve the living conditions of the inmate, but a poor widow was highly unlikely to have a wealthy benefactor willing to assist her in this manner. Once released it would be extremely difficult for her to regain custody of her children as they had likely been apprenticed or sent to another household.

Women with adult children may be able to rely on their goodwill for support, depending on the wealth the children had accrued themselves or the financial situation their father had left them in. If circumstances allowed, the widow may move to reside with one of her adult children; she could in turn then support with childcare or managing the household if able or required. Widows in this situation tended to move in with, or near to, their daughters who usually took the responsibility for the welfare of their mother if she were widowed. The Act for the Relief of the Poor in 1601, firmly placed the burden of maintaining elderly, poor, or those otherwise unable to maintain themselves primarily on the children, assuming the elders' parents had passed already:

And be it further enacted, That the Father and grandfather, and the Mother and Grandmother, and the children of every poor, old, blind, lame, and impotent person, or other poor person, not able to work, being of a sufficient ability, shall at their own charges relieve and maintain every such poor person in that manner, and according to that rate, as by the Justices of peace of that County where such sufficient persons dwell, or the greater number of them, at their general quarter

Sessions shall be assessed, upon pain that every one them shall forfeit twenty shillings for every month which they shall fail therein.[9]

Elderly women, including widows, without adequate family support, were considered as the model recipients for parish alms, and support, particularly if they had not been a burden previously. The parish alms for the elderly acted as an informal pension, it was not guaranteed. The value of alms depended on the wealth of the parish who were reliant on the donations received from inhabitants, fayres, or bequests to the parish from those who left a donation in their last will and testament for distribution to the poor. Most communities had no objections to assisting the elderly inhabitants with chores and ensuring they received sustenance. To continue to receive the alms from the parish, a widow's behaviour had to remain respectable, else the parish would disapprove and begin to withhold any support, forcing elderly women to beg for coin, food and drink. The aristocracy and the royal family commonly distributed alms, especially around celebratory events or holy days. Religious institutions including churches, convents and monasteries were the main distributers of alms for the poor. Following the dissolution of the monasteries and convents, the dispensation of alms was reduced. Women in need would have been impacted immensely by this, particularly those widows who had become too old to secure any other type of income.

Widows gained the power to make decisions as to whether she wished to remarry. And if she chose to do so, she may choose her own groom, although in theory there were some exceptions to this. The monarch had the prerogative to arrange a marriage for a widow of one of their tenants in chief, usually women of the nobility. These widows had to swear not to remarry without the monarch's permission in order to obtain their dower rights. In reality, if one of these widows wished to remarry, she required a licence of approval. If granted, she was free to go ahead. The licence incurred a charge but could be granted without fee as a show of favour from the monarch. Part of the reasoning behind this feudal law was to ensure the lands of the nobility were protected. Agreements could be made between a widow and the monarch where land would be transferred to the Crown in exchange for their permission to remarry. Couples who risked waiting until after they were married to approach the monarch may find themselves making a trip to the Tower. Widows could also make matches for their children and negotiate marriage settlements for herself and on behalf of her children. The exceptions were when a guardian had been appointed to the children through wardship. In these circumstances, the guardian could decide on a match, but the majority of guardians would at least consult the mother. Widows often remarried following a mourning period of a year or two. Society expected a widow to remain single for a year, although some did remarry before this time, some as little as four months or even earlier in the case of Lady Margaret Hoby, who married her second husband within a fortnight of becoming a widow. This would most certainly have been frowned upon by some.

There were various factors for a widow to consider when deciding whether to remarry; her wealth, the age of herself and her children and whether she wished to improve her social standing. Approximately one third of marriages were remarriages, indicating the number of marriages that took place after the death of a first or subsequent spouse.[10] For some, they felt they had little choice. Remarriage was a survival technique for those who would otherwise find themselves faced with poverty, loss of property, and possibly ostracised from their social circle. Another factor that could influence women to remarry was the preference to have the support of a husband in legal battles. A man's assistance could be particularly helpful where a widow was facing claims against her children's inheritance or an heir attempting to negate her claims upon the estate. A new husband, one that had influence and rank, could be the perfect solution to any legal issues and ensure the rest of her children were protected. A husband could assist with securing bequests for her children, keeping dowries safe until they were required, and help his wife to carry out her duties as executor to her previous husband. To assist his wife in securing bequests for her children actually helped the husband if the children were still dependents. Any annuities and life-time grants to property and income meant he would benefit from that until the children came of age, so it made it worthwhile to support his wife for this reason also. A widow did have to consider that the opposite effect was a possibility and there could be issues between her children, stepchildren and her husband. On remarrying, a woman was once again under the control of her husband. Her property became his and any plans she may have had for property, land and moveable goods could be completely destroyed. For this reason, many aristocratic women sought favourable remarriage arrangements, which acted as a form of pre-nuptial agreement. A husband would also be in control of any property his wife was holding for dependent children until they came of age, so it could become a difficult situation if there was no agreement made beforehand either between the couple or through a grant from the monarch.

Fraught relationships could also occur with any children the new husband had from previous marriages if they saw themselves at a disadvantage to their stepsiblings as a result of their new stepmother trying to protect her children's inheritance. Men who remarried would often ensure their will was explicit in stating that the goods belonging to his stepchildren were theirs. This not only protected his wife and her children but also avoided any claims by stepchildren against his estate. For all of these reasons, age played a factor in a woman's decision to remarry. For older women, their children were likely already grown and independent, not requiring her assistance in regard to their inheritance. If a widow could maintain herself or had received a generous jointure with no protest from her husband's family, it would be a much simpler life and therefore, a husband was more of a choice for companionship than necessity. Older widows were more likely to remain single than their younger counterparts who were still of childbearing age and who possibly required assistance with inheritance and the maintenance of herself and her children. Some younger widows chose to marry an older man, perhaps as his children were grown and she would not be required to care for them, or maybe because it was simply a good match for both parties. Widowers differed in some cases as they would aim to marry a younger woman in the hopes of having more children, particularly if they were still seeking a male heir.

Remarriage could result in huge, blended families with both partners bringing their children from previous marriages, and then possibly having their own together. Women were expected to take up the role of stepmother naturally, many being referred to as 'mother' by their stepchildren. Margaret Donnington, a wealthy heiress, who had been widowed twice, married John Bourchier, 2nd Earl of Bath in 1548. When making arrangements for their marriage, Margaret ensured she remained in control of her property and was at liberty to dispose of it as she wished. She also insisted that the earl's five daughters were not to reside with them at their home; the beautiful Hengrave Hall, which remains today. Hengrave had been part of Margaret's inheritance after the death of her first husband. Her own four daughters, three fathered by Sir Richard Long and one by Sir Thomas Kitson were to live with them.[11] This seems unreasonable but Margaret went even further by insisting that the earl's heir, John Bourchier, Lord Fitzwarn, marry her daughter, Frances Kitson, and the couple were married alongside their parents.

Those who had no children of their own would still be expected to act in a motherly role to her husband's children. Rank did not matter in this situation; Jane Seymour and Kateryn Parr both took on the role of acting as a mother to the children of Henry VIII. Kateryn Parr had previously been widowed and had no children of her own. In his will, her husband Lord Latimer had requested Kateryn take responsibility for ensuring the income from property allocated to his daughter Margaret was used to maintain Margaret and to pay for her dowry when she married. Kateryn seemingly maintained a close relationship with her stepdaughter who later left Kateryn much of her own estate when she died.[12] Younger widows were more likely to remarry in order to have further opportunity for more children and maintain their economic and social standing or to regain the security a husband could bring. Young widows who remarried older men faced the possibility of being rejected as a stepmother, especially if she were of a similar age to her husband's children. She would be likely to outlive her husband and therefore impose on their inheritance much longer than an older widow, through her jointure and any bequests her husband made to any children she had brought to the marriage.

Through smart matches it was possible for a woman to rise in social status. The most notable woman during the Tudor era to do this successfully was Elizabeth Hardwick, later known as Bess of Hardwick. Bess became the richest woman in England after Elizabeth I, largely as a result of her advantageous marriages. To accomplish this, a woman required an understanding of her legal rights as a widow, or someone to advise her, usually a male relative. Bess married a total of four times, each time increasing her wealth and influence. Her birthdate is unknown but thought to be c.1527. She was the daughter of a gentleman, John Hardwick and his wife Elizabeth Leeke. Bess lost her father when she was only 7 years old and inherited 40 marks, equivalent to £26.[13] She met her first husband, Robert Barlow and married him in 1543. A few months later in December 1544, Barlow, who was still a young teenager, died leaving Bess a young widow. Her dower rights were disputed but after a lengthy battle she won her claim, inheriting Barlow's lands including profitable lead mines. She remarried in 1547, becoming Lady Cavendish through her marriage to Sir William

Cavendish. Cavendish was much older than Bess, being 42 at the time of their marriage, whilst she was approximately 20 years old. It was during this marriage that Bess became the lady of the household of Chatsworth. Cavendish died a decade later and Bess was widowed once again. This time Bess inherited the responsibility of Cavendish's two daughters, the six surviving children she conceived during their marriage, and a large debt owed to the Crown. Bess succeeded in managing to convince the courts to award her the estates, stating they should remain with her and Cavendish's heirs. Her third marriage took place only two years later in 1559, when she became Lady St Loe upon marrying Sir William St Loe. Her third husband was an extremely wealthy courtier who was the Chief Butler of England and Captain of the Guard to Elizabeth I. He used his wealth and influence to not only have Bess' debt reduced but also paid it himself. This was the marriage that gave Bess the bulk of her fortune. When St Loe died a few years later, Bess was the sole beneficiary, inheriting an annual income of approximately £60,000 (around £20 million in today's economy).[14] This vast wealth and her youth made her a prime target for those seeking a wealthy wife. Her final husband was George Talbot, 6th Earl of Shrewsbury, vaulting Bess into the nobility and making her Countess of Shrewsbury. The couple furthered the family ties by marrying two of Talbot's children to two of Bess' children, one of the marriages being that of Talbots's heir, ensuring the estates would remain within Bess' family as well as Talbot's. The marriage of Bess and Talbot would eventually break down, possibly due to the impact of having to host Mary Queen of Scots in their estates for fifteen years. Talbot died in 1590, after which Bess retained a lot of his estates to the chagrin of his heir. She is remembered for the beautiful buildings of Chatsworth and Hardwick Hall but is also an incredible example of how high a woman could rise through marriage during the Tudor era.

If a widow chose to remarry, her priority was to ensure she protected her property and her own interests. Widows who made the decision to remarry had an advantage, if they wished to pursue it. They could choose whether any property they held was to be held by her new husband 'in right of his wife' or whether she wished to grant the property to a joint tenure. Any property held 'in right of his wife' could only be used by the husband for the term of the marriage. If the marriage ceased for any reason it would revert to the woman or her heirs if she had died. This was a shrewd method for ensuring her property was protected, particularly if there were doubts around actions the husband may take if he acquired the land. It also safeguarded the inheritance of any children the woman had from a previous marriage. This assurance that their land and property was safeguarded is perhaps a factor in why almost fifty per cent of aristocratic women chose to remarry.[15] For some women of rank, remarriage was not a decision based on wealth or security, it was a love match. Katherine Willoughby married her Master of Horse, Richard Bertie, after being widowed from Charles Brandon, Duke of Suffolk. In comparison to her first husband, Bertie could offer little but Katherine was an heiress in her own right, not needing anything in the form of wealth or security from a husband.

Other widows with substantial wealth chose not to remarry and instead retired from public life and whilst they may not take vows, some would lead a very pious, modest and humble life for their remaining years. Of course, widows wishing to take this path did not require substantial wealth, merely enough to maintain themselves but the additional wealth could certainly help, especially those who chose to increase their charitable donations. Widows who chose to lead a more pious life were likely to endow schools for poor children or donate food and alms to those in need within their local communities. Not all chose to retire from public life but still refused to remarry. Agnes Howard, Dowager Duchess of Norfolk was the widow of the second Duke of Norfolk. As a widow she controlled vast estates with a very generous income, making her one of the wealthiest women in England at the time. Although she was widowed, she remained an active part of court life, travelling to participate in celebrations and events. Her home also became a popular household for young girls to be sent for education and to learn the art of becoming a respectable Tudor lady. The dowager duchess accepted many girls into her home, providing tutors, accommodation and practise in singing and dancing for them. The girls shared dormitory-like accommodation and many of her large, extensive family sent their female relatives to live there, including Lord Edmund Howard who sent his daughter, Catherine Howard.

Widowhood could be difficult, desertion even more so. Women who found themselves deserted by their husband were not able to claim their dower and could not remarry. Abandoned women had no choice but to try and earn enough to maintain herself and her family. As with most aspects of Tudor life, the experience of widowhood was not the same for all. Some became influential women, patrons of the arts, whilst others struggled to survive and relied on parish alms and charity to maintain themselves.

## Chapter Nine

# Wills of Women

Death was the final life-stage, and whether this occurred early or late in life, women would prepare themselves with prayers, giving blessings to those in attendance at her deathbed, and if single, widowed, or permitted by her spouse, the making of her last will and testament. For those who were literate, preparation for her death may also include writing a collection of advice, recipes or religious snippets which she would leave for her daughter or other female kin.

As married women could not execute a will without the consent of her husband, they are much less common and most of the wills that have survived were made by men. The *Statute of Wills* was introduced in 1540, establishing the common law right to bequeath land by will; the legislation excludes married women from being able to do so.[1] There was also a much larger proportion of women who were illiterate and so if they wished to write a will they would have to rely on family, friends or the services of a scrivener to make an account of their wishes on their behalf. A widow's authority to bequeath her property partly relied on the contents of her husband's will, what he had left to her specifically and the terms of those bequests, as well as her own personal property. Women who could afford to do so often left bequests to charitable causes, varying from alms to the local church to distribute, gifts for specific poor families or for the endowment of charitable institutions.

Those who believed their death was nearing would attend church to receive holy communion. Alternatively, if they were too sick or unable to travel to the church, they could ask for a priest to attend upon them at home for a blessing and to make their final confession. Some parishes employed the services of a poor woman to sit with the dying, providing comfort in their final hours and ensuring they did not die alone if they had no companions. They would later wash the body ready for burial. The church bells would usually toll for a dying person to show respect and notify the parish someone was dying. They would then toll again to signal the funeral.

Following a death, the funeral rites would begin to take place. A woman's funeral was one of the few aspects of her life where she could express her preferences. Even the poorest women could request a specific burial place, though with the cost often being met by the parish, in many cases their wishes could not be met. They were however, accorded a respectful burial within the parish. Wealthier women could certainly choose the place of their burial, along with ideas for the design of their tomb if this had not already been completed by a husband. They also had the resources to pay for prayers to be said for their soul after her death. Amongst the aristocracy, the rituals around funerals were much more complex and lengthier. The College of Heralds was responsible for controlling the funerals of the aristocracy and would follow the precise rites, including the period of lying-in rest, for which embalming was required. Some abhorred the idea of embalmment or the thought of their corpse being laid out for all to see once they had passed, and therefore requested a swift burial.[2]

A funeral began with a procession, originating from the deceased's home or in the case of others, from the place where they had lay in rest. Once the procession reached the church, it would be met by the priest who would begin with prayers before accompanying the mourners into the church for prayers and a sermon before the mourners moved to the gravesite. Others proceeded directly to the gravesite, omitting a service inside the church. Once at the graveside further prayers were said before the corpse was placed into the ground. Those attending were invited to throw soil into the grave as the priest spoke: 'Forasmuch as it hath pleased almighty God of his great mercy to take unto himself the soul of our dear brother here departed: we therefore commit his body to the ground, earth to earth, ashes to ashes, dust to dust, in sure and certain hope of resurrection to eternal life, through our Lord Jesus Christ: who shall change our vile body that it may be like to his glorious body, according to the mighty working, whereby he is able to subdue all things to himself'. The congregation would then say a short prayer before a sermon of the first Epistle is read.[3] The sermon read during the funeral of a woman would include recognition of her charitable acts and piety. If she had been married and had children, it would also note how she had been a good mother and obedient to her husband.

A last will and testament was not just a method of dispensing with belongings. For the Tudors it was also a way to atone for sins. Prior to the Reformation and under the reign of Mary I, the majority of wills would contain a reference to an offering for prayers to be said for their soul. Many wills also included donations to religious houses and the endowment of chantries. This was all in an effort to reduce the time a soul would spend in purgatory after death. Mary I left several bequests to religious houses including £500 each to the convents of Sion and Sheen as well as bequests to the Observant Friars at Greenwich, the Black Friars of St. Bartholomew's and for the 'pore Nunns of Langley'. She also bequeathed large amounts for prayers to be said for her soul. Mary continued her will with several charitable bequests for those in need.

> 'I will and geve for and to the relefe of the pore Scolers in either of the said Universities the Summe of 500li the which summe I will that my Executors shall delyver within oon yere next after my decesse unto the Chancellors and others of the most grave & wisest men of the same Universities, to be distributed and geven amongst the said pore Scolers, from tyme to tyme as they shall thynke expedient for ther relefe and comfort, and specially to such as intend by Godds grace to be Religious persons and Priests. And whereas I have by my warrant under my Signe Manuell assigned and appointed londs, tenements, and hereditaments of the yerly valewe of 200li and somewhat more to be assur'd unto the Master and Brotherne of the Hospitall of Savoy, fyrst erected and founded by my Grandfather of most worthy memory Kynge Henry 7.'[4]

The will continues with a bequest for the endowment of a manor or house, specifically for the relief of poor and aged soldiers who had no income or pension, and requested the residents were cared for, specifically those who had been injured during the cause of war on behalf of the realm. Mary does not forget her servants, leaving a sum of money to be shared amongst them, and asking her executors to consider their length of service when distributing the funds.

Wills of Tudor women contain many personal belongings which had been accumulated over their lives. Even the poorest of women would have belongings they wished to pass on to family or friends. Bedding, including sheets and bed hangings were common bequests along with other textiles such as cushions, napkins, table coverings and sleeves. One of the most unusual wills is that of widow Margaret Browne. Margaret left her home in

Colchester to her five children. The will is very specific in how the property is to be shared: 'to John Browne the hall house of the tenement with the entry; to Richard and Joan his wife the chamber over the parlour, in which chamber he now dwelleth, for their lives, and after their deceases, to John; to Anne now wife of John Glascock of St. Osyth the kitchen of the tenement; to Oliver the parlour (in which he now dwelleth); and to Katherine wife of Robert Symon of Colchester weaver the shop with the little buttery in the entry. If any of my children be not contented with the division, he or she shall have 40s, given by the rest in lieu and not hereafter have any part'. Margaret then specifies her wishes for her garden: 'also equally divided between my 5 children (I have already divided the same by stakes), viz. that John shall have 1 of the 'knottes' [laid out gardens] within, Oliver the other, Richard the green place by the 'knott' wherein the peartree standeth, and the other green yard shall be divided between my 2 daughters, and the stoney yard shall be divided equally between John and Richard. All my children shall have liberty to go and come from the well'.[5] Margaret was not the only one who left a very detailed will. Alice Boughtell was a widow when she wrote her will in 1572. She first requested that she be buried next to the monument in the churchyard of Great Sampford, where her late husband was buried. Her bequests then largely consist of furniture and dishware and are very detailed. She bequeathed her daughter Joan numerous gifts including a featherbed, her best brass pot, kettle, pewter platters, two porringers, four saucers, two candlesticks, a pewter cup, a pewter pint pot, a flaxen tablecloth, three painted cloths, one towel, a half bushel, a great tub, a peck, three holland kerchers, one holland rail, one flaxen rail, a train gown, her red kirtle, her sleeves, violet cassock, trundle bedsteads, one oaken stool, three cushions, her best silver pin, and three beasts. It is apparent from this that Alice wished to ensure her daughter received the very specific items intended for her. It is interesting that her son Richard is left a hutch, one sheep and one lamb, though her son likely received the family estate from his father when he died.[6]

Aristocratic women often had numerous works of literature to bequeath. Cecily Neville, Duchess of York and mother to Edward IV and Richard III, died in 1495 leaving various books in her will. The gifts, which were likely to have been beautifully illuminated copies, included a psalter for Elizabeth of York. Copies of *Golden Legend* which told of the visions of St Matilda and the life of St Catherine were left to Bridget of York, who was a Dominican nun. And St Bridget's *Revelations* was bequeathed to Anne de la Pole who was the prioress of the Bridgettine house at Syon. Elizabeth of York, Bridget and Anne de la Pole were all granddaughters of Cecily but they were not the only recipients of gifts. Margaret Beaufort was also listed as a beneficiary, and was gifted a breviary which is a liturgical book of prayers, psalms and hymns to be used during the canonical hours, a gift the pious Margaret would surely have greatly appreciated.[7]

Lady Mary Grey, after spending seven years under house arrest, did not have the possessions one would expect from someone of royal status but when she fell ill in 1578, she wrote her will leaving her jewels to her stepgrandmother Katherine Willoughby. The jewels had once belonged to her mother Frances Brandon, the eldest daughter of Mary Tudor and Charles Brandon. Lady Mary had spent two years of her house arrest under the supervision of Katherine and this request is an indication that she was treated with kindness during that period of her incarceration. She also asked Katherine to gift something to her daughter Susan Bertie, Countess of Kent, who Mary had spent time with when she was under house arrest and who would be the chief mourner at Mary's funeral. To friends she left silver and gold tankards and plate. Her servants were not forgotten, they were left horses whilst a serving boy was gifted an apprenticeship in a respectable trade, a valuable gift. Her stepdaughter Jane was bequeathed her bed whilst Jane's daughter, Mary, would receive the greater part of her money.[8] This is particularly interesting considering the outcome of Mary's marriage to Thomas Keyes, as discussed in Chapter Three.

Wills can highlight how women perceived others and the respect they felt towards other women. Midwives were sometimes remembered in the wills of women. In 1584, Jane Magham included a bequest in her will of four sheep to her midwife. This is a valuable gift as the sheep could benefit the midwife, providing wool and of course meat if she chose to have them slaughtered. This bequest clearly shows the gratitude of Tudor women towards those who helped them in their most vulnerable travails.[9] It was common for women with the resources to do so, to leave a bequest for the poor women of the parish. The bequest would be managed by the churchwardens and were intended to pay for the marriages of those who otherwise could not afford to marry. Dame Joan Thurcross, in 1523, left a bequest of thirteen white gowns for thirteen poor women. This was just one of many bequests; other gifts indicate Dame Joan was pious, leaving funds for building works at White Friars, £35 for a priest to sing for her and her family's souls for a period of seven years and £30 for the purchase of new vestments for her parish church. Gifts were also made to nuns residing at Sixhills convent and funds bequeathed to a priest to perform an obituary at the convent of St Leonard's in Grimsby.[10]

Women will-writers were commonly generous towards their female kin, particularly sisters and nieces. Some women had spent their lives serving a sister in some capacity, so they likely formed a close bond. Some bequests may have been in recognition of this bond. Others were an attempt to provide their sister with sufficient inheritance to assist with their maintenance after the will-writer died, especially if she had been the one to maintain her sister within her household. Margaret Ayloffe, who was widowed three times, left the bulk of her estate to male kin but made specific bequests to her sister Jane and her niece Agnes.[11] Alice Clarke, a widow, gave gifts of a bedstead, trundle bedstead and two featherbeds, amongst other gifts of plate, to her granddaughter, Thomasine. All of the inheritance other than a petticoat was to remain in the hands of Alice's kinsman John Fryse until Thomasine reached 18 years old or married. Alice also left her servant, Joan, a new frieze gown and a russet petticoat, two neck kerchiefs and four kerchiefs. These are indications that Alice appreciated her servant; giving a new gown was not as common as gifting one's own gowns.[12]

Amongst the wealthy, their wills are evidence that they were attempting to ensure the next generation of their family were secure and they made bequests very carefully. Women who owned property in their own right, that was not part of their jointure, often left it to non-inheriting children rather than the heir. It can be assumed that this was to provide them with their own household rather than illustrate any negative feelings towards the heir. By leaving property to her other children, a widow reduced the burden on the heir of maintaining their siblings. If they died without children, the property of an heiress would pass to her natal kin rather than her husband or his heirs. This safeguard allowed aristocratic families to retain their inheritance and family estates. For others, it meant they could ensure their daughters received adequate inheritance.

It was not unheard of for widows to appoint their daughter as an executor of their will rather than rely on male kin. In 1578, Agnes Brett appointed her daughter Joan, as her sole executrix. She bequeathed Joan half of her goods 'for her pains' in carrying out her wishes. The remaining half of her goods were to be split equally between her two sons, William and Edmund. Interestingly, Agnes leaves her rights in the manor of Walton Hall to be equally divided between all three children but instructs that her freehold land which is bequeathed to William is given with the condition that he pays her daughter an annual fee of 20s for ten years. This ensures Joan not only has a place of residence but also an income for at least ten years following the death of her mother.[13] Another who wished to ensure her female relatives were provided for was Katherine Beryff. Katherine was a widow when she made her will in 1584/5. She left her home and surrounding outbuildings to her daughter, Margaret Woodd, for the term of her life and then to Katherine's grandson, John. A further bequest was made to Margaret, 'my term of years, leases and lease grounds which I hold of Sir Thomas Lucas knight and his wife'. It is possible that Katherine's goddaughter, also named Katherine, was also her granddaughter or at least an in-law, as she shares the surname of Eyles with the grandson John. It is feasible that the benefactors were all residing at the family property, as the goddaughter is left the stable room, shop and fish house which adjoined the property. These bequests ensure both her daughter and goddaughter receive an income and in the case of the goddaughter, a business opportunity. Curiously, despite these generous gifts to one of her daughters and her goddaughter, Katherine leaves her other two daughters only a bedstead each. Margaret leaves other gifts to family and concludes that all her remaining goods are to be sold and the funds divided between named members of her family; the two daughters receiving a bedstead are not included.[14]

The wills of those who were affected by the dissolution of the religious houses give an indication of how much they valued their earlier life and their fellow sisters. From ten wills of former nuns, there are over twenty bequests made to those the women had shared a life with in a convent, prior to their dissolution. Some may not have had anyone else to leave their chattels too, but it is conceivable that the women would have formed close bonds and that they wished to recognise that fact after death.[15] At the time of her death, Elizabeth Lord, previously the prioress of Wilberfoss and afterwards, the owner of the site, had an estate that included over £50 in cash. Elizabeth's bequests are a clear indication that she still cared for those she had previously shared her cloisters with. She left specific bequests of money to four of her previous sisters, specifically noting 'which was sisters with me in the house of Wilberfoss'. She also left £4 for the priests who attended her funeral to pray for her. Another former nun left her home to another woman she had lived with during her time in her convent and had later resided with in friendship.[16]

An interesting aspect of wills is that women made intelligent use of them to recover debts owed to them. Elizabeth Arnolde, when writing her will in 1584 noted a debt of £8 that was owed to her by her son-in-law, Thomas Beckwell. Elizabeth asked that it be repaid to her two grandchildren at £3 each, saving Thomas £2. The payment was to be made upon their twenty-first birthday or when they married, whichever came first. If either of the grandchildren were to die before that, their portion was to be paid to Elizabeth's daughter, Margaret. Her remaining bequests to her children were made up of livestock, furniture and various items of cookware such as a frying pan and a butter churn. In addition to a cow, a large hutch chest and bees, Margaret was to receive items of clothing. Elizabeth's remaining pewter was to be divided equally amongst her children.[17] Margery Almon also used her will to recover debts owed to her estate. Writing her will in 1585/6, Margery left generous gifts of £11 to her granddaughter, Joan Cleyton, and £10 to another granddaughter, Bridget. Both granddaughters were to receive their inheritance at the age of 16. Joan was also given two cows and six sheep. A cousin, Alice, was to receive money and a petticoat and Margery's maid, Thomasine, received money, one cow and four sheep. Her bequest to her son, Henry Almon, was the debts he owed her. Lastly, she bequeathed funds for repair works of her parish church and to be used as alms for the poor. Another son of Margery, William Almon, is not referred to in her will but it is possible he predeceased his mother as his own will was written in 1582. William bequeathed £10 to his niece, Joan Cleyton, the same Joan who was due to inherit £11 from her grandmother. The sum was to be paid either when she married or at age 20. He left his mother, Margery, his mare, a colt, two cows and all of his sheep, which according to the will were already on her lands. William rather interestingly left his mother's maid, Thomasine, a bequest of 40s to be paid either when she married or when she reached age 21. Mother and son left the exact same amounts for church repairs and for the poor, being 3s 4d and 10s respectively. After a couple of other small bequests, William left the remainder of his estate to his brother Henry. It appears Margery had replicated her sons will to an extent and was ensuring both his and her own wishes were fulfilled.[18]

Single women had the legal right to write a will and bequeath their goods as they wished. Those of aristocratic families who had inherited property and land to generate an income to fund their maintenance after the death of their parents, may be leaned upon to bequeath this back to the family in their will, but could not be forced. This did not include any property that was left for their life term as this automatically reverted back to the estate. Any moveable goods they owned were theirs to do with as they wished. Amongst the wealthy and the aristocracy, single women who never married were often the beneficiaries of generous bequests from their mothers. They had usually received funds for a dowry or maintenance from their father, but mothers also added to this to ensure their daughters were kept in the manner they were accustomed to.

Wills certainly give insight into the property and relationships held dear by Tudor women but unfortunately, they represent a small proportion of the female population at the time. Married women are underrepresented through wills as they could not create a will without the express consent of their husband. However, that does not mean most husbands refused to give consent. Some likely agreed but died prior to their wife executing a will of her own, resulting in her not having a will until she was widowed. Others included their wife's wishes in their own will; this is a clear way of stating they fully supported her wishes. Even if they do not explicitly state that some of the bequests are the wishes of their wife, it is plausible that those who had a happy, loving relationship discussed these matters, and agreed them beforehand, making the will of a wife irrelevant. The majority of the female population had little to bequeath, but what they did own was not subject to the pressures and customs faced by wealthy and aristocratic women. Mothers likely passed on their own collection of recipes, books and advice to daughters, along with household goods, jewellery if they had any, and clothing. Poorer families with only a single daughter would assume she would take ownership or the lease of the family home. Death for Tudor women was the final life stage in a series of events, ending their journey from a maiden to a wife, a mother and possibly a grandmother. They spent their lives honouring their role as dutiful daughters and wives, caring for their family, observing their faith and preparing the next generation for adulthood and their life without parents. Their wills are testament to their value of family and an understanding of the hardships faced by women as a result of customs such as primogeniture.

# Chapter Ten
# Conclusion

Much of family life and the roles of family members were dictated by religion, law and custom. From a young age, children were treated as miniature adults, from their clothing, behaviour and of course, because many of them had to work for a living. Life could be very difficult for some children and society felt it best they faced the reality, rather than being sheltered from it. The harshness of life was closely entwined with a female's wealth and status. Young girls effectively began training for the next stage of their life as a wife and mother as early as possible. All females received an education of some description, for some this may be as basic as learning her prayers and some recipes by rote directly from her mother or female relative, whilst the most fortunate received an exemplary education. Female education was primarily practical, they did not require the same academic achievements as their male counterparts if they could not enter the same professions as them. It may appear that housewifery is not much of an education at all, but to those who lived in the Tudor era it was not only important but extremely hard work. Women had to learn how to keep accounts for her household, budget for food and drink as well as other necessities, manage servants and tenants where required, as well as ensure her household was managed effectively on a daily basis. It was therefore a very practical but necessary education for Tudor women.

Throughout the period education and religion remained closely interlaced, religion being the primary focus of early education for all children irrespective of wealth, class or prospects. At a time when the Renaissance was sweeping across Europe, humanist scholars such as Desiderius Erasmus, Juan Luis Vives and Richard Mulcaster argued that females should be educated. Their reasons were not to make them intellectual equals to their male counterparts, but instead they should be educated in a manner which could benefit their position in the domestic household and most importantly, to allow them to read religious texts and moral philosophy. It is perhaps the influence of these scholars amongst others, that encouraged the advancement of females studying Latin. If women were capable of reading and understanding religious texts then they had the ability to later teach their children the fundamentals of religion. This resulted in a few exceptionally educated females, including but not limited to the daughters of Sir Anthony Cooke and Sir Thomas More, Lady Jane Grey and her sisters, Mary I, and Elizabeth I. There will have been others who received an impressive education similar to these females but it remains apparent that although formal education increased in importance, it remained predominantly a benefit for men and elite women in Tudor England.

Regardless of the opinions of men like Vives, Erasmus and Mulcaster, and those parents who promoted female education, it meant little to the lower classes. For this social group, education was largely unimportant in the grand scheme of things and earning an income was vital. The middle classes and lower ranks of the aristocracy also had no reason to bestow a humanist education on their daughters. For those families, the aim of education remained practical; to prepare them for their future as a wife and mistress of her household. For the majority of women who could read, the skill opened up a vast range of literature. Literacy levels did increase during the period, influenced by the availability of printed material as a result of advancements in the printing press. The evolution of, and an increase in printing, made books and pamphlets much more affordable, meaning more people could use them to learn to read, sometimes teaching themselves. Once they were able to read, they could also teach themselves to write using the available literature on handwriting and model letter books. For women, literature remained focused on devotional works, moral philosophy, conduct and books of domestic recipes, needlework and housewifery. There were no restrictions on women purchasing their own material from the booksellers in St Paul's or the pedlars travelling across the country, though married women may face the disapproval of her husband depending on her choice of literature. They could take advantage of educational manuals, learn new languages or subjects they had not yet studied or delve into Arthurian legends. Books of romance and fiction were also aimed at women but remained frowned upon by scholars as immoral and a waste of valuable time. There was also religious material which was printed primarily for women; Thomas Bentley created his *Monument of Matrones* in 1582 which compiled a wealth of prayers, mediations and psalms specifically for women. The tome includes prayers for expectant mothers, times of sickness, marriage and those created for society to pray for their monarch, Elizabeth I.

With an increase in literacy and affordability of reading material, reading became a pastime of more than just the very wealthy. Despite the Renaissance and an increase in humanist learning, the Reformation, through the dissolution of the convents and chantries, impacted the education of Tudor girls. These institutes had previously provided the opportunity for children to receive an education, some very basic, some much more accomplished but this ended with their dissolution. Free education decreased, though privately endowed schools increased.

Most aspects of a female's life were affected by her socio-economic status; from her education, how old she was when she left home, the age she married, the number of children she bore, whether she breast fed or not and even the type of job she could gain, if she required one at all. The lives of wealthy women appear to have less in common with their male counterparts than the lives of poorer classes. Married couples of the humbler classes worked together as a unit to sustain themselves, their family and their household. Marital status also affected women's lives, primarily their legal status but also everyday life. Those who were married or widowed took priority in the front pews of the church whilst single women had to sit in the rows behind them. Family, particularly men could impact women's wealth, status and rank. Although the elite and unmarried but successful businesswomen could assert their independence much more easily than poorer counterparts, all were limited in their freedoms to an extent. They were also more welcome to move to other parishes. Unmarried women without the financial means to support themselves were rarely welcome to a new parish without a job secured. This was due to the concern she would require alms to support herself, especially if she were to end up with a child outside of wedlock. Amongst the female population, it was widows that commanded the most autonomy whilst married women had the fewest legal rights of the differing marital statuses. Widows had a level of independence that single and married women did not, especially those with financial security who could live as they chose and had no obligations towards any man. It was rare for a female born to a poorer family to improve her social rank and wealth but, it was not impossible if she found herself in the right situation and was noticed by a suitor who could improve her prospects. Thomasine Bonaventure was one such woman who married above her station. Thomasine was born to a humble family but married three wealthy men, one being Sir Thomas Percival, Lord Mayor of London. From each of these marriages she would have received a dower or jointure but after the first marriage, Thomasine possibly had to pay a dowry herself in her subsequent marriages.[1]

With socio-economic status impacting the lives of women, the experiences of women varied drastically between the classes. Women born into wealthy families had longer childhoods and greater access to formal education but little opportunity in terms of employment. The poor were forced to work from as young as possible and had little choice in job roles, accepting whatever work was available, whilst the middle classes had the ability to run businesses themselves, asserting an independence neither the wealthy nor the poor had. Although there was no formal benefits system, the Tudors did not neglect those in need. Impoverished individuals and families had more access to alms and opportunities of receiving food if they resided in towns rather than rural areas. Extremely wealthy homes such as the royal court would allow servants access to some of the food following the clearing of the table but most of the remains were to be taken to the gates and distributed amongst the poor. Those living in the country had fewer options of wealthy homes to wait outside for food, though there would also be more people to feed in towns. Most parishes ensured the poorest in their communities were at least provided with grain to sustain themselves through periods of hardship. This was extremely important, especially in times of famine caused by bad harvests. Irrespective of rank and wealth, all women in some way or another, tried to preserve whatever produce they were able to. Many food types including meat and fish were preserved by pickling in vinegar, salting or smoking. Pickling was another way in which Tudor women sought to avoid waste, using ale that had been left until sour as a type of vinegar. Herbs and flowers were dried for use in cooking, medicine and the making of scents. Fruit was preserved by either drying or making preserves, for use through the winter. Butter and cheese resources were stocked ahead of the colder months. The grandest of homes were no different. In a society where famine could mean the death of many, all were conscious of not being wasteful. This was the reality for the majority of housewives and those in service to them. They constantly strived to keep their households sufficiently fed whilst trying to secure a winter store.

Although there were defining life-stages for Tudor women, these stages could not be specified to ages. Poor young females grew up much faster, they could be working with their family from as young as 4 years old, apprenticed at 7 and spend the rest of their lives working whilst the wealthy and aristocratic females enjoyed a much longer childhood but usually married earlier. Although the aristocracy were keen to secure advantageous matches for their children and contracts could be made before the age of consent, it was becoming much rarer, though they often still married earlier than their humbler counterparts. The classes also had differing experiences of courtship, marriage, motherhood and widowhood. For the aristocracy, there was a lot more at stake when arranging marriages than for those of the poorer classes. For this reason, the aristocracy spent large sums of money and made great efforts to ensure their daughters were accomplished in the skills that would be noticed by an advantageous suitor. Girls whose families could afford a dowry for them grew up with the knowledge that she was entirely dependent on her parents to provide her with a good dowry and therefore, a suitable marriage. A good marriage could result in favour, wealth and extend the influence of the bride's family. The possibility of these benefits not being achieved, if she did not consent, placed pressure on aristocratic women to agree to a match recommended by her family. That is not to say they had no choice; marriage was based on consent but the consequences for refusal could be dire. Women could make their own suggestions for a match and parents may perhaps agree, providing the potential spouse was from a suitable family and would not disgrace the family in any way. In a society where disobeying your parents was a sin, the additional threat that a girl may lose her inheritance and have no legal protection if she were to become widowed, ensured that the majority made the decision to accept the choice made on their behalf, rather than marry against their parents' wishes. Once a match had been made and courtship followed, it could be a lengthy affair for all classes; the wealthy needed time to negotiate financial matters whilst the humbler classes had to save for their wedding and the setting up of their household.

When married, the household was the woman's domain, regardless of wealth and rank. Women were designated the responsibility for the running of their household, childcare and the care of the sick and infirm.

Although they shared the same accountability, the experience in meeting these responsibilities were of course wildly different. Wealthy households had the resources to employ others to complete the tasks on the woman's behalf whilst she maintained a supervisory position. Poorer counterparts not only had to complete much of the work themselves, but also often had to secure further income from secondary employment in order to survive. The majority of work undertaken by females leaves few records, though managing their household could be a huge amount of work, was unpaid, and yet was expected of them due to the expectations of society. Women were also required to be subordinate to men, good wives and daughters.

Women were also actively involved in the life events of their family: birth, marriage and death. One of those life events where the experience was shared amongst all the classes, was that of childbirth. Those with wealth may have been able to afford a sumptuous confinement beforehand and lying-in afterwards, whilst those mothers with little financial support found themselves taking as little time as possible away from work. Despite the difference, all had to contemplate the fear of death during childbirth. Most women recovered, but with the lack of medical care we have today, those who faced a difficult labour had a much lower chance of surviving than today. Midwives, if fearing for the life of the mother may have had to use metal hooks to remove the child, often resulting in the death of the child, harm to the woman and increasing the chances of the woman's death. Regardless of rank and wealth, the threat of death was an ever-present possibility to all Tudor women experiencing pregnancy. The lack of reliable contraception meant women struggled to control conceiving a child. In situations where the family were struggling financially, the birth of more children could place them in a dire situation, unable to support their family. The aristocracy, however, would continue conceiving, always striving for a male heir and spares.

The aristocracy could be assumed to be uncaring parents due to the supervisory role they played rather than being actively involved in their children's lives. To think they did not care for their children would be a mistake. Mothers would petition for wardship of their own children rather than leave them to be brought up by another. The fact they cared is also evident through the wills of women who tried to ensure their daughters and un-inheriting sons were taken care of after their death. Society placed expectations on women to return to their duties as a wife as soon as possible following childbirth, and those appointed within the royal court would be expected to return. That some sent their children to reside in the country is not an indication that they did not want them near, it shows they were attempting to keep them healthy by providing what they perceived to be healthier surroundings. The role of an aristocratic woman meant spending much time away from her children and her husband. As a mother, her aim was to secure advantageous marriages and preferments for her children when they came of age. For those with large and blended families, this could take a lot of resources, and required the woman to use all of her social contacts to make matches. As a wife, a woman was to ensure the household was managed effectively, her husband's interests protected and where she could, use her connections to improve his prospects and preferments, particularly if they involved the royal court.

All women regardless of class also faced the prospect of an unhappy marriage. Some who may not have been initially keen on the match chosen for them, grew to love their husband or at least, have a successful marriage. As women's property became that of their husband's upon marriage it was almost impossible for women to leave a husband, even if he were mistreating her. The extremely wealthy may be able to rely on family for support, who in turn could perhaps exert influence over the husband in exchange for better treatment, or possibly an agreement that the couple reside largely separate lives. If she were to leave him completely, and begin a new life with another man, she would lose all of her rights to whatever property had once been hers. For those reliant on their husband for financial matters they had no choice but to persevere through the marriage or lose everything. Others chose to avoid this possibility all together by remaining single. Women who could maintain themselves through inheritance or business had no pressures, other than possibly their family, to marry. Marriage is not the aim for many women today, and there were Tudor women who felt the same way, instead choosing a life of independence.

The genders of the humbler population worked together much more closely than those of the higher ranks where the work of women was a separate entity to that of men. Lower class women would think nothing of joining their menfolk in the fields earning wages, whereas a wealthy woman would maintain her role of supervising others. Women had to make the best of their location. Those in the country would focus on the provision of food for her family, selling the excess for additional income, just as those near the sea may try to sell oysters and other seafood. Those in towns and cities would more likely be involved in some kind of manufacturing, whether this be assisting in a merchant shop, working as a silk woman or spinning for her wages. Residing in a town or city also created the possibility of women being able to set up as a tradeswoman on her own. If she were married and her parish allowed it, she would be required to apply to be a *femme sole* and obtain her husband's consent. Single women and widows could set up their own business in areas with higher populations, providing a further opportunity that those in rural areas did not have. This did mean there was a lot of competition for trade and even if she could set herself up, that did not mean she would succeed, and was at risk of finding herself in debt, possibly jail, if she could not pay her debtors. Despite the risks, there were some very successful businesswomen during the Tudor era. Roles also changed with the economy, demand from abroad for certain products meant the workforce fluctuated with the demand.

Technology also affected women. They were initially the primary gender in brewing ale, but during this period, equipment was introduced to improve the brewing process and men began to take an interest. Brewing became a more lucrative process as the brewing of beer, which kept fresh longer, could be profitable. This meant women were slowly pushed out of the role, having to find alternatives to make an income. This new brewing process likely benefitted some women who now found themselves with more time on their hands now that they no longer had to brew ale daily for their household.

Wealthier women did not need to concern themselves with their location as their estate and husband usually provided the majority of the income. This did not mean she did not have to work, she was still required to understand the costs of running and maintaining her household, particularly if her husband was absent and she was responsible for ensuring the accounts were correct. Those in service had vastly different experiences. Some were expected to complete all manner of tasks, sometimes with the assistance of casual labourers brought in to help with specific jobs such as laundering or charwomen, whilst others would be responsible for more personal tasks, working closely with their mistress and focusing more on her than on more laborious tasks.

For working women, it is apparent that domestic service was one of the most secure job roles. During the Tudor era, inflation caused wages to increase. Women became a much more attractive prospect to employ as servants as they were paid less than men. Initially, the employment of men was not only preferred due to the number of labour-intensive tasks but was also seen as a status symbol. The wealthy wanted all to know they could afford to employ mostly men, but all would eventually increase the number of female servants as an alternative, in roles that would allow it. They were given bed and board, clothing, and some were even paid when sick. Many were given substantial gifts of dowries, which a father may have been unable to provide. Some were also given additional gifts, and those who made a lifelong career were sometimes lucky enough to receive a pension until their death, with the benefit of still being invited into the household to visit their mistress on occasion. The less fortunate were forced to beg or rely on alms from their local parish or other community institutions who aimed to support the poorest inhabitants by providing food, drink, clothing and the opportunity to work if possible. The lives of these poor women were far from the glittering royal court of the Tudor monarchs but for some, being sent away as a child to serve in another household was an improvement upon their home life. They were at least guaranteed a bed and food, whereas at home, the poor may struggle to provide even the basics for their children. For these women, every day was a fight for survival for themselves and sometimes their children, with no formal way of improving themselves through education or opportunity to secure a professional occupation. Society treated lower class women and children as cheap labour and they were poorly paid for their work especially in comparison to their male counterparts. It is apparent women worked in a wide variety of jobs during the Tudor era but it is also evident that despite how long and hard they worked, it was much more difficult for women to earn a sufficient living than men. Even if they wished to remain single, it would prove almost impossible for a working-class single woman to earn enough to set herself up in her own household and maintain herself without male assistance. Only those who found a position in one of the wealthier households had the opportunity to secure herself a lifelong career with a kind mistress and even then, it was not guaranteed.

Another similarity between the classes is that they all spent considerable time on needlework and textiles, though with differing aims. The quality of the thread and fabrics they were working with was the main difference between the classes. For humble women, needlework was a way of providing clothing and bedding for her family and earning a wage. They would usually be working with dull colours of a rough texture. For the wealthy, although the primary aims were similar, they would be working with more vivid and expensive threads and fabrics. Wealthy women would be busy creating embroidered items of clothing, gifts for friends, family and the Church, donations for those in need, or luxury items to afford herself some privacy in bed. Even women of the highest ranks, including queens, would spend time on needlework, both for the purpose of clothing, gifting or charitable purposes. Katharine of Aragon was accomplished with a needle and would make shirts for Henry VIII, continuing to do so even during the period when Henry was attempting to annul their marriage.[2] The middling classes could make a profitable venture from textile trades, whether a woman acted as a *femme sole* or continued with her husband's trade following his death. The textile trades were one of the most popular occupations for females, following that of domestic service.

The Reformation affected all, some more than others, but the whole of society was affected to some degree. The convents had provided women with an alternative to marriage whether by her own choice or through the influence of her family. They had also provided an alternative for widows who wished to withdraw from society. Their closure resulted in women who may have wished to take vows, having to face the choice of either marrying or attempting to survive alone or with the goodwill of friends and family. This was an unenviable decision considering the patriarchal society they lived in. It also had financial implications for families with multiple daughters. They no longer had the option to send one of their daughters to a convent within England and therefore would be required to fund a dowry or find an alternative future for them. Alternatively, women could still choose a religious vocation. Women were able, if they had the resources, to travel abroad and enter a convent where there were still many opportunities. In addition, towards the end of the sixteenth-century English Benedictine and Augustinian convents were founded in Brussels and Louvain, which may have tempted more to leave the shores of England to pursue a life of piety.

Life-stages were largely met with some kind of church service, for example, marriage, baptism and churching. Most services became entangled in the ongoing debates surrounding religious policy. For the majority who were illiterate it meant a change in some parts of religious services, but the celebratory element of each service continued for the most part, unaffected. In terms of literacy, for those who were illiterate, this would have been a time of turmoil; they could not read pamphlets, and had little idea on the latest way they should observe religion, other than the exchange of news passed by word of mouth. The attitude towards aspects of services that were deemed superstitious affected women on a grander scale. They were no longer supposed to follow certain traditions or use items such as holy relics that could cast a shadow over them. Women remained active participants in religious changes following the Reformation. Despite the fact women were meant to be obedient, there was no shortage of women willing to speak out, or in some cases, remain silent, in defence of their faith. Women were not exempt from the law when it came to religious practice. They could be arrested and burned at the stake for practising the wrong form of religion, known as heresy. What constituted the 'wrong form' was determined by who sat on the throne at the time. Fines could be imposed on those who regularly missed church services. For some, this was no deterrent due to the fact that if they were married, they had no money of their own anyway, so a fine had little effect. The wealthy could afford to pay the fines and continue with secret masses held in their homes. If a woman chose to proceed with voicing her views after being informed this was heresy, her husband could also face punishment as he was technically in charge of his wife and therefore, should control her behaviour. Others did not speak out directly but refused to give up on their faith and resorted to more covert methods to observe their faith and practices. There are those who would assist in hiding Catholic seminary priests within their homes, others were fined repeatedly for non-attendance at church.[3] Margaret Clitherow was one such woman, who despite being imprisoned numerous times, faced a charge of harbouring priests in 1586. Margaret refused to plead and was sentenced to *peine forte et dure* (pressed to death). Her execution was a gruesome affair, she was made to lay down with a single rock under her back, and the door of her own home was placed on top of her. Rocks and stones were piled on top of the door. The weight of the rocks would cause her back to break on the rock that had been placed underneath her. There is no doubt this was a horrific way to die, but it displays the strength of faith Tudor women had; they were willing to risk their lives for their beliefs. John Foxe's *Book of Martyrs* gives plenty of examples where women were persecuted for their beliefs.

For most people, when we think of the Tudors we think of beautiful palaces, jewels, gowns, dancing and of course the well-known Tudor monarchs and the wives of Henry VIII. The reality is that most women worked extremely hard, maintaining their homes and caring for their families. The working lives of women is almost a world away from the experience of most women today. Women in the Tudor era were evidently incredibly resilient, hard-working and vital to both society and the economy. Aristocratic women were fundamental to the success and survival of their family lineage and estates. Their humbler counterparts were also essential to a family's survival but in a much more practical way as they physically laboured for their family's maintenance. Without women, the men would not be able to work as they did without the ability to rely on their female counterparts, whether this be family, labourers or even the local wise woman. The skills of these wise women are often underestimated; these women concocted remedies using ingredients that in some format, or at least a derivative of them, are still in use today. Ergot was used to ease labour pains and remans in use today in a derivative form. Rosemary and lavender are also common plants that were used in herbal remedies by many and are still used today. The experience of these wise women was the result of many years of practice and the passing on of recipes, and it is apparent that they were rather successful, even without access to the scientific research we have available today. Women provided valuable services in medicine, housewifery and the progress of education. Even those who did not have what we would refer to as an occupation, were rarely idle, they would keep themselves occupied with their household matters and charitable works. Although they remained subordinate to men, Tudor women showed themselves to have amongst their number successful businesswomen, patrons of the arts and they used their influence to their advantage, wherever possible. It is strange to think that Tudor women were able to petition the Privy Council or Court of Chancery on behalf of their husband, and could act as sole executors for extremely wealthy, complex estates, but without the consent of their husband, married women could not commence legal proceedings on their own and could not write a will. Wives appear to be recognised as an extension of their husband rather an individual in their own right.

It would be easy to assume with the reigns of Mary I and Elizabeth I, that women would find themselves in a less subordinate position to men, but Tudor England remained a fundamentally patriarchal society. Women faced certain disadvantages from their birth, regardless of their capabilities. There were of course exceptional women who demanded respect from males for their intellectual capacity but for the majority of women, two queen regnants did little to affect how they were regarded by the majority of men in society. Even with a queen as the head of state and head of the Church of England, many men still viewed women as inferior subjects. The Tudor era ended with women still unable to attend university, join the ranks of the Church, enter legal and other professional occupations and they remained on lower wages than their male counterparts. Instead, their expected roles remained predominantly that of a dutiful daughter, an obedient wife and mother, or a respected widow. Women had the responsibility for ensuring her husband was happy, his wishes catered for, children were cared for and educated, particularly in religion, and that her household was managed effectively. The reality was that despite the expectations, women proved themselves to be intelligent, independent and extremely accomplished. Whilst they may have been submissive when it came to their husband heading their household, they were more than capable of knowing their own minds. Working-class women laboured just as effectively as men, whilst aristocratic women managed their estates during the regular absences of their husband. Women kept extensive accounts, managed hundreds of staff, used their initiative and developed a trusting relationship with their husband, who in turn treated their wives as close to equal partners as possible.

Attitudes of society and customs such as primogeniture and coverture attempted to keep women in a subordinate position. Women of the aristocracy, however, show that they were not the subservient women we may expect. As daughters the majority accepted the authority of their parents in their chosen marriage partner. As wives, they commanded authority across their estates, within the royal court, and amassed wealth and power through the successful management of their estates. Widows also successfully managed vast estates, made desirable matches for the children and were respected within society. Women of all ranks kept themselves occupied through hard work, charity and devoted themselves to their family and households, whatever the size of their estate. Tudor women were pivotal in the education of their children, maintaining land ownership, and protecting the inheritance of their children. They became patrons of schools, printshops and benefactors of religious and charitable institutes. Some of the buildings still standing today exist as a result of a Tudor woman. That is an incredible legacy and shows they were not the timid, quiet, obedient women Aristotle thought they should be.

# Notes

**Introduction**
1. Flower, A, *Tudor Women's Legal Rights 1485–1603*, Stuart Press, Bristol, (2006), p. 6.
2. Norton, E, *The Lives of Tudor Women*, Head of Zeus, London, (2017), pp. 10–11.
3. Values are based on the National Archives Currency Converter and the Bank of England Inflation Calculator, along with information from Measuring Worth (https://www.measuringworth.com/index.php). It should also be noted that when discussing wages across the era, consideration should be given to the fact that England's currency was much weaker during the reign of Elizabeth I than it was during her father's reign. £1 during the reign of Henry VIII was worth over £600, whilst at the end of the century it was worth less than half that amount.

**Chapter One: Growing Up**
1. Norton, E, *The Lives of Tudor Women*, Head of Zeus, London, (2017), pp. 58–9.
2. Rhodes, H, *The boke of Nurture, or Schoole of good manners (1577)*, printed within, Russell, J, *The boke of Nurture*, J. Childs & Son, (1867), pp. 259–50.
3. Norton, E, *The Lives of Tudor Women*, Head of Zeus, London, (2017), p. 57.
4. McElroy, A, *Educating the Tudors*, Pen and Sword, Barnsley, (2023), p. 108.
5. Ibid, p. 92.
6. Eales, J, *Women in Early Modern England 1500–1700*, Routledge, Oxon, (1998), p. 38.
7. Becon, T, *The Catechism*, ed. Ayre, J, Cambridge University Press, Cambridge, (1844), p. 377.
8. McElroy, A, *Educating the Tudors*, Pen and Sword, Barnsley, (2023), p. 148.
9. Ibid, p. 25.
10. 1601: 43 Elizabeth 1 c.2: Act for the relief of the poor, (See online sources).

**Chapter Two: Adolescence**
1. Lady Lisle also sent quails to Jane Seymour when she craved them during her pregnancy. *The Lisle Letters*, St Clare Byrne, M, (ed), Penguin Books, Middlesex, (1983), p. 360.
2. Ascham, R, *English Works*, edited by Wright, W.A., Cambridge University Press, London, (1970), pp. 201–202.
3. McElroy, A, *Educating the Tudors*, Pen and Sword, Barnsley, (2023), p. 87.
4. Hogrefe, P, *Tudor Women, Commoners and Queens*, Iowa State University Press, Iowa, (1975), pp. 8–9.
5. Cross, Claire, *The Religious Life of Women in Sixteenth-century Yorkshire*, (Presidential Address), Studies in Church History, 27, (1990), p. 311.
6. Bullinger, H, *The Christen State of Marriage (1541)*, quoted from Sim, A, *The Tudor Housewife*, The History Press, Stroud, (2010), p. 36.

**Chapter Three: Tudor Brides**
1. Harris, B.J., *English Aristocratic Women 1450–1550: Marriage and Family, Property and Careers*, Oxford University Press, Oxford, (2002), p. 62.

2. Eales, J, *Women in Early Modern England 1500–1700*, Routledge, Oxon, (1998), p. 62.
3. Mountfield, D, *Everyday Life in Elizabethan England*, Liber, Barcelona, (1978), p. 29.
4. Cleaver, R, *A godly forme of houshold government for the ordering of priuate families, according to the direction of Gods word: wherunto is adioyned in a more particular manner, the seuerall duties of the husband towards his wife, and the wiues dutie towards her husband, the parents dutie towards their children, and the childrens towards their parents, the maisters dutie towards his seruants, and also the seruants duty towards their maisters / first gathered by R.C. ; and now newly perused, amended and augmented by Iohn Dod and Robert Cleuer*, R, Field, London, (1621), page unnumbered.
5. Harris, B.J., *English Aristocratic Women 1450–1550: Marriage and Family, Property and Careers*, Oxford University Press, Oxford, (2002), p. 53.
6. PROB/11/32/514.
7. Houlbrooke, R.A., *The English Family 1450–1700*, Longmans, Harlow, (1992), p. 40.
8. See image 9.
9. If the father had passed away or was otherwise unavailable, this could also be paid by a male relative, master or the executor of the father's estate if she had received her dowry as a bequest.
10. Harris, B.J., *English Aristocratic Women 1450–1550: Marriage and Family, Property and Careers*, Oxford University Press, Oxford, (2002), p. 45.
11. Ibid, p. 45.
12. *LPFD*, ed. J.S. Brewer, J. Gairdner and R.H. Brodie, London, (1862–1932) Vol. 12 (2): 137, 1018, 1019 & Vol. 13 (2): 448.
13. Harris, B.J., *English Aristocratic Women 1450–1550: Marriage and Family, Property and Careers*, Oxford University Press, Oxford, (2002), p. 45.
14. Cressy, D, *Birth, Marriage & Death*, Oxford University Press, Oxford, (1997), p. 269.
15. Sim, A, *The Tudor Housewife*, The History Press, Stroud, (2010), pp. 10–11.
16. Katherine was only 14 years old; Brandon was 47.
17. *The Form of Solemnization of Matrimony, The Book of Common Prayer*, (1559), printed in *Liturgical Services of the Reign of Queen Elizabeth*, Cambridge University Press, Cambridge, (M.DCCC.XLVII), p.219.
18. Cressy, D, *Birth, Marriage & Death*, Oxford University Press, Oxford, (1997), pp. 337–340. The liturgy and vows from before the Reformation can be read in *Sarum Missal in English*, The Church Press Company, London, (1868). The Catholic liturgy had referred to 'if the holy church will it ordain' where the Protestants spoke 'according to God's happy ordinance'.
19. *The Form of Solemnization of Matrimony, The Book of Common Prayer*, (1559), printed in *Liturgical Services of the Reign of Queen Elizabeth*, Cambridge University Press, Cambridge, (M.DCCC.XLVII), pp. 223–4.
20. Hodder, S.J., *The York Princesses: The Daughters of Edward IV and Elizabeth Woodville*, Chronos Books, Alresford, (2021), p. 124.
21. Eales, J, *Women in Early Modern England 1500–1700*, Routledge, Oxon, (1998), p. 89.
22. Cross, Claire, *The Religious Life of Women in Sixteenth-century Yorkshire*, (Presidential Address), Studies in Church History, 27, (1990), pp. 313–4.
23. *The Lisle Letters*, St Clare Byrne, M, (ed), Penguin Books, Middlesex, (1983).

### Chapter Four: Lives of Wives
1. Harris, B.J., *English Aristocratic Women 1450–1550: Marriage and Family, Property and Careers*, Oxford University Press, Oxford, (2002), p. 63.

168  Women's Lives in the Tudor Era

2. NRO,LEST/P3–Anne,wife of Sir Thomas Le Strange,Household Accounts,1533–1545.
3. Cleaver, R, *A godly forme of houshold government for the ordering of priuate families, according to the direction of Gods word: wherunto is adioyned in a more particular manner, the seuerall duties of the husband towards his wife, and the wiues dutie towards her husband, the parents dutie towards their children, and the childrens towards their parents, the maisters dutie towards his seruants, and also the seruants duty towards their maisters / first gathered by R.C.; and now newly perused, amended and augmented by Iohn Dod and Robert Cleuer*, R, Field, London, (1621), page unnumbered.
4. Ibid, page unnumbered.
5. Eales, J, *Women in Early Modern England 1500–1700*, Routledge, Oxon, (1998), p. 26.
6. During this period trusts were referred to as 'uses'.
7. Hogrefe, P, *Tudor Women, Commoners and Queens*, Iowa State University Press, Iowa, (1975), p. 31.
8. Ibid, pp.11–12.
9. Ridley, J, *The Tudor Age*, Constable &Robinson Ltd, London, (2002), pp. 165–6.
10. Sim, A, *The Tudor Housewife*, The History Press, Stroud, (2010), p. 50.
11. If they wanted to bleach or brighten the clothes, they would leave them in the sun and wet them, allowing the sun to bleach them or perhaps adding urine to the lye to bleach the clothes. Sim, A, *The Tudor Housewife*, The History Press, Stroud, (2010), p. 53.
12. There were public baths near London and in Chester until the mid-sixteenth century.
13. Goodman, R, *How to be a Tudor, A dawn-to-dusk guide to Everyday Life*, Penguin, London, (2015), p. 180.
14. Ibid, p. 35.
15. Sim, A, *The Tudor Housewife*, The History Press, Stroud, (2010), pp. 79–81.
16. Tusser, T, *Five Hundred Points of Good Husbandry*, with intro by Grigson, G, Oxford University Press, Oxford, (1984), p. 91.
17. Ibid, p. 116.
18. Marital rape was not considered a crime until 1991.
19. Mendelson & Crawford, *Women in early Modern England*, Clarendon Press, Oxford, (1998), p. 128.
20. Harris, B.J., *English Aristocratic Women, 1450–1550: Marriage and Family, Property and Careers*, Oxford University Press, Oxford, (2002), p. 19.

**Chapter Five: Motherhood**
1. Cressy, D, *Birth, Marriage & Death*, Oxford University Press, Oxford, (1997), p. 43.
2. *As For the Deliverance of a Queen: Articles ordained by King Henry VII for the Regulation of his household, 31st December, 1494*, within *A Collection of ordinances and regulations for the government of the royal household, made in divers reigns: from King Edward III to King William and Queen Mary*, Society of Antiquaries of London, London, (1790), p. 125.
3. Rösslin, E, *The Birth of Mankynde: Otherwyse named the Woman's Booke*, Richard Jugge, London, (1565), p. 166.
4. Eagle stones featured a stone within a stone and were reported to originate initially from Cyprus and Africa. They were certainly available in London and likely other towns during the Medieval and Tudor periods.
5. Sim, A, *The Tudor Housewife*, The History Press, Stroud, (2010), pp. 17–18.
6. *Sarum Missal in English*, The Church Press Company, London, (1868), p. 568.
7. Cressy, D, *Birth, Marriage & Death*, Oxford University Press, Oxford, (1997), pp. 80–81.
8. Rösslin, E, *The Birth of Mankynde: Otherwyse named the Woman's Booke, The Third Booke, Fol. Ci*, Richard Jugge, London, (1565), pp. 244–45.

Notes 169

9. *The Ministration of Public Baptism, The Book of Common Prayer*, (1559), printed in *Liturgical Services of the Reign of Queen Elizabeth*, Cambridge University Press, Cambridge, (M.DCCC.XLVII), pp. 202–03.
10. *Sarum Missal in English*, The Church Press Company, London, (1868), pp. 164–5.
11. *The thanks giving of women after child birth commonly called the Churching of Women, The Book of Common Prayer*, (1559), printed in *Liturgical Services of the Reign of Queen Elizabeth*, Cambridge University Press, Cambridge, (M.DCCC.XLVII), p. 237.
12. Ibid, p. 238.
13. Cleaver, R, *A godly forme of houshold government for the ordering of priuate families, according to the direction of Gods word: wherunto is adioyned in a more particular manner, the seuerall duties of the husband towards his wife, and the wiues dutie towards her husband, the parents dutie towards their children, and the childrens towards their parents, the maisters dutie towards his seruants, and also the seruants duty towards their maisters / first gathered by R.C. ; and now newly perused, amended and augmented by Iohn Dod and Robert Cleuer*, R, Field, London, (1621), page unnumbered.
14. Cressy, D, *Birth, Marriage & Death*, Oxford University Press, Oxford, (1997), p. 73.
15. Mendelson & Crawford, *Women in early Modern England*, Clarendon Press, Oxford, (1998), pp. 148–9.
16. Eales, J, *Women in Early Modern England 1500–1700*, Routledge, Oxon, (1998), p. 64.

**Chapter Six: Working Women**

1. Mendelson & Crawford, *Women in early Modern England*, Clarendon Press, Oxford, (1998), p. 86.
2. Eales, J, *Women in Early Modern England 1500–1700*, Routledge, Oxon, (1998), p.77.
3. Wright, S, *'Churmaids, Huswifes and Hucksters': The Employment of Women in Tudor and Stuart Salisbury* in Women and Work in Pre-Industrial England, ed. Charles, L & Duffin, L, Croomhelm, London, (1985), pp. 109–10.
4. A sum was paid to a poor woman for bringing apples on more than one occasion though her identity is not recorded so it is not known if it was the same woman. *PPE Princess Mary*, (ed.) Madden, F, William Pickering, London, (1831), p. 224, 236.
5. Sim, A, *Food and Feast in Tudor England*, Sutton Publishing Ltd, Stroud, (1997), pp. 47–51.
6. These amounts are approximations based on the National Archives calculator and the Bank of England inflation calculator. It should also be noted that when discussing wages across the era, consideration should be given to the fact that England's currency was much weaker during the reign of Elizabeth I than it was during her father's reign. £1 during the reign of Henry VIII was worth over £600 whilst at the end of the century it was worth less than half that amount.
7. Eales, J, *Women in Early Modern England 1500–1700*, Routledge, Oxon, (1998), pp. 77–78.
8. Wright, S, *'Churmaids, Huswifes and Hucksters': The Employment of Women in Tudor and Stuart Salisbury* in Women and Work in Pre-Industrial England, ed. Charles, L & Duffin, L, Croomhelm, London, (1985), p. 104.
9. The Statute of Artificers' (1563), 5 Eliz., c.4, in Mendelson & Crawford, *Women in early Modern England*, Clarendon Press, Oxford, (1998), p. 96.
10. *The Norwich Census of the Poor 1570*, (ed.), Pound, J.F., NRO, (1971), p. 16.
11. *PPE Princess Mary*, (ed.) Madden, F, William Pickering, London, (1831), p. 15.
12. *A Collection of Ordinances and Regulations of the Royal Household from King Edward III to King William and Queen Mary*, Society of Antiquaries, London, (1790), p. 215.

170  Women's Lives in the Tudor Era

13. Sim, A, *Food and Feast in Tudor England*, Sutton Publishing Ltd, Stroud, (1997), p. 32.
14. Evans, V.S., *Ladies-in-Waiting: Women Who Served at the Tudor Court*, Independently Published, (2014), p. 3.
15. The role of Maid of honour became Maid of the privy chamber under the reigns of Mary I and Elizabeth I.
16. Evans, V.S., *Ladies-in-Waiting: Women Who Served at the Tudor Court*, Independently Published, (2014), p. 49.
17. Harris, B.J., *English Aristocratic Women 1450–1550: Marriage and Family, Property and Careers*, Oxford University Press, Oxford, (2002), p. 50.
18. *PPE Elizabeth of York*, (ed.) Sir Nicholas Harris Nicolas, William Pickering, London, (1830), pp. 99–100.
19. *LPFD, Henry VIII, 1509–47*, ed. J.S. Brewer, J. Gairdner and R.H. Brodie, London, Vol. 1, (iii): 1651, London (1862), p. 243.
20. *A Collection of Ordinances and Regulations for the Government of the Royal Household, made in divers reigns: from King Edward III to King William and Queen Mary, also receipts in ancient cookery*, Society of Antiquaries of London, London, (1790), p. 164.
21. Evans, V.S., *Ladies-in-Waiting: Women Who Served at the Tudor Court*, Independently Published, (2014), p. 40.
22. Mendelson & Crawford, *Women in early Modern England*, Clarendon Press, Oxford, (1998), p. 271.
23. Hogrefe, P, *Tudor Women, Commoners and Queens*, Iowa State University Press, Iowa, (1975), p. 53.
24. Cleaver, R, *A godly forme of housbold government for the ordering of priuate families, according to the direction of Gods word: wherunto is adioyned in a more particular manner, the seuerall duties of the husband towards his wife, and the wiues dutie towards her husband, the parents dutie towards their children, and the childrens towards their parents, the maisters dutie towards his seruants, and also the seruants duty towards their maisters / first gathered by R.C. ; and now newly perused, amended and augmented by Iohn Dod and Robert Cleuer*, R, Field, London, (1621), page unnumbered.
25. McElroy, A, *Educating the Tudors*, Pen and Sword, Barnsley, (2023), p. 27.
26. The Court Leet in 1589, Manchester, ordered that no single woman could keep a house/room, sell bread, ale or work in trades. Mendelson & Crawford, *Women in early Modern England*, Clarendon Press, Oxford, (1998), p. 172.
27. Hogrefe, P, *Tudor Women, Commoners and Queens*, Iowa State University Press, Iowa, (1975), p. 46.
28. Dale, K, 'The London Silk women of the Fifteenth Century', The Economic History Review, Vil. 4, (1933) p. 325.
29. Rösslin, E, *The Birth of Mankynde: Otherwyse named the Woman's Booke*, Richard Jugge, London, (1565), p. 165.
30. Mendelson & Crawford, *Women in early Modern England*, Clarendon Press, Oxford, (1998), p. 284.
31. *Injunctions for the Diocese of Salisbury (1538)*, Frere, W.H., & Kennedy, W.M., (eds), *Visitation Articles and Injunctions of the Period of the reformation, Vol 2*, Church of England, London, (1910), pp. 58–9.
32. Strype, J, *Annals of the Reformation and establishment of religion, Vol. 1*, B. Franklin, New York, (1968), pp. 242–43.
33. Mendelson & Crawford, *Women in early Modern England*, Clarendon Press, Oxford, (1998), p. 318.

34. Ibid, pp. 379–80.
35. Hogrefe, P, *Tudor Women, Commoners and Queens*, Iowa State University Press, Iowa, (1975), pp. 28–29.
36. Cross, Claire, *The Religious Life of Women in Sixteenth-century Yorkshire*, (Presidential Address), Studies in Church History, 27, (1990), p. 314.

## Chapter Seven: Recreation
1. *PPE Princess Mary*, (ed.) Madden, F, William Pickering, London, (1831), p. 3, 10–11.
2. Report of Sebastian Giustinian, the Venetian ambassador on his first visit to England, 'Henry VIII: July 1519, 16–29', in *Letters and Papers, Foreign and Domestic, Henry VIII, Volume 3, 1519–1523*. Ed. J.S. Brewer, London (1867), pp. 136–148.
3. McElroy, A, *Educating the Tudors*, Pen and Sword, Barnsley, (2023), p. 154.
4. Sim, A, *Pleasures & Pastimes in Tudor England*, Sutton Publishing, Stroud, (1999), p. 88.
5. *PPE Princess Mary*, (ed.) Madden, F, William Pickering, London, (1831), p. 6, 13.
6. Ibid, pp. 442–3.
7. McElroy, A, *Educating the Tudors*, Pen and Sword, Barnsley, (2023), p126.

## Chapter Eight: Woes of Widowhood
1. PROB 11/32/514.
2. Charles Brandon and Sir Francis Walsingham were also amongst those who chose their wives to administer their will on their behalf.
3. In the late fifteenth and early sixteenth century, 77% of the nobility chose their wife as the sole executor of their will. This is reported from Erickson, A.L., *Women and Property in Early Modern England*, Routledge, London, (1993), p. 156.
4. LPFD, *Henry VIII, 1509–47*, ed. J.S. Brewer, J. Gairdner and R.H. Brodie, London, Vol. 1, (iii): 1777, London (1862), p. 267.
5. Alvarez, A.D., *A Widow's Will: Examining the Challenges of Widowhood in Early Modern England and America*, Dissertations, Theses, & Student Research, Department of History, 57, University of Nebraska, (2013), p. 43.
6. Harris, B.J., *English Aristocratic Women 1450–1550: Marriage and Family, Property and Careers*, Oxford University Press, Oxford, (2002), p. 52.
7. Ibid, p. 131.
8. LPFD, *Henry VIII, 1509–47*, ed. J.S. Brewer, J. Gairdner and R.H. Brodie, London, Vol. 1, (iii): 1624, London (1862), p. 240.
9. 1601: 43 Elizabeth 1 c.2: Act for the Relief of the Poor, (See Online sources).
10. Laurence, A, *Women in England, 1500–1760, A Social History*, Phoenix Press, London, (1996), p. 46.
11. Harris, B.J., *English Aristocratic Women 1450–1550: Marriage and Family, Property and Careers*, Oxford University Press, Oxford, (2002), p. 122.
12. Ibid, p. 122.
13. £26 in the Tudor era is equivalent to around £20,000 in 2022. This amount could purchase five horses or the labour of a tradesman for 866 days. Calculation based on Currency converter: 1270–2017 (nationalarchives.gov.uk).
14. Calculation courtesy of the Inflation calculator: www.bankofengland.co.uk/monetary-policy/inflation/inflation-calculator.
15. 45% of aristocratic women remarried between 1450–1550. Harris, B.J., *English Aristocratic Women 1450–1550: Marriage and Family, Property and Careers*, Oxford University Press, Oxford, (2002), p. 10.

## Chapter Nine: Wills of Women

1. Harris, B.J., *English Aristocratic Women, 1450–1550: Marriage and Family, Property and Careers*, Oxford University Press, Oxford, (2002), p. 18.
2. Mendelson & Crawford, *Women in early Modern England*, Clarendon Press, Oxford, (1998), p. 198.
3. *The Order for the Burial of the Dead, The Book of Common Prayer*, (1559), printed in in *Liturgical Services of the Reign of Queen Elizabeth*, Cambridge University Press, Cambridge, (M.DCCC.XLVII), pp.233–34.
4. J.M. Stone, *The History of Mary I: Queen of England*, Sands & Co, London, (1901), pp. 507–520. The will is from a transcript *Harlean MSS (6949)* which is sadly no longer in existence.
5. *Essex Wills, The Bishop of London's Commissary Court 1578–1588*, Emmison, F.G., (ed.), Essex Record Office, Essex, (1995), p. 28.
6. Ibid, p. 13.
7. Eales, J, *Women in Early Modern England 1500–1700*, Routledge, Oxon, (1998), p.39.
8. De Lisle, L, *The Sisters who would be Queen, The tragedy of Mary, Katherine & Lady Jane Grey*, Harper Press, London, (2009), pp. 289–90.
9. Cressy, D, *Birth, Marriage & Death*, Oxford University Press, Oxford, (1997), pp. 72–3.
10. Cross, Claire, *The Religious Life of Women in Sixteenth-century Yorkshire*, (Presidential Address), Studies in Church History, 27, (1990), p. 307.
11. PROB 11/72/1.
12. *Essex Wills, The Bishop of London's Commissary Court 1578–1588*, Emmison, F.G., (ed.), Essex Record Office, Essex, (1995), p. 44.
13. Ibid, p. 16.
14. Ibid, pp. 33–34.
15. Sim, A, *The Tudor Housewife*, The History Press, Stroud, (2010), p. 125.
16. Cross, Claire, *The Religious Life of Women in Sixteenth-century Yorkshire*, (Presidential Address), Studies in Church History, 27, (1990), pp. 314–15.
17. *Essex Wills, The Bishop of London's Commissary Court 1578–1588*, Emmison, F.G., (ed.), Essex Record Office, Essex, (1995), p. 4.
18. Ibid, p. 2 & 8.

## Chapter Ten: Conclusion

1. Hogrefe, P, *Tudor Women: Commoners and Queens*, Iowa State University Press, (1975), p. 13.
2. Evans, S.J., *Ladies in Waiting: Women Who Served at the Tudor Court*, Independently Published, (2014), pp. 58–9.
3. There are still houses with remaining priest holes within England. Harvington Hall, Worcestershire and Speke Hall, Liverpool are amongst those where you can glimpse a priest hole and imagine what those men experienced if they had to hide.

# Bibliography

**Abbreviations**
LPFD – Letters & Papers Foreign and Domestic in the Reign of Henry VIII
NRO – Norfolk Record Office
PPE – Privy Purse Expenses
PROB – Probate – National Archives
SP1 – State Papers – Henry VIII

**Online Sources**
http://statutes.org.uk/site/the-statutes/seventeenth-century/1601-43-elizabeth-c-2-act-for-the-relief-of-the-poor/
https://www.bankofengland.co.uk/monetary-policy/inflation/inflation-calculator
https://www.nationalarchives.gov.uk/currency-converter/#
https://www.measuringworth.com/index.php

**Journals/Theses**
Alvarez, A. D., *'A Widow's Will: Examining the Challenges of Widowhood in Early Modern England and America'*, (Dissertations, Theses, & Student Research, department of History. 57. University of Nebraska – Lincoln, 2013).
Cross, C, *The Religious Life of Women in Sixteenth-Century Yorkshire*, (Studies in Church History, 27, 307–324, 1990) doi: 1017/50424208400012134.
Dale, M. K., *The London Silkwomem of the Fifteenth Century*, (The Economic History Review, Vol. 4, No. 3, Oct 1993).
Daybell, J, *Gender, Obedience, and Authority in Sixteenth-Century Women's Letters*, (The Sixteenth Century Journal, vol. 41, no. 1, 2010), pp. 49–67. *JSTOR*, www.jstor.org/stable/27867637.
Harding, V, *'Families in Later Medieval London: Sex, Marriage and Mortality'. Medieval Londoners: Essays to Mark the Eightieth Birthday of Caroline M. Barron*, (ed) New, E. A. and Steer, C. (University of London Press, 2019), pp. 11 36. *JSTOR*, www.jstor.org/stable/j.ctvc16qcm.10.
Harris, B. J. *Property, Power, and Personal Relations: Elite Mothers and Sons in Yorkist and Early Tudor England.* (Signs, vol. 15, no. 3, 1990), pp. 606–32. *JSTOR*, www.jstor.org/stable/3174430.
Harris, B. J. *Defining Themselves: English Aristocratic Women, 1450—1550*, (Journal of British Studies, vol. 49, no. 4, 2010), pp. 734–52. *JSTOR*, www.jstor.org/stable/23265721.
Hogrefe, P, *'The Legal Rights of Tudor Women and their circumvention by men and women'*, (Sixteenth Century Journal 3, 1972).
Holmes, R. E, *A Widow's Will: Adapting the Duchess of Amalfi in Early Modern England and Spain*, (Studies in Philology, vol. 116, no. 4, 2019), pp. 728–57. *JSTOR*, www.jstor.org/stable/26786848.

Howey, C. L. *Dressing a Virgin Queen: Court Women, Dress, and Fashioning the Image of England's Queen Elizabeth I*, (Early Modern Women, vol. 4, 2009), pp. 201–08. *JSTOR*, www.jstor.org/stable/23541582.

Humphries, J, & Weisdorf, J, *The Wages of Women in England, 1260–1850*. (The Journal of Economic History, vol. 75, no. 2, 2015), pp. 405–47. *JSTOR*, www.jstor.org/stable/24550938

Jarrett, S, *By Reason of Her Sex and Widowhood: An Early Modern Welsh Gentlewoman in the Court of Star Chamber*. Star Chamber Matters: An Early Modern Court and Its Records, (ed) by Kesselring, K. J & Mears, N, (University of London Press, 2021), pp. 79–96. *JSTOR*, www.jstor.org/stable/j.ctv24w62j4.10.

Karras, R. M., *The Regulation of Brothels in Later Medieval England*, (Signs, vol. 14, no. 2, 1989), pp. 399–433. *JSTOR*, www.jstor.org/stable/3174556.

Macek, E. A., *Ghostly Fathers' and Their 'Virtuous Daughters': The Role of Spiritual Direction in the Lives of Three Early Modern English Women*, (The Catholic Historical Review, vol. 90, no. 2, 2004), pp. 213–35. *JSTOR*, www.jstor.org/stable/25026570.

McNabb, J, *She Is but a Girl: Talk of Young Women as Daughters, Wives, and Mothers in the Records of the English Consistory Courts, 1550–1650*, The Youth of Early Modern Women, (ed) by Cohen, E. S, & Reeves, M, (Amsterdam University Press, 2018), pp. 77–96. *JSTOR*, https://doi.org/10.2307/j.ctv8pzd5z.6.

Milsom, J, *Songs and Society in Early Tudor London*, (Early Music History, vol. 16, 1997), pp. 235–93. *JSTOR*, www.jstor.org/stable/853804.

Scott, B, *The Dissolution of the Religious Houses the Tudor Diocese Meath*, (Archivium Hibernicum, vol. 59, 2005), pp. 260–76. *JSTOR*, https://doi.org/10.2307/40285208.

Sharpe, J. A. *Domestic Homicide in Early Modern England*, (The Historical Journal, vol. 24, no. 1, 1981), pp. 29–48. *JSTOR*, www.jstor.org/stable/2638903.

Whittle, J, *Inheritance, marriage, widowhood and remarriage: a comparative perspective on women and landholding in North-East Norfolk, 1140–1580*, (Continuity and Change, Vol. 13, 1998).

### Primary Sources
PROB 11/32/514 *Will of Sir Anthony Denny of Cheshunt, Hertfordshire.*
PROB 11/72/1 *Will of Margaret Ayloffe.*

### Printed Primary Sources
*Articles ordained by King Henry VII for the Regulation of his household, 31st December 1494*, printed within *A Collection of Ordinances and Regulations for the Government of the Royal Household, made in divers reigns: from King Edward III to King William and Queen Mary, also receipts in ancient cookery*, (Society of Antiquaries of London, London, 1790).

Ascham, R, *English Works*, edited by Wright, W.A., (Cambridge University Press, London, 1970).

Becon, T, *The Catechism*, ed. Ayre, J, (Cambridge University Press, Cambridge, 1844).

Bentley, T, *The monument of matrones conteining seuen seuerall lamps of virginitie, or distinct treatises; whereof the first fiue concerne praier and meditation: the other two last, precepts and examples, as the woorthie works partlie of men, partlie of women; compiled for the necessarie vse of both sexes out of the sacred Scriptures, and other approoued authors*, (H. Denham, London, 1582). Available from: http://name.umdl.umich.edu/A08610.0001.001

Castiglione, B, *The Book of the Courtier*, translated by Opdycke, L.E. (Dover Publications, 2003).

Cleaver, R, *A godly forme of houshold government for the ordering of priuate families, according to the direction of Gods word: wherunto is adioyned in a more particular manner, the seuerall duties of the husband towards his wife, and the wiues dutie towards her husband, the parents dutie towards their children, and the childrens towards their parents, the maisters dutie towards his seruants, and also the seruants duty towards their maisters / first gathered by R. C.; and now newly perused, amended and augmented by Iohn Dod and Robert Cleuer*, (R, Field, London, 1621).

*Essex Wills, The Bishop of London's Commissary Court 1578–1588*, Emmison, F.G., (ed.), (Essex Record Office, Essex, 1995).

*Injunctions for the Diocese of Salisbury (1538)*, Frere, W.H., & Kennedy, W.M., (eds), *Visitation Articles and Injunctions of the Period of the reformation, Vol 2*, (Church of England, London, 1910).

*Letters and Papers, Foreign and Domestic, of the Reign of Henry VIII*, ed. J.S. Brewer, J. Gairdner and R.H. Brodie, 21 vols in 32 parts, and Addenda (London, 1862–1932).

Markham, G, *The English Housewife*, (ed.) Michael, R. Best, (McGill-Queen's University Press, London, 1986).

Moody, J, (ed.), *The Private Life of an Elizabethan Lady, The Diary of Lady Margaret Hoby 1599–1605*, (Sutton Publishing, Stroud, 1998).

*Privy Purse Expenses of Elizabeth of York: Wardrobe Accounts of Edward the Fourth: With a Memoir of Elizabeth of York*, (ed.) Nicholas H. Nicolas, (William Pickering, London, 1830).

*Privy Purse Expenses of the Princess Mary, Daughter of King Henry the Eighth, Afterwards Queen Mary*, (ed.) Madden, F, (William Pickering, London, 1831).

Rhodes, H, *The boke of Nurture, or Schoole of good manners (1577)*, printed within, Russell, J, *The boke of Nurture*, J. Childs & Son, (1867).

Rösslin, E, *The Birth of Mankynde: Otherwyse named the Woman's Booke*, (Richard Jugge, London, 1565).

*Sarum Missal in English*, (The Church Press Company, London, 1868).

Strype, J, *Annals of the Reformation and establishment of religion: and other various occurrences in the church of England, during Queen Elizabeth's happy reign: together with an appendix of original papers of state, records and letters, Vol. 1*, (B. Franklin, New York, 1968).

*The Lisle Letters*, ed. St. Clare Byrne, (Penguin, London, 1985).

*The Norwich Census of the Poor 1570*, (ed.) Pound, J.F., (Norfolk Record Society, 40, 1971).

Tusser, T, *Five Hundred Points of Good Husbandry*, (Oxford University Press, 1984) Originally published in 1557 as *A Hundreth Good Pointes of Husbandrie* and enlarged in 1573, becoming *Five Hundreth Pointes of Good Husbandrie*.

Vives, J.L, *The Education of a Christian Woman: a sixteenth century manual*, edited and translated by Fantazzi, C, (University of Chicago Press, 2000, initially written 1523).

### Secondary Sources

Borman, T, *Elizabeth's Women*, (Vintage, London, 2010).

Borman, T, *The Private Lives of the Tudors*, (Hodder & Stoughton, London, 2017).

Cressy, D, *Birth, Marriage and Death, Ritual, Religion, and the Life-Cycle in Tudor and Stuart England*, (Oxford University Press, Oxford, 1997).

De Lisle, L, *The Sisters who would be Queen, The Tragedy of Mary, Katherine & Lady Jane Grey*, (Harper Press, London, 2009).

Denny, J, *Katherine Howard*, (Portrait, London, 2005).

Dodd, A. H, *Life in Elizabethan England*, (John Jones Publishing, Ruthin, 1998).

Du Boulay, F. R. H., *An Age of Ambition, English Society in the late Middle Ages*, (Thomas Nelson and Sons Ltd, London, 1970).
Eales, J, *Women in early modern England, 1500–1700*, (Routledge, Oxon, 1998).
Erickson, A.L, *Women & Property in Early Modern England*, (Routledge, Oxon, 1995).
Evans, V. S., *Ladies-in-Waiting: Women Who Served at the Tudor Court*, (Independently Published, 2014).
Flower, A, *Tudor Women's Legal Rights 1485–1603*, (Stuart Press, Bristol, 2006).
Goodman, R, *How to be a Tudor*, (Penguin Random House, London, 2015).
Harris, B. J., *English Aristocratic Women 1450–1550: Marriage and Family, Property and Careers*, (Oxford University Press, Oxford, 2002).
Hodder, S.J., *The York Princesses: The Daughters of Edward IV and Elizabeth Woodville*, (Chronos Books, Alresford, 2021).
Hogrefe, P, *Tudor Women, Commoners and Queens*, (Iowa State University Press, Iowa, 1975).
Houlbrooke, R. A., *The English Family 1450–1700*, (Longman, Harlow, 1984).
Jones, J, *Family Life in Shakespeare's England, Stratford-Upon-Avon 1570–1630*, (Sutton Publishing Ltd, Stroud, 1996).
Laurence, A, *Women in England, 1500–1760, A Social History*, (Phoenix Press, London, 1996).
Leyser, H, *Medieval Women, A Social History of Women in England 450–1500*, (Phoenix Press, London, 1996).
McElroy, A, *Educating the Tudors*, (Pen & Sword History, Barnsley, 2023).
McGrath, C, *Sex and Sexuality in Tudor England*, (Pen & Sword History, Barnsley, 2022).
Mendelson, S & Crawford, P, *Women in Early Modern England*, (Clarendon Press, Oxford, 1998).
Mountfield, D, *Everyday Life in Elizabethan England*, (Liber, Barcelona, 1978).
Norton, E, *The Lives of Tudor Women*, (Head of Zeus, London, 2017).
O'Hara, D, *Courtship and Constraint: Rethinking the Making of Marriage in Tudor England*, (Manchester University Press, Manchester, 2000).
Picard, L, *Elizabeth's London, Everyday Life in Elizabethan London*, (Weidenfeld & Nicolson, London, 2003).
Pollock, L, *With Faith and Physic, The Life of a Tudor Gentlewoman, Lady Grace Mildmay 1552–1620*, (Collins and Brown Ltd, London, 1993).
Pound, J, *Poverty and Vagrancy in Tudor England*, (Longman Group Ltd, Harlow, 1986).
Power, E, *Medieval People*, (Penguin Books, Harmondsworth, 1937).
Read, S, *Maids, Wives, Widows, Exploring Early Modern Women's Lives 1540–1740*, (Pen & Sword, Barnsley, 2015).
Ridley, J, *The Tudor Age*, (Constable & Robinson Ltd, London, 2002).
Sim, A, *Food and Feast in Tudor England*, (Sutton Publishing Ltd, Stroud, 1997).
Sim, A, *Masters and Servants in Tudor England*, (Sutton Publishing, Stroud, 2006).
Sim, A, *The Tudor Housewife*, (The History Press, Stroud, 2010).
Stone, J.M., *The History of Mary I: Queen of England*, (Sands & Co, London, 1901).
Stone, L, *The Family, Sex and Marriage in England 1500–1800*, (Penguin Books, London, 1979).
Stone, L, *Road to Divorce, England 1530–1982*, (Oxford University Press, Oxford, 1992).
Watkins, S.B., *Lady Katherine Knollys*, (Chronos Books, Winchester, 2015).
Willis, A. J. (F.R.I.C.S.F.S.G), *Church Life in Kent being Church Court Records of the Canterbury Dioceses 1559–1565*, (Phillimore & Co Ltd, London, 1975).
Wright, S, *'Churmaids, Huswyfes and Hucksters': The Employment of Women in Tudor and Stuart Salisbury* in Charles, L & Duffin, L (ed.), *Women and Work in Pre-Industrial England*, (Croom Helm, London, 1985).

# Index

Abortion, 87
*Act for the Relief of the Poor*, 137
Adolescence, 15, 19, 24, 94
   Lower class, 16
   Upper class, 18
Adultery, 67, 69
Aesop, 21
Alewifery, 92–93
   *See also*, Brewing
Alms, 6, 45–46, 48, 67, 96, 111, 113, 127, 136, 138, 143, 151, 155–156, 161
   *See also*, Charitable causes
Anne of Cleves, 99
Apprenticeships, 11–12, 15, 65, 103, 106–107, 129, 136–137, 148, 157
   Contract, 34, 90, 94, 128
   Education, 12–13, 108
   Parish, 90
Aquinas, Thomas, xiv
Aristotle, xiv, xv, 123, 165
Ascham, Roger, 22
Ashley, Kat, 2, 105
Askew, Anne, xvi

Baptism, 1, 80, 109, 110, 162
   Godparents, 28, 79–80
Basset, Anne, 17, 49
Beaufort, Lady Margaret, 11, 26, 126, 148
Becon, Thomas, 9, 52
Bentley, Thomas, 154
Betrothal, 23, 25, 29, 33–36, 86
Boleyn, Anne, 21, 28
Boleyn, Mary, 21, 28
Boleyn, Thomas, 21
*Book of Common Prayer*, 42, 82–83
Brandon, Charles (Duke of Suffolk), 37–38, 55, 89, 127, 143, 148
Brandon, Frances, 140
Bray, Elizabeth, 67

Breastfeeding, 71, 78, 84, 105, 155
   *See also*, Wet nurse
Brewing, 14, 57, 60, 93, 97, 112, 160
Bridget of York, 45, 147
Brothels, 93
Bourchier, Anne (7th Baroness Bourchier), 67, 147

Castiglione, Baldassare, 99
Caxton, William, 123
Cecil, William, 89
Charitable causes, 20, 41, 48, 62, 67, 85, 162, 165
   Bequests, 127, 144, 146
Chatsworth, 142
Childbirth, 48, 70, 72, 75, 86
   Confinement, 70, 73–75, 79, 81–82, 102, 158
   Death, 74, 78, 158
   Lying-in, 81–83, 158
   Pain relief, 76, 164
   *See also*, Pregnancy
Church, 40, 51, 57, 67, 113, 118
   Children, 5, 8
   Courts, 67, 69, 93
   Services, 25, 34–35, 43, 80, 144–145, 162
Churching, 80, 82–84, 162
Cicero, 21, 123
Clitherow, Margaret, 163
Clothing, 4, 20, 59, 61–62, 72, 94, 97, 103
   Bridal, 41
   Sumptuary Laws, 3, 41
Contraception, 87, 158
Convents, 9, 45, 148–149
   Charity, 45–46, 138, 149–150
   Dissolution, 9, 45–46, 112, 138, 150, 155
   Education, 8–9, 24, 45, 155
   Vocation, 24, 44–45, 47, 113, 162
Convocation of Canterbury, 8, 26
Cooke, Sir Anthony, 154

# 178   Women's Lives in the Tudor Era

Cooking, 17, 56–57, 156
   Employment, 56, 111
Courtly love, 18, 124
Courtship, 28, 33–34, 157
Crime, xvi, 69
   Sexual Crimes, xvi, xvii, 69, 87, 109
Cromwell, Thomas, 31

Dance, 28, 44, 100, 116, 118–121, 125, 164
   Training, 11, 18, 20, 143
De la Pole, Anne, 148
De la Tour, Geoffrey, 123
Dean, Agnes, 101
Denton, Elizabeth, 105
Divorce, 67
   Annulment, 39, 67–68, 162
Domestic violence, 69–70
Dormer, Jane, 2
Dowry, 23, 27, 29, 31, 36, 45, 47–48, 132, 152, 156–157, 161
   Gift, 101, 103
   Negotiations, 27, 30, 32,
Dowers, 29, 31, 41–42, 53, 69, 134, 143, 156
   Widows, 127, 131–133, 138, 141
Drama, 121, 124
   Masques, 28, 119, 122, 124
   Mumming, 121
   Theatre, 121–122
Duwes, Giles, 11

Education, xv, xviii, 3–5, 7–11, 19–21, 65, 79, 85, 104, 153–154, 164
   Languages, 8, 10, 20–21, 154
   Needlework, 6, 20
   Religion, 5–7, 11, 45, 80, 85
   *See also*, Schools
Edward IV, 147
Edward VI, 3, 57, 82
Elizabeth I, xv, 10, 38, 96, 105, 120, 141, 155, 164
   Education, 6, 21, 123, 154
   Household, 2, 89, 98, 101–102, 106, 142
Elizabeth of York, 11, 45, 74, 78, 101, 126, 147
Erasmus, Desiderius, 10, 123, 153–154
Executions, 118, 163

Fitzherbert, Master, 55–56, 58
Food, 3, 58, 92, 102, 116
   Feast, 44
   Preservation of, 57
Fools, 47, 122
Foxe, John, 20, 163
Funerals, 126, 144–145

Galen, xv, 63, 72
   *See also*, Medicine
Gardens, 12, 65, 95
   Herbal, 46, 64
Godparents, *see* Baptism
Grey, Lady Jane, 10, 14, 21–22
Grey, Lady Katherine, 38
Grey, Lady Mary, 38, 148
Guilds, 107, 121, 128

Hardwick, Elizabeth, 141–142
Hardwick Hall, 142
Heiresses, 23, 32, 37, 48, 53, 149
Hengrave Hall, 140
Henry VII, 11, 26, 126
Henry VIII, 17, 27, 37–38, 45, 68, 93, 97, 101, 108–109, 162
   Childhood, 10–11, 105
   Recreation, 57, 117, 122, 125
Hoby, Lady Margaret, 63, 85, 111, 139
Hone, William, 11
Hospitals, 111, 127
Housewifery, 13, 16, 65–66
   Hospitality, 13, 17, 19, 45, 48, 56, 116
Howard, Agnes (Duchess of Norfolk), 16, 143
Howard, Catherine, 16, 143
Hubberd, Anne, 101
Humanism, 10, 21, 153–155
Hygiene, 3, 13, 56
Hyrde, Richard, 123

Illegitimacy, 38–39, 69
Infancy, 13, 126
Inheritance, 127, 130, 133, 140, 149, 159
   Issues, 36, 39, 54, 86, 132, 157
   Receiving, 29, 30, 37, 48, 149
   *See also*, Primogeniture,

Jointure, 29–31, 43, 51, 53, 101, 127, 131–132, 134, 140, 149
   Issues, 36, 69, 132–133

Katharine of Aragon, 99, 101, 103, 108, 162

Ladies-in-Waiting, 62, 97
   Royal court, 18, 37, 98, 100
Laundry, 16, 58–59, 75, 92
   Launderess, 96, 101, 105, 111
Law, 1, 11, 138
   Common, 31, 53–54, 69, 106, 134, 144
   Ecclesiastical, 30, 36, 67
Lisle, Bridget, 49
Lisle, Elizabeth, 48–49
Lisle, Lady Honor, 17, 21, 48
Lisle, Lord Arthur, 17, 48
Literacy, 5, 7, 9, 55, 85, 88, 108, 144, 154, 162
Literature, xiv, 8, 10–11, 20–21, 25, 99, 111, 120–121, 123–124, 147, 154
Louis XII, of France, 21

Margaret, Queen of Scotland, 11, 105, 116
Mary, Queen of France, 11, 21, 28, 37, 148
Mary I, 3, 10, 67, 74, 92, 96, 101, 105, 117, 122, 145
   Will, 146
Mary, Queen of Scots, 143
Markham, Gervase, 65
Marriage, 36, 41–42
   Consent, 25–26, 30, 37, 39
   Dispensation, 28, 30, 35, 40
   Impediments, 28, 34–35
   *See also*, Betrothal
Medicine, 17, 46, 63–64
   *See also*, Galen
Midwives, 68, 71, 75, 77, 83, 87, 112, 148, 158
   Baptism, 77, 79, 109
   Training, 108–110
   Wage, 80, 110–111
Mildmay, Lady Grace, 64
More, Sir Thomas, 22, 154
More-Roper, Margaret, xv, 22, 123
Mulcaster, Richard, 153–154
Music, 19, 44, 100, 116, 119–121, 125
   Training, 11, 18, 20, 22, 24

Needlework, 62, 124, 161
   Embroidery, 20, 41, 62, 116, 124

Neville, Cecily (Duchess of York), 147–148
Nunneries *see* Convents

Parr, Kateryn, 14, 67, 108, 123, 141
Parr, William (Marquess of Northampton, 67
Parry, Blanche, 2
Patronage, 6, 100, 143, 164
Pensions, 46, 101, 112–113, 138, 146, 161
Plantagenet, Arthur *see* Lisle, Lord Arthur
Plato, 22
Poetry, 124
Poppincourt, Jane, 11
Pregnancy, 39, 71
   Confinement, 73–74
   Pleading the belly, 110
   Symptoms, 71
Primogeniture, 1, 23, 31, 132–133, 135

Rape, *see* Crime
Reading, 5, 8, 20, 22, 116, 122–124, 154–155
Reformation, 40, 46, 68–69, 76, 112, 119
   Education, 5, 8, 155
   Services, 42, 80, 82–83
   Relics, 76, 163
Religion, 4–5, 7, 9–10, 40, 118–119, 153
   *See also*, Education, Reformation,
Remedies, 17, 63–64, 72, 76, 82, 87, 111, 115, 164
   *See also*, Medicine
Renaissance, 21, 153, 155
Richard III, 147
Rösslin, Eucharius, 108–109

Schools, 8–9, 127, 143
   Dame, 6, 104
   Needlework, 6
   Petty, 7, 8, 10
   *See also*, Tutors
Servants, 2, 15, 55–56, 86, 119
   Domestic service, 16, 82, 94–96, 103
   Wages, 61–62, 94, 102
Seymour, Jane, 78, 141
Shrewsbury, Earl of, *see* Talbot, George
Silkwomen, 107–108, 160
Spinning, 8, 81, 124
   Employment, 104–105, 111, 136, 160
   *See also*, Needlework

St Bridget, 72, 147
St Catherine, 147
St Jerome, xiv
St Loe, Sir William, 142
St Matilda, 147
*Statute of Wills*, 144
Stuart, Mary, *see* Mary, Queen of Scots
Suffolk, Duke of, *see* Brandon, Charles
Swaddling, 17, 72, 77, 84
Syon Priory, 148

Talbot, George (6th Earl of Shrewsbury), 142
Treason, xvi, 31, 37, 67, 70
    *See also*, Crime
Tudor, Edmund (Earl of Richmond), 26
Tudor, Elizabeth, *see* Elizabeth I
Tudor, Margaret, *see* Margaret, Queen of Scotland
Tudor, Mary, *see* Mary I

Tudor-Brandon, Mary, *see* Mary, Queen of France
Tusser, Thomas, 58, 64
Tutors, 8, 10–11, 22, 143

Vives, Juan Luis, 26, 123, 153–154

Wages, 46–47, 68, 90–91, 94–95, 101–102, 165
Walsingham, Our Lady of, 72
Wardship, 23, 36, 135, 158
    Guardian, 23, 37, 139
Wet nurse, 71, 78, 105
Wheathill, Anne, 123
Willoughby, Katherine, 37–38, 54, 89, 101, 143, 148
Woodville, Elizabeth, 101

York, Bridget, *see* Bridget of York
York, Elizabeth, *see* Elizabeth of York